LOOKS AND FRICTIONS

PERSPECTIVES

Series editors: Colin MacCabe and Paul Willemen

LOOKS AND FRICTIONS

Essays in Cultural Studies and Film Theory

PAUL WILLEMEN

INDIANA UNIVERSITY PRESS

Bloomington and Indianapolis

BFI PUBLISHING

First published in 1994 by the
British Film Institute
21 Stephen Street, London W1P 1PL
and the
Indiana University Press
601 North Morton Street, Bloomington, Indiana 47404

The British Film Institute exists to encourage the development of film, television and video
in the United Kingdom, and to promote knowledge, understanding and enjoyment of the
culture of the moving image. Its activities include the National Film and Television
Archive; the National Film Theatre; the Museum of the Moving Image; the London Film
Festival; the production and distribution of film and video; funding and support for
regional activities; Library and Information Services; Stills, Posters and Design; Research,
Publishing and Education; and the monthly *Sight and Sound* magazine.

British Library Cataloguing in Publication Data
A catalogue record for this book is available from the British Library.

ISBN 0–85170–398–4
       0–85170–399–2 pbk

US Cataloging data available from the Library of Congress.

Cover still from *Dyn Amo* (Steve Dwoskin, 1972).

Typeset by Fakenham Photosetting Ltd, Fakenham, Norfolk

Printed in Great Britain by
St Edmundsbury Press Ltd, Bury St Edmunds, Suffolk

In memory of Claire Johnston

Contents

Brasschaat–Bombay:
A Way of Inhabiting a Culture

Meaghan Morris

These three film-makers [Nelson Pereira dos Santos, Ousmane Sembene and Ritwik Ghatak] exemplify a way of inhabiting one's culture which is neither myopically nationalist nor evasively cosmopolitan. ... Their way of inhabiting their cultures ... founded the search for a cinematic discourse able to convey their sense of a diagnostic understanding (to borrow a happy phrase from Raymond Williams) of the situation in which they worked and to which their work is primarily addressed.

'The Third Cinema Question'

In other words, what I feel energised enough to try to theorise, the issues I feel compelled to address and the terms in which I address them, are significantly determined by the situation in which I live and work. In my case, that is contemporary Britain. While this is a readily acknowledged truism for most intellectuals, it is also something rarely taken into account in the actual formulation of our work.

'Bangkok–Bahrain–Berlin–Jerusalem: Amos Gitai's Editing'

I

Paul Willemen is probably most familiar to film students in Britain and the United States today for his work on 'Third Cinema', a project that emerged, or re-emerged, in the 1980s with an aim of rearticulating the radical internationalist traditions of Latin American, Soviet and European cinemas to contemporary concerns with neocolonialism, multiculturalism and national-historical experience. The *Questions of Third Cinema* anthology (1989)[1] which Willemen co-edited with Jim Pines has helped to shape a revival of interest in comparative cinema studies, and to encourage new film scholarship devoted to 'expelling the Euro-American conceptions of cinema from the center of both film history and critical theory'.[2]

In an international frame, however, the scope and significance of Willemen's work far exceeds one recent influential anthology. Paul Willemen is not an orthodox academic. He is a well-known scholar and critic of Indian cinema,[3] and his major essays in film history and critical theory have contributed to the development of cinema studies for over twenty years. So has his work as an editorial board member (1972–80) of the innovative British film theory journal *Screen*, and as an editor (1981–88) of the comparative cinema journal *Framework*. Employed by the British Film Institute since 1976, he has also worked in many countries across every aspect of film culture: funding, production, festival politics and promotion, archival work, critical discussion, teaching, writing and publishing. Above all, he has acted as a travelling interlocutor for film-makers, theorists, critics, historians, cultural activists and policy workers involved in diverse Asian, European, African and Australian cinemas.

So it should be easy to introduce new readers to the essays in *Looks and Frictions* simply by placing them historically in the context of their author's complex commitments, and in relation to what Willemen modestly calls 'the situation in which I live and work'. It is certainly easy for me to begin by paying tribute to the acuity and brilliance of his criticism, since I have benefited from it personally; I find no difficulty in prefacing work to which I owe a major intellectual debt. I do mean an *intellectual* debt, in the fullest sense of the term. It is not simply that a dialogue with Willemen's writing has inflected my own theoretical priorities as an Australian cultural critic, and that a sometimes 'frictive', but always productive, engagement with his politics has helped me define, on many occasions, my own commitments and views. The debt I have in mind is even more fundamental; it bears on my sense of what it can mean to 'live and work' *as* an intellectual 'inhabiting' a culture, and it is a debt that I share with many others of his interlocutors elsewhere.

When I was living and working as a film critic trying to support independent Australian cinema through a newspaper column in the early 1980s, I learned two things from Paul Willemen that I have never forgotten. Both are practical strategies which mark the arguments and the rhetorics of this book, and both, I think, are wisdoms which go against the grain of professionalised practice in the metropolitan (in Australia, US-based) humanities academy today. One is that it is crucial to put '*how?*' questions, in cultural studies, to every theoretical argument and to each political claim: this is a way of developing one's social aims beyond shaping a career in 'critique'. The other is that it is just as important to *listen* as it is to speak in any comparative exchange: this is a way of making connections with others by learning to recognise 'the many-layeredness' ('The Third Cinema Question') and even the otherness ('The National') of one's own 'cultural-historical formation'.

Conditions in the academy today make both these activities difficult. As Willemen points out in 'Bangkok–Bahrain–Berlin–Jerusalem', it is one thing to admit that 'theory and criticism are intellectual
practices very much tied to specific historical moments and geographical locations', but quite another to let this affect 'the *actual
formulation* of our work'. Travelling theorists routinely do the
former in a prefatory way ('this paper was originally written for an
American context about conditions in the US') before going on to
universalise the significance of their work ('but I'm not going to
change it for you'). Along with the worsening institutional conditions
which most teachers and critics now face, 'time pressures' on those
elite personnel who can circulate in global metropolitan space (that is,
our involvement in the over-production of intellectual goods by the
conference and publishing industries) ensure that *listening* to others is
an ethic much more talked about than practised. The result is a mode
of conduct, and a genre of theory, that Willemen calls 'cosmopolitan'.
It is an 'evasive' mode because, in its spatial-historical abstractedness
and its miserly use of time, it organises an academic culture in which
'*how?*' questions – *political* questions about particular social aims –
need never be confronted in realistic and reciprocal ways.

Working as a travelling interlocutor (rather than 'theorist')
involves a contrary form of address that Willemen calls 'diagnostic
understanding' (after Raymond Williams), or 'creative understanding' (after Mikhail Bakhtin). This isn't necessarily a polite and restful
process: if Willemen always listens, he often expresses 'other'
opinions about one's own cherished cultural concerns. This refusal of
what he calls, in 'The National', *ventriloquism* ('the monopolist-
imperialist's guilty conscience') has a certain potential for friction: my
own past moments of myopically nationalist feeling suggest that there
are few things more irritating to a nationally-oriented critic than
losing an argument to a foreigner (let alone, in my situation, to a
'British film theorist') who actually follows all the intricacies of multi-
layered local debates – and still presumes to differ. Yet this is why
Willemen's diagnostic is so helpful, his labour of understanding so
creative in suggesting what an interactive comparative criticism might
be able to achieve. In his essay on 'An Avant-Garde for the 90s',
Willemen emphasises Brecht's 'argument for the things artistic practice should be able *to do*'; in much the same way, I read *Looks and
Frictions* as an argument for developing the positive capacities of
criticism.

II

That much is easy to say. If I find it more difficult to place Willemen's
theoretical work on cinema in (as I think he would wish) particular
historical contexts, it is not, therefore, because I do not live and work
in Britain, but because a metropolitan narrative about the recent

history of film theory immediately gets in the way. The essays in *Looks and Frictions* were written between 1971 and 1990. The narrative I have in mind is organised by a stark opposition between 'the 1970s' and 'the 1980s' and it supports a professional fiction of disciplinary development and of generational/*national* succession which could serve as a grid for dividing these essays *chronologically* – rather than historically – into two distinct 'periods', respectively typified by *Screen* (Parts One and Two) and *Framework* (Part Three).

In the 1970s, the story goes,[4] Anglophone cinema studies fell under the sway of a hyper-speculative and jargon-ridden discourse known as 'British Film Theory', primarily disseminated by *Screen*. While intellectual gains were made, especially for feminism, by the introduction of semiotics, Marxist aesthetics and Lacanian psychoanalysis to film culture in this period, an overemphasis on 'Language' as opposed to 'Society' and 'History' combined with an exclusive focus on sexual difference to marginalise issues of race, class and colonialism. At the same time, the punitively difficult style of writing favoured by *Screen* combined with its focus on 'classic Hollywood' (that is, on canonical texts) to doom the whole project to an 'academic' elitism.

In the 1980s, things looked up. The productive base of cinema studies moved to the United States. Serious film scholars reaffirmed the need for empirical work, some staging a return to History. New critical movements began to articulate race, class and nation to gender and sexuality, some through ethnographic and social research based on concepts of cultural identity, some by elaborating 'difference' theories. There was a revival of interest in community-oriented and political film traditions, and a surge of Anglo-American scholarly research into some non-Western cinemas. Firmly installed in the publishing arms of the 'global' US academy, critical writing became less *academic*. At the same time, its objects became more 'popular': work on television, advertising, music video, new image technologies and contemporary commercial films enabled a born-again cinema studies to claim its market share of the boom in '*cultural* studies'.

The professional value of such fiction is clear enough: US cultural studies is not the first humanities project to use a little old-historicist triumphalism to legitimate the story of its own miraculous birth. There is also some descriptive value in this academic family romance. Paul Willemen himself writes eloquently about the 'suffocating ethnocentrism' of 1970s film theory ('The National') and the 'abstract, ahistorical notion of subjectivity' that secured its failure to realise a 'theory of the articulation of text and history' ('An Avant-Garde for the 90s'). While his essays are not, in fact, presented here in the order of their first publication (the oldest material is in Chapter 3, 'The Sirkian System', and the first chapter dates in its final form from 1981), there is also a difference in style between Part Three and the rest of the book. *Looks and Frictions* is a text of decreasing surface

4

difficulty, and readers new to the dense polemics of Willemen's contributions to *Screen* may well find it more rewarding to begin at the end and work backwards.

It is important, however, to arrive at the beginning and those taxing, innovative essays that make the later work on Third Cinema both possible and theoretically rich today for political work in cinema. If period-myth has its uses, the chronology that sustains it has no analytical value; brought to bear on *Looks and Frictions*, its first consequence would be to marginalise as 'archival' half the argument of this book – in my view, the very half that has most to contribute to 'contemporary' cultural studies. For example, 'Cinematic Discourse: The Problem of Inner Speech' (1975/81) is a theory of *translation* that takes as its premise the constitutive heterogeneity of all psychic *and* cultural activity, and works towards an account of the ways in which the subjective and the social articulate in complex historical experience; 'Notes on Subjectivity' (1978) extends this study of the 'carrying over' of meaning to a theory of ideology as an institutional practice.

In other words, a critique of the conditions of ethnocentrism is fundamental to *Looks and Frictions* from the first to the last essay in the book.[5] So is one of that critique's immediate corollaries: the refusal of any model of an abstract subjectivity 'constructed' by 'the text' or by a monolithic 'language'. This is why 'Notes on Subjectivity' – a brilliant essay which now risks dismissal for its intricate argumentation as well as its publishing period – is able to derive a critique of the 'projective appropriation' ('The National') of Japanese films to Western modernism from an extended and unequivocal demonstration that 'real readers are subjects in history, living in given social formations, rather than mere subjects of a single text'. This is now an orthodox claim in cultural studies; its implications for film analysis have rarely been so rigorously drawn out.

If Willemen's essays from the 1970s offered only a prescient glimpse of a cultural studies to come, then metropolitan chronicles might still be justified in leaving them aside. Of course, they were actually arguments put forward in a many-sided debate about history and subjectivity that linked work in film theory throughout the decade to feminism, to socialist thinking and to British cultural studies; serious accounts now place the project of *Screen* (and Willemen's highly critical position within it) historically in that context of debate.[6] My concern here, however, is that the useful originality of his theoretical work is actually made unreadable by the populist professionalism that dominates cultural studies today.

There are at least two reasons for this concern. One is that Willemen's analysis of the 'unbridgeable gap between "real" readers and authors and inscribed ones' never gave rise, as it has in cultural studies, to an equation of real readers with *consumers* and of their

5

'pleasure' with purchasing power. He maintains an intensely critical distance from 'celebrants of shopping and devotees of the short-term, rapid turnover (cultural) investment strategy characteristic of contemporary finance capitalism' ('Bangkok–Bahrain'), and he argues for 'a fighting', rather than a market, 'notion of popularity' ('The Third Cinema Question'). In other words, he requires us strongly to imagine a difference between the popular and the corporate – and the future and the present – precisely at a time when academic thinking is strongly pressured to accept that critical activity is always already *contained* by market forces. In this context, the fighting element of Willemen's work is most easily dismissed as *not*-popular, and thus as 'other' to the marketing self-image of academic cultural studies – that is, as academic.

The other reason is more serious. *Looks and Frictions* does not simply offer a negative account of ethnocentrism and the 'realities' of finance capitalism. On the contrary: from the first essay, the book provides a positive framework for comparative cultural analysis that transforms many assumptions about 'language', 'society' and 'history' sustaining cultural studies. As a theory of thinking, 'Cinematic Discourse: The Problem of Inner Speech' is unique in recent film theory (and it was certainly eccentric to the prevailing concerns of *Screen*). It can be difficult, even strange, on first reading, because its frame of reference is unorthodox (drawing on little-read work by Eikhenbaum, Vygotsky and Luria) and its guiding questions heretical: exactly *how* are 'the psychoanalytic subject' and 'the subject in history' bound in the hybridising process of inner (or unenunciated) speech?; what *kind* of 'speech' is this, and are there really any grounds for attributing separate 'specificities' to 'language' and 'the image'?; can any cultural politics dispense with thinking about what happens as people think, and is psychoanalysis entirely sufficient to that task?

Professionalism is a corporatist ethos, unresponsive, on the whole, to destabilising bursts of originality; it prefers to regulate 'change' consensually through the rise and fall of reputations and seasonally adjusted shifts of emphasis of the kind advertised by the 1970s/80s story: *this* is the historical context in which I would like to place *Looks and Frictions*. Since I think that the conceptual difficulty of some of the chapters derives as much from Willemen's steadfast disrespect for professionalism as from their 'style', I want to map the conceptual coherence of the book rather than the shifts between the essays. One way to do this is to tell another story about a way of living and working in the 1970s as a British film theorist.

III

Born in Brasschaat, near Antwerp, Paul Willemen emigrated from Belgium to Britain in February 1968. It wasn't a simple crossing or a

6

cosmopolitan glide. Emigration is a frictional experience; to *inhabit* another language as well as a different culture is not only to encounter barriers, resistances and gaps, but to live and work, every day, in a chafing proximity, *with* them. For Willemen, landing in London as a Flemish-speaking, French-reading cinephile, one such abrasion was a stimulus to thought. On his own account, the immediate context of his early theoretical work was 'the shock of discovering a culture – English – which did not have a trace of surrealism in it'.

Before emigrating, Willemen spent two years working for the Belgian Cinémathèque: in 1967 he organised the first women's film programme ever screened (showing 90 films by women directors) and he worked on the Knokke Le Zoute Experimental Film Festival which took place at the turn of that year. For a Belgian coming out of the vital film culture and the turbulent political climate of Europe in the late 1960s, part of the shock of the unsurreal was an alien formation, The Literary – 'the ruling English ideology described so vividly in all its suffocating decrepitude in Tom Nairn's classic essay on "The English Literary Intelligentsia"'[7] – powerful enough to shape the practices of 'dissident' as well as 'compliant' intellectuals ('The Third Cinema Question'). An energy derived from this discovery lends zest throughout *Looks and Frictions* to Willemen's acerbic analyses of English intellectual life. One feature of the English ideology, however, was particularly disconcerting to someone who had grown up on the border between Belgium and Holland just after World War Two. With its history of imperial *and* populist pretensions to a common-sense universality, the confidently boundless insularity of The Literary was (and in Willemen's view, still is) that of a country – *England* rather than 'Britain' – never occupied by foreign forces in living memory.

Two explicit and entangled consequences of Willemen's discovery of 'English' can be traced in *Looks and Frictions*. One has to do with the insistence of 'borders', on *montage* and on the problem of translation in his writing, to which I will return. The other has to do with a method of working *in between* particular fields of cultural activity and, since this method informs his themes and arguments as well as his concept of cultural politics, I want to situate it briefly in the wider context of his 1970s work.

As a self-taught intellectual with a background in cinephilia, Willemen began to collaborate on *Screen* with literary academics. The composite text of any significant journal is defined as much by the conflicts developing within it as it is by its differences from other publications; some of Willemen's major pieces (including, from this volume, 'Cinematic Discourse', 'Notes on Subjectivity' and 'Letter to John') were embedded critiques of the work of other contributors or of the journal's general direction. At the same time, he continued to work for the independent film culture active then in Britain; 'The

Fourth Look', a dialogue with Laura Mulvey's work on visual pleasure (1976), and '*Photogénie* and Epstein', an argument with David Bordwell (1981), were first published in the London magazine *Afterimage*. With the feminist critic Claire Johnston, he also organised a series of special events at the Edinburgh Film Festival throughout the decade, including influential retrospectives and publications on Roger Corman (1970), Douglas Sirk (1972), Frank Tashlin (1973), Raoul Walsh (1974), Jacques Tourneur (1975), Brecht and Cinema (1975) and Max Ophuls (1978).

These events formed critical spaces of the kind that professionalism now projects as 'outside' the academy, and then wonders wistfully where they went. For Willemen and Johnston, the point was not to situate criticism either inside *or* outside a single institutional space but to develop a triangular practice oriented towards *cinema*, not literary, institutions, and capable of linking their theoretical work to festival culture on the one hand and independent cinema on the other; in other words, to ensure that film theory could engage with work going on in film exhibition, distribution and production contexts as well as with secondary and tertiary education. In this spirit, Willemen organised National Film Theatre seasons on Hammer films (focusing on Terence Fisher) in 1971,[8] and on the films of Frank Borzage in 1975.

Willemen's Edinburgh Festival publications can also be read as critiques of the 'literary' tendencies of *Screen*, primarily because most of them were resolutely focused on single films and directors[9] at a time when the journal was destabilising both of these figures. In an essay later published elsewhere ('Remarks on *Screen*'),[10] he notes that while 'this dissolving of the industrially and ideologically imposed boundaries of the text as it is circulated by the industry and journalism' was important for theorising cinema as 'signifying practice', it seriously impeded *Screen*'s ability to stay in touch with the dominant institutions of cinema and film studies at that time; 'theoretical "advances" were bought at the price of a tendency towards institutional isolation'.

This remark is of more than archival interest for contemporary cultural studies. It suggests that the tendency of *Screen* or of any theoretical project to veer off into what Willemen poetically calls 'the deep space of academia' may be accelerated less by a particular intellectual style than by the delinking of academic research and pedagogy from other institutional practices that professionalism now promotes. If this assumes that 'theory' is not a self-sufficient activity (as most practitioners happily accept), it also assumes that a rhetorically populist cultural studies can equally find itself in deep space if it has no practical rather than gestural links to organised institutional forces 'other' than its own. It follows that a cultural politics needs something that a radical rhetoric does not; namely, a realistic way of negotiating differences between *overlapping* social spaces, combined

8

with a willingness to work in contact (however chafing) with 'the main institutions and forces shaping film culture' at any given time.

A comparable approach to cultural studies has recently taken the form – at least in Australia, Britain and Canada – of a turn to cultural *policy* rather than populism. The strength and resilience of Willemen's version, however, is suggested by the speed with which some proponents of this turn have hurtled off into *administrative* deep space by disconnecting cultural policy from 'critique'.[11] Theirs might be called a romantic pragmatist argument. While accepting the professionalist move to institutional isolation (a condition often confused with the limited, local authority ascribed by Foucault to 'specific' intellectuals), it rediscovers the universalising power of the Literary academic – not in the common-sense corporate popular but in the specialised discourse of the bureaucrat.

Willemen's way of working differs from this. He could be called a thoroughly pragmatic utopian. By asking *how* to move particular forces in a socialist direction ('An Avant-Garde for the 90s'), he values what Foucault called the 'lateral connections across different forms of knowledge and from one focus of politicisation to another' that make it possible, Foucault claimed, 'to rearticulate categories which were previously kept separate'.[12] As much through his work as an interlocutor as in his theoretical divergence from *Screen* and his Third Cinema projects, Willemen has argued for over twenty years that cultural politics is a *relational* 'profession'. For professional critics, this means taking into account 'in the actual formulation of our work' the ways in which a practice carried over or *translated* from one area of culture to another will change its value and its direction in the process of 'lateral connection'; a practice *becomes* oppositional only when it is mobilised in relation to something else, and made intelligible as an alternative to others available at any particular 'focus'.

This *montage* method of 'responsible intervention'[13] assumes (unlike cosmopolitan travel) that the borders between spaces are real and that they make a difference, and it affirms (against defensive nationalism) that borders can be crossed in both directions and that the spaces between borders are open and diverse. The border is a dense and busy place in Willemen's writing; he uses it to organise various linguistic, institutional, social, cultural and national orders of reality, and again to map the comings and goings between them. In a sense, what allows him intellectually to inhabit, even to *occupy* the insular terrain of 'English' – at home as he is in the culturally mixed 'contemporary Britain' described in his essay on Amos Gitai – is the conviction he shares with Bakhtin that 'the most intense and productive life of culture takes place on the boundaries of its individual areas and not in places where these areas have become enclosed in their own specificity' ('The Third Cinema Question').

Looks and Frictions is a book about this border-life in cinema: from the first chapter, refusing the rigid division between verbal and visual 'language' sustaining cinematic modernism, to the third section on radical cinema in an economy of globalisation, Willemen's work examines boundaries and limits, affirming their historical reality while contesting their political power. His passion for a translative practice is shared by many activists and writers ('How many people today', Deleuze and Guattari asked in 1975, 'live in a language that is not their own?'[14]) Widely shared, too, is his belief that 'a sense of non-belonging, non-identity with the culture one inhabits' is indispensable to those intense and productive aspects of cultural life. The special force of this book, however, is to frame its exposition of a politics of becoming (Part Three) with a substantial revision of the models of subjectivity, looking, and cinematic specificity which have dominated work in film theory for over twenty years (Parts One and Two). In the process, *Looks and Frictions* makes central to film history and critical theory the concerns of cultural struggles too often called 'marginal' or 'minor' by transforming (rather than dismissing or ignoring) the 'major' Euro-American theories of film spectatorship.

IV

Some of the argumentation of *Looks and Frictions* uses what can be, for students of cultural studies, a slightly unfamiliar syntax. Willemen follows Bakhtin in conjoining a concern for the 'interconnection and interdependence' of diverse areas of culture with a strong mistrust for what Bakhtin in 1970 called, 'our enthusiasm for specification'.[15] Work in cultural studies more usually assumes that 'diversity' and 'specificity' logically go together; we can even, logically, predicate an infinite diversity of plural specificities, and then declare a need for coalition.

There is a complication here. Bakhtin's term 'specification' refers both to a formal method seeking to establish 'the specific features of literature' *and* to historicist techniques for encapsulating works in particular epochs or periods ('in their own contemporaneity'). Willemen's usage more widely embraces both a modernist aesthetic ideology *and* 'attempts to enclose cultural practices within class or ethnic or gender specificities' ('The Third Cinema Question'). Cultural critics now engaged in either version of the second activity do not always see themselves as committed to the first. Perhaps very few would do so; for reasons as much to do with the burden of The Literary in the United States as in England, a principled rejection of 'formalism' is often taken to be crucial to the development of an identity politics on the one hand, and to historical research on the other.

The deep ungrammaticality of *Looks and Frictions* is to argue that all these enthusiasms are, in work on cinema, historically interconnected and interdependent; *'specificity as fetish'* ('An Avant-Garde for the 90s') is one of the chief critical targets of the book. Willemen never denies particularity or rejects individuation, and he is himself meticulous in making distinctions (demonstrating in 'The National', for example, that the governmental, industrial and financial frames of film production make cultural specificity in cinema primarily a national issue). Nor does he accept that formalism (or any other aesthetic) is *intrinsically* undesirable: he stresses its practical value for charting trajectories in a social formation ('Cinematic Discourse') and even its political value for some institutional occasions ('Notes on Subjectivity'). His polemic is against a particular *notion* of specificity that mimics, in writing about the cinema, the fetishistic 'regime of split belief' ('I know ... but nevertheless') in which cinematic looking is said to be caught, and against the *consequences* of this 'mimicry' in the history of film theory (*'Photogénie* and Epstein').

For example, in his discussion of the 1920s French impressionist ideal of *photogénie* – 'that mysterious, indefinable something present in the image which differentiated cinema from all other arts' – he notes that these first theoretical writings on cinema put in place a *viewer's aesthetic* that works to distinguish viewers 'sensitive' to *photogénie* from those who are not. Sensitive viewers recognise that something fundamental to cinema is at stake in their fantasies of a 'purely' visual plenitude, but they also want it to remain *unspoken*; 'the price of this theoretical insight is that it must be relegated to the unspeakable'. Paradoxically, this something-indefinable relentlessly attracts attempts at definition which spiral around the 'forever unreachable focal point' that they designate and contain. Willemen traces the spiral of this 'wished-for refusal of the fall into language' through to some aspects of the semiotics of Christian Metz, and in the 'audio-visual fantasy' (shared with Metz by many film-makers, critics and theorists) of two rigorously distinct homogeneous blocks that may be juxtaposed or combined in a 'psychodramatic confrontation of the figure and the word', but never *merged* 'in hybrid forms of signification, interpenetrating each other' ('Cinematic Discourse').

Several essays ('Cinematic Discourse', 'The Fourth Look', 'Letter to John', 'An Avant-Garde for the 90s') examine the problems that follow from this splitting of the cinematic operation in the viewer's aesthetic. Since a desire to repress language is a desire to repress difference, any attempt to differentiate cinema on the basis of an 'indefinable something' is doomed theoretically to fail. But it does succeed institutionally in producing the repetitive spirals of discourse that sustain the profession of the 'sensitive viewer' as critic. Film studies, for example, divides into two distinct fields, one organised by the text as a self-enclosed object separated from the viewer, the other by the psychology of the spectator; locked into opposition, 'text' and 'viewer' become the poles of an unresolvable, and thus interminable, 'debate'. As a traditional idealist machine for endlessly generating discourse, this 'debate' is carried over in cultural studies as a confrontation between textual analysis and ethnographic research.[16]

'An Avant-Garde for the 90s' examines the slippage that the term 'specificity' allows between its descriptive and evaluative uses. A descriptive definition of cinematic specificity is indiscriminate; it must be able to cover all films without exception, from blockbusters to 'industrial training loops'. An evaluative usage singles out particular films for drawing attention to the *features* of that specificity. These features, however, are the products of a reading practice and, in most cases, of a particular professional training; they are made available by a viewer's learned ability to distinguish them. So when critics find that texts are 'ever so cinematically specific . . . chock-a-block with contradictions directing attention to processes of enunciation and requiring active readers', we simply transmute the value of our own theoretical competence into the value of a film (another exercise repeatable across an infinite number of texts). This is one reason why formalist and populist approaches to film have much so in common for Willemen; in practice, both require cultural practices to repeat the *terms* of a specificity which is rendered ahistorical. A formalist reading for signs inscribing cinematic specificity *and* a populist reading for signs soliciting viewer activity are equally engaged in valuing texts on classic modernist terms: that is, 'according to their high art value, which is no more than the value of the consumer's social and educational status delegated to the object'.

Most of Willemen's disagreements in the 1970s with positions dominant in *Screen* can be related to his mistrust for 'specificity'. 'Notes on Subjectivity' makes some of these explicit. Willemen rejected the prescriptive aesthetics that attacked realist strategies wherever they appeared, and he contested the 'discourse theory' that precluded any mixing of Marxism with psychoanalysis by enclosing each in the immanent specificity of its field. In his powerful analysis of the rhetoric of subject construction, he argues for a theory of discursive practice that can engage with ideology and with the role of institutions; with the historical variability of the enunciative processes and the traditions of representation enabling different modes of cinematic discourse, as well as of the aesthetic techniques which any cinema may usefully explore; and thus with the 'cumbersome extra-textual' created and excluded by the process of specification. This argument lays the basis for his later critique of Stephen Heath's more complex account of cinema as a specific signifying practice, insofar as it *postpones* history for 'a still to be theorised articulation with an elsewhere of the cinema' ('An Avant-Garde for the 90s').

'Notes on Subjectivity' is an intense and illuminating argument linking the institutional practices of literary modernism to the problem of ethnocentrism in film studies. Written in response to an essay by Edward Branigan on Oshima's *The Story of a Man who Left his Will on Film* and Fellini's $8^{1}/_{2}$, it shows how the categories of 'point of view' (POV) and 'character' (terms deriving from the study of the nineteenth-century novel) carry with them into film studies the 'ahistorical persons' put in place by the *communication* model that a psychoanalytic theory of the subject was supposed to displace. For Willemen, only a universalising use of European concepts of person-hood and perspective makes it possible for Branigan, first, to pull *The Story of a Man who Left his Will on Film* and $8^{1}/_{2}$ into the same space of analysis, and, second, to *contrast* them in terms of their formal structures of subjectivity. The result of Branigan's formalism is that Oshima's film emerges as 'the negation, the reverse side of Fellini's film' (and as a breakthrough to modernism) rather than as opening up a 'radically different approach to signifying practices' in which the literary concept of character 'is not redefined, it is made irrelevant'.

Two related lines of argument follow. One examines the complicity between information theory and the viewer's aesthetic in splitting the cinematic operation. A formal 'twinning' of the author/sender and the reader/receiver confirms the division of the object of film study by, on the one hand, ignoring the cultural history of authorship, and, on the other, by enabling 'the reader' to figure as the locus of truth, 'the point at which the productivity of the text stops'. The other argument bears on the ethnocentric pull exerted by the literary practice of close reading that informs cinematic studies of POV. As a professional protocol, close reading insists that evidence be drawn from the phenomenal aspects of a text (or, from our own theoretical competence delegated to the text). In the process, it evacuates from the field of pertinent evidence such historical resources as, in this instance, the differences between 'European monocular perspective, Japanese systems of perspective and Byzantine lack of perspective', and the cultural histories of different framing procedures, modes of spatial layering and so on.

Close reading creates an 'outside' of the text consisting of precisely the 'discourses in struggle' to which, for Willemen, the concept of subjectivity should be referred. His method is neither to mirror the formalist move by taking the part of the reader, nor to prolong 'the paranoid game' of inside/outside by deconstructing its terms, but to conceptualise enunciation as a *discursive* process, not a textual 'feature', that occurs in historical time; it involves 'a multiplicity of I's and You's' pulled provisionally into coherence as much by institutional strategies and conventions as by a reader's production of subjectivity via the text. On this account, any text is 'a profoundly unstable economy of discourses' while 'readers, like texts (and for that matter characters within texts), are always sites where pluralities intersect'. This solution to the problem of articulating texts to history is by no means unique to Willemen; it simply derives directly from the

linguistic theory of enunciation as a *temporal* production of rhetori-
cal coherence and referential power, rather than reducing 'enunciation' (as Anglo-American literary theory is wont to do) to a way of
reading the personal pronouns, and thence a 'point of view', marked
in a text. However, it is a solution always ignored by re-formulations
of a text/context, form/history debate for cultural theory – on the
interminability of which the critical industry thrives.

V

Willemen's theoretical framework emphasises *looking*, rather than
'the gaze', and *frictions*, not subject 'positions'. Instead of a viewer's
or consumer's aesthetic, he proposes a politics of cultural production
(film-making, viewing, reading) that refers for its theory of consumption to Bakhtin's model of reading as a profoundly social practice.
Willemen does not discard semiotics and the study of film language,
or psychoanalytic work on viewing pleasure. Instead, he involves
them both in asking *how* the experience of the subject in language
and cinema is '*transformed* into an analysis of the experience of the
subject in history' ('An Avant-Garde for the 90s').

Willemen develops his ideas casually, almost anecdotally, as a particular argument proceeds. His concepts gather force irregularly in
the movement of a reading; *Looks and Frictions* is not a thesis, but a
book of notes and reflections by an essayist committed to an activist
model of research and experimentation. Nevertheless, several organising concepts do carry over from essay to essay and from one context
of argument to another, and of these the most important are *inner
speech* and *the fourth look*, theoretical concepts dealing with the
relations between heterogeneous orders of experience; and *double
outsidedness* and *the in-between*, methodological concepts addressing
the 'how?' of cultural politics.

'Inner speech' and 'the fourth look' are two processes that explain
how the interweaving of the textual and the social may be traced in
relation to the viewer ('Letter to John'). Each participates simultaneously in the textual, and in the social situations within which the
textual arises 'as production or as reading'. Inner speech is the discourse of thought or 'attention': it works with heterogeneous signifiers ('images, phonemes, fragments of images, fragments or blocks of
writing, schemata, mathematical symbols') to bind the subject of
psychoanalysis and the subject living in history; it functions 'as a
locus of condensation, a site where the two overlap' ('Cinematic
Discourse'). The fourth look is described by Lacan as a gaze which is
not seen but *imagined* by me in the field of the Other. In the filmic
process, it is a look that can constitute the viewer as a *visible* subject,
raising the possibility of being 'overlooked' in one's voyeuristic
pleasure. Directly implicated in both the psychic and the social
aspects of censorship and the law, the fourth look 'introduces the

social into the very act of looking, while remaining an integral part of the textual relations' ('The Fourth Look').

In Willemen's terms, both inner speech and the fourth look are border operations involving mechanisms of translation. Citing C. S. Peirce's description of inner speech as 'a dialogue between different phases of the ego', Willemen notes that the subject of inner speech is both split and *sustained* in the force field of this split '*as* the tension between "I" and "other"', thus enabling social discourse to cohere: inner speech is a 'frontier creature' mediating pressures exerted by conscious, unconscious and preconscious psychic systems, and 'lining' any process of meaning production. 'The Fourth Look' foregrounds the *interactions* of looks at play in the filmic process. These are excluded from most definitions of cinematic specificity just as the fourth look is suppressed by aesthetic strategies allowing viewers to imagine ourselves invisible. In fact, we are 'caught in a complex interaction of different looks from different places', rather than having '*a*' point of view; Amos Gitai's films show that we are mobilised not through point-of-view shots, but through the 'differences between one point of view and another, even within the one shot' ('Bangkok–Bahrain').

Again, the conditions of social discourse are at issue in Willemen's stress on an *interdependent* multiplicity. In the cinema, Eikhenbaum claimed, film metaphor is lined by verbal metaphor for which we must find correspondences (usually without translating again from inner to enunciated speech) in order to understand the film. For Willemen, the lining function of inner speech, rather than an Edenic fantasy of an unsullied visuality, explains the *excess* of images over verbal language. From this he derives a principle that follows through to the project of Third Cinema: if the 'infinite polysemy' of images always produces untranslated or unanalysed material, there can be no *unanalysable* material; no *photogénie*, no ineffable Difference; all languages have their unspoken, but languages do overlap. On the side of the fourth look, our textual mobilisation is always regulated by institutional constraints and incitements. Public concern about pornography, for example, involves 'the institutionalisation of the fourth look within a social formation', while games of taste and cultural distinction entail hierarchical valuations: if shame is attached to those caught looking at porn, 'some would even go so far as to want to be seen looking at an Altman film' ('Letter to John'). To these examples, we could add political conflicts about ethnic and sexual representations whose public circulation is 'overlooked' by the people to whom they claim, or presume, to refer.

Inner speech and the fourth look are frictional processes for Willemen, and they also overlap in his thinking; together, they map something like a theory of cinematic *experience*. Inner speech acts as a 'cement' between text, subject and the social, while the textual and social regulation of the fourth look participates in the ideological process whereby 'bundles of discourses in struggle' are pulled into coherence through institutions. Ideology ('the mode of coherence of a discursive formation') is never treated in *Looks and Frictions* as a purely imaginary play of relations, still less as a message or structure smoothly transmitted from 'texts' to 'subjects'. Ideologies are the everyday product of the mundane, grating labour of institutions. In cinema, inner speech and the fourth look enable this endless unifying labour, this production of cohesion, to continue. At the same time, their translative force ensures that coherence is an unstable process, not a static condition, and that unities take a fragile and provisional form. This is why social formations are dynamic and contestable, and why an effective cultural politics must engage with institutions.

This is also why Willemen's theory of experience is not a theory of cinematic specificity, but a theory of historical *particularity*; a theory not of the consumption of cultural goods but of the production of social change. Just as inner speech is a 'locus of condensation' where different modes of subjectivity overlap, so group as well as individual identities for Willemen are 'riven as well as constituted' by the processes-in-tension that ceaselessly challenge or consolidate social formations: 'identities are the names we give to the more or less stable figures of condensation located at the intersection of psycho-social processes' ('The National'). In the logic of *Looks and Frictions*, it is impossible to oppose 'language' to 'society and history' or to displace one term by the other; there is no such thing as a transcultural or transhistorical 'gaze' to which a twist of difference theory and identity politics must somehow then be applied.

In the theory of looking in Part One, for example, any 'subject production' effected by a film must pass through inner speech to interact with the social and psychoanalytic histories combining 'to produce that particular "individual" in that place at that time'. Part Two examines different social and aesthetic strategies used by filmmakers (Douglas Sirk, Steve Dwoskin, Max Ophuls) who formally explore identities by soliciting a complex interaction with a particular *culture* of 'looking', which they work to inflect or modify in different directions. The essays in Part Three use Bakhtin's concept of the chronotope ('time-space articulations characteristic of particular, historically determined ways of conceptualising social existence') to develop a comparative analysis of the ways that nationally as well as aesthetically diverse cinemas use particular cultural spaces (as representation) to make histories intelligible *for* particular cultural spaces (as a mode of address).

'Complex seeing', a phrase taken from Raymond Williams, is one name for this process of diagnostic understanding that binds filmmaking to film viewing in an interactive mode; as a way of inhabiting a culture, it is irreducible to either pole, 'text' or 'subject', of the

16

viewer's aesthetic. In Willemen's own work on film's ability 'to make us recognise spaces in which history can be seen at work', he represents cinema not primarily as staging a drama of the subject in process, as Stephen Heath has suggested, but as engaging people's experience of *history* in process ('An Avant-Garde for the 90s'). In this space of analysis, an avant-garde cinema is not involved in reproducing the routine shock of the new, but in working to direct and to intensify cinema's power to connect: it is 'a cinema that doesn't just ask the question of cinema historically, but the questions of history cinematically'. It follows that formal research and experimentation are – like careful critical analysis – vital aspects of production for Willemen. Released from the spiral of modernism's search for a redundant specificity, experiment and criticism are fundamental to a cinema that seeks to render 'a particular social situation intelligible' *for* a particular culture; that is, they are fundamental to a responsive and realistic cultural politics.

'*In-between*' is a term which Willemen uses to describe a double movement of translation between aesthetic and social strategies, and cinematic and historical modes of understanding. First sketched in his study of the 'peculiar in-between strategies' of the films of Max Ophuls (in which 'the look is simultaneously subjected to two forces pulling it in different directions'), the idea of an 'in-between' *mode of address* is most explicitly developed in his essay on Amos Gitai's editing. Editing, he notes, is traditionally used and discussed as a way of limiting ambiguity, whereas in cinema it might more accurately be called 'the *orchestration* of meaning'. Like the work of Sembene, Ghatak, Chantal Akerman and David and Judith McDougall, Gitai's films work *with*, as well as upon, the viewer's knowledges and skills, in a register that is 'in-between intellectual and mood manipulation'; orchestrating meanings as an argument, not an order, addressed to the viewer, Gitai's is a 'nudging, essentially friendly kind of discourse' in which the authorial voice is neither authoritarian (as in 'social concern' documentaries) nor effaced (as in 'community' video).

Willemen comments that this method is hard to describe, and he often presents it initially as a *neither/nor* proposition: Gitai's cinema is neither realist nor modernist, neither populist nor formalist, and neither assumes a 'bogus neutrality' nor resorts to the 'flashy enunciation strategies' of stylistic innovation. The descriptive struggle in these passages testifies to the immediacy with which this cinema mobilises Willemen's own sense of the need for film theory to disengage from the dualisms that dominate its history; *Looks and Frictions* is at least partly a book about the inadequacy of current critical rhetorics for engaging with creative contemporary cinema. At the same time, his own rejection of 'neutral' and 'flashy' enunciative modes carries his conviction that a cultural politics must work positively as well as polemically with the culture it presumes to address.

Willemen's authorial voice is never neutral, and he does not engage in the critic's equivalent of the routine pursuit of the new. He uses the conceptual stock-in-trade of metropolitan critical culture (including our interest in borders and translation) in order to nudge his analyses *through* the moment of neither/nor to find another way of thinking about familiar issues.

His work on 'the national' is exemplary. Arguing in-between the poles of the debate traditionally opposing internationalism to nationalism, he frames the issue of national *cinema* as 'primarily a question of address'. On the one hand, he reminds us that the fiscal, legal, and educational systems put in place by national governments have consequences both for social power relations and the kind of cinema they enable; people's lives are shaped by histories made 'nationally specific' by the boundaries that frame the terrain of a particular government's writ. On the other hand, the economic facts of cinematic life dictate that an industrially viable cinema must follow one of two cultural logics: it must either address an international market ('multinational' cinema) or a very large domestic market (a 'national film industry' attuned to the project of nationalism).[17] Both of these logics are homogenising. It follows that only a marginal, poor, dependent and *non*-nationalist cinema can critically engage with the 'multidimensional and multidirectional tensions' of actual social life. So Willemen concludes that a marginal cinema is now, ironically, the *only* form of national cinema available; 'the only cinema which consciously and directly works with and addresses the materials at work within the national cultural constellation'.

The internationalism of Third Cinema and of avant-garde cultural practice can then be rethought in terms of a shared methodological field, not a unifying aesthetic, and a comparative, rather than a common, politics of culture. *Double-outsidedness* connects the otherness involved in inhabiting one's culture (non-belonging, non-identity) to the 'outsidedness' involved in creatively understanding *another* culture. This again entails a movement across borders in two directions, and in-between the poles of a neither/nor: double-outsidedness is neither an act of identification with an image of 'one's own' people (the invisibility option for intellectuals), nor a projective appropriation of identities elsewhere (ventriloquism); the analyst must 'relate to his or her own situation as an other' on both sides of a given border ('The National').

This is why the project of displacing Euro-American conceptions of cinema from the centre of film history and critical theory does not confront them with 'globalised other' imagined as *non*-Euro-American; Third Cinema for Willemen is not an Oshima—Fellini contrast writ large. Nor does it exclude the relations of otherness and the internal histories of political and cultural suppression constituting 'Europe' and 'America' as metropolitan states of mind.[18] The shared

18

methodological field is organised by unequal power relations as well as by cultural difference; for Western critics studying cinemas which are *not* European or American, a doubly-outside position entails a responsibility for the potential effects of their criticism as it circulates back to the national space of those cinemas. Willemen's essay on melodrama and industrialisation, 'The Sirkian System', links up with 'The National' in discussing the example of Western readings of Indian cinema.

Along with its major organising concepts, *Looks and Frictions* also offers practical ways of organising comparative cinema studies as a project of transformation. One is to investigate '*the mode of attention*' proposed by particular films, or scenes in films, in interaction with the actual social constraints, the institutional demands, and the personal as well as cultural practices of looking that any text may encounter. This is a way of displacing 'the subject', 'the gaze' and 'the text' as privileged terms of analysis by asking a different question about historical experience in cinema. When Willemen argues that 'films are read unpredictably, they can be pulled into more or less any ideological space' ('Notes on Subjectivity'), he does not do so in the name of the abstract liberty of the consumer. A mode of attention is always negotiated *in-between* a film and the inner speech of subjects looking (not always only at film) in a real, densely layered social space. An emphasis on inner speech requires film theory to take account of attention (thought) itself as a *mobile* process that 'allows for various degrees of intensity, from day-dreaming to focused concentration' ('Cinematic Discourse').

To do this is to conceptualise cinema in terms of energy, time and mobilising power; in Willemen's vocabulary, filmic utterances are *corridors*, rather than artefacts or vehicles of a singular personal expression. His studies of Sirk, Dwoskin, Ophuls, Gitai and films such as *Maeve* and *So That You Can Live* draw out the descriptive implications for film analysis. Unlike most theorists of consumption, Willemen does not erase the labour and desires of film-makers from his account of cultural practice. He elaborates their efforts to affect the social contexts and historical moments that their work will unpredictably encounter. A corresponding evaluative way of examining cinema's capacity for transformation is provided by the notion of *trajectories* in meaning production. This is what Willemen calls '*the question of directionality*', as distinguished from the question of specificity, in cinema ('An Avant-Garde for the 90s'), and, from 'The Sirkian System' to 'The National', it comes down in practice to asking: in which direction do these discourses seek to *move* their viewers and readers?

The same question can be put to the project in which it arises; to use a phrase from 'The Sirkian System', it has a rebounding, or a boomerang, critical trajectory. *Looks and Frictions* seeks to move its readers away from the search for specificity in part because of the incapacity this induces (even in the sophisticated form of a theory of disarticulated subjectivity) to formulate social and political directions; it supports a movement *away* from the question 'how to speak?' and *towards* a critical practice that begins by asking 'how to understand social existence?'. Taken seriously, this question seeks to move academic film studies towards an engagement with the open historical conflicts taking place on the boundaries of culture *and* in-between institutions. As 'An Avant-Garde for the 90s' makes clear, however, the choice of a direction in these conflicts is never a matter, for Willemen, of an *aesthetics* of transformation for transformation's sake: 'because the social can change in a number of different directions, many of which are not especially desirable'.

VI

To map the coherence of *Looks and Frictions* is difficult only in the sense that it means following the logic of a project that pushes as far as possible our understanding of cinema as a dynamic and creative cultural force. Cinema for Willemen is a mode of action as complex and as varied as the lives of the people who make films and the people whom films address. To acknowledge this energy and complexity is easily, even readily, done; to take it into account in the actual formulation of our work is a much more difficult task. *Looks and Frictions* makes intense demands on academic readers, if only because it asks us to question the formulation, as well as the direction, of our own professional practice.

In this respect, *Looks and Frictions* may well be an untimely publication. As a partial outsider to academic film study, Willemen has the same passionate commitment to the value of criticism, to the ethic of social responsibility, and to the *pleasure* of intellectual work, that he treasures in the Third Cinema manifestos of the 1960s. This commitment is not always shared today by professional academics. As he notes in 'The National', the constant reference to pleasure in discussions of popular culture in Britain and the US has its own restrictive force: the pleasures of *understanding* 'are nearly always outlawed or stigmatised'. On the other hand, any suggestion that intellectuals have a responsibility to exercise their knowledges and skills in the analysis of their social formations can be dismissed as 'elitist' ('Bangkok–Bahrain'). Australian cultural critics are in a slightly different situation. We are encouraged to accept responsibility, even to enjoy analysis, as long as our work has a clear and constructive 'nation-building' purpose; in this context, the value of critique ('unconstructive') is itself called into question by professional critics.

I think that Willemen may be right to see in these developments a movement of de-skilling, and I am persuaded by his rage against the class self-hatred that makes it easy for intellectuals to acquiesce in the denial of their knowledges (a process that many of us protest in a gendered or a racialised context), and even to seek virtue in acquiescence. Among the many things I love about *Looks and Frictions* is Willemen's own love of 'critical lucidity': his struggle, not least between languages, to achieve it by responding with care, with *pleasure*, to a difficult problem or an intricate phase of someone else's thinking; his humour as well as his anger about the ethical and political frailties of 'compliant' intellectual conduct; his refusal to accept that the only way out of academic deep space is a 'malevolently paranoid anti-intellectualism'; his devotion to cinemas that strain our powers of translation and intensify our understanding of social life; his irrepressibly active internationalism; and his practical intelligence in finding ways for the lucidity he values to survive an everyday, grating involvement with cultural institutions.

Untimely or not, *Looks and Frictions* has a practical as well as a lucid contribution to make to the present moment in film studies. As the 1970s/80s story consolidates its power as the dominant professional myth, another spiral of discourse is beginning to take shape: in journals and corridors, there are stories of an overemphasis 'in the 1980s' on Society and History; whispers of a formalist revival, fond memories of 'the signifier'; a restless impatience with literary celebrations of 'the self' parading as political interventions, and a yearning for textual analysis that 'makes the film read like a film'.[19] Willemen's work does not give support to this (or any other) '*back to ...*' movement of redoubling in the disciplinary saga. It does offer a lucid account of the pressures shaping the saga itself, and a set of practical alternatives for thinking cinematic discourse, society and history together.

Instead of adopting a comfortless cynicism about the cycles of academic fashion, Willemen reminds us that 'specificity as fetish' *institutionally* imposes an endless pursuit of lost objects: when Text is the privileged object of analysis, we discover that subjectivity has been lost; once the Subject becomes the favourite term, we find that its history has been lost; with History enshrined as the hottest thing, we complain that textuality has been lost. Deleuze and Guattari call this kind of spiral a *tragic regime of infinite debt*: 'Nothing is ever over and done with in a regime of this kind. It's made for that'.[20] Like their work in philosophy, however (with which *Looks and Frictions* shares a careful reading of Bakhtin), Willemen's revision of film theory challenges that regime's practical capacity to petrify thought in cinema. His effort to think heterogeneity as constitutive at every level of cinematic activity is also an effort to show how a direct engagement with questions of cultural difference and social identity can accompany, and also *sustain*, a rigorous as well as a distinctive theoretical project. Willemen's way of inhabiting a culture is unrepentantly critical as well as irreducibly political. I think we need that right now.

Notes

1. Jim Pines and Paul Willemen (eds), *Questions of Third Cinema* (London: British Film Institute, 1989). This publication followed a conference held in Edinburgh in 1986.
2. See p. 190 below.
3. See Paul Willemen and Behroze Gandhy (eds), *Indian Cinema* (London: British Film Institute, 1980), and Ashish Rajadhyaksha and Paul Willemen, *Encyclopaedia of Indian Cinema* (London and Delhi: British Film Institute and Oxford University Press, 1994).
4. See, for example, Jane Gaines, 'White Privilege and Looking Relations: Race and Gender in Feminist Film Theory', in *Cultural Critique* no. 4 (Fall 1986), pp. 59–79; Judith Mayne, *Cinema and Spectatorship* (London: Routledge, 1993); Norman N. Holland, 'Film Response from Eye to I: The Kuleshov Experiment', in Jane Gaines (ed.), *Classical Hollywood Narrative: The Paradigm Wars* (Durham, NC: Duke University Press, 1992).

    Critical accounts of this story are given in Patrice Petro, 'Feminism and Film History', in *Camera Obscura* no. 22 (1990), pp. 9–26, and in Lesley Stern, 'Remembering Claire Johnston', in *Framework* no. 35 (1988), pp. 114–22.
5. See also Paul Willemen, 'The Films of Akira Kurosawa', in *Screen Education Notes* no. 1 (1971), pp. 34–5, and 'Haile Gerima Interview' in *Framework* nos. 7/8 (1978), pp. 31–5.
6. See Anthony Easthope, *British Post-Structuralism* (London and New York: Routledge, 1998), and Nicholas Garnham, 'Subjectivity, Ideology, Class and Historical Materialism', in *Screen* (London) vol. 20 no. 1 (1979), pp. 121–33.
7. Tom Nairn, 'The English Literary Intelligentsia', in *Bananas*, Emma Tennant (ed.) (London: Blond & Briggs, 1977), pp. 57–83.
8. See Tom Milne and Paul Willemen, *The Aurum Encyclopaedia of Horror* (London, Aurum Press, 1986), and Willemen's contributions to *The Aurum Encyclopaedia of Science Fiction*, Phil Hardy (ed.) (London: Aurum Press, 1984).
9. See Mike Wallington, David Will and Paul Willemen (eds), *Roger Corman: The Millenic Vision* (Edinburgh: Edinburgh International Film Festival, 1970); Claire Johnston and Paul Willemen (eds), *Frank Tashlin* (Edinburgh, EIFF, 1973); Paul Willemen, 'The Fugitive Subject', in *Raoul Walsh*, Phil Hardy (ed.) (Edinburgh: EIFF, 1974); Claire Johnston and Paul Willemen, (eds), *Jacques Tourneur* (Edinburgh: EIFF, 1975); Paul Willemen (ed.), *Pasolini* (London: British Film Institute, 1977); Paul Willemen (ed.), *Ophuls* (London: British Film Institute, 1978).
10. Paul Willemen, 'Remarks on *Screen*', in *Southern Review* (Adelaide), vol. 16 no. 2 (July 1983), pp. 292–311.
11. See Tony Bennett, 'Putting Policy into Cultural Studies', in *Cultural Studies*, Lawrence Grossberg, Cary Nelson and Paula Treichler (eds) (New York and London: Routledge, 1992); Stuart Cunningham, 'TV Violence: the challenge of public policy for Cultural Studies' in *Cultural Studies*, vol. 6 no. 1 (1992), pp. 97–115; Tom O'Regan, '(Mis)taking policy: notes on the cultural policy debate' in *Cultural Studies*, vol. 6 no. 3 (1992), pp. 409–23.
12. Michel Foucault, *Power/Knowledge: Selected Interviews and Other Writings 1972–1977*, Colin Gordon (ed.) (London: The Harvester Press, 1980), p. 127.
13. 'Remarks on *Screen*', p. 298.
14. Gilles Deleuze and Felix Guattari, *Kafka: Toward a Minor Literature*, trans.

Dan Polan (Minneapolis: University of Minnesota Press, 1986), p. 19; *Kafka: Pour une littérature mineure* (Paris: Minuit, 1975).

15. Mikhail Bakhtin, *Speech Genres and Other Late Essays*, trans. Vern W. McGee (Austin: University of Texas Press, 1986), p. 2.

16. See Virginia Nightingale, 'What's "ethnographic" about ethnographic audience research?', in *Australian Cultural Studies: A Reader*, John Frow and Meaghan Morris (eds) (Urbana and Chicago: University of Illinois Press, 1993), pp. 149–61.

17. See Paul Willemen, 'The Making of an African Cinema', in *Transition*, no. 58 (1992), pp. 138–50.

18. On 'Europe', see Ien Ang, 'Dismantling "cultural studies"', in *Cultural Studies*, vol. 6 no. 3 (1992), pp. 311–21, and Dipesh Chakrabarty, 'Provincializing Europe: postcoloniality and the critique of history', in *Cultural Studies*, vol. 6 no. 3 (1992), pp. 337–57.

19. Toby Miller, '(How) Does Film Theory Work?', in *Continuum*, vol. 6 no. 1 (1992), pp. 186–211. See also Geoff Mayer, 'A Return to Form – Russian Formalism and Contemporary Film Practice', in *Metro*, no. 93 (1993), pp. 18–29.

20. Gilles Deleuze and Felix Guattari, *A Thousand Plateaus*, trans. Brian Massumi (Minneapolis: University of Minnesota Press, 1987), p. 113; *Mille Plateaux* (Paris: Minuit, 1980), p. 142.

Part One

Chapter 1

Cinematic Discourse:
The Problem of Inner Speech

The interdependence of the verbal and the visual in the cinema has been asserted, denied and generally commented upon by film theorists. Yet film theory has tended to avoid the issues that such a recognition of interdependence might raise. The problems are indeed extremely complex, and the implications of their investigation could prove to be far-reaching for the ways in which we understand and write about cinema as well as for the production and making of films. Moreover, as I will try to suggest, consideration of the verbal-visual nexus inevitably touches on the status of cinema as an ideological practice, which in turn opens up a host of further problems.

In the face of this, the safest option would be to avoid the problem altogether, or, if the problem cannot be avoided, to regard the orders of figuration and of verbal discourse as irrevocably separate. In this way, no existing notions about the cinematic fact or institution need be upset and theorists need not venture out on a limb too far for comfort.

The common-sense position, shared by dominant and even highly elaborated theoretical discourses, is that language and image shall be regarded as entirely separate, each with its own regimes of specificity. Those who contest the reductionist definition of cinema implicit in the terms 'motion pictures' or 'movies', and who insist on the importance of language as an integral part of cinema, nevertheless maintain a rigorous distinction between the two registers of signification, reducing each to its phenomenal, empirical manifestations.

This chapter starts from the recognition firstly that 'language is the symbolic expression *par excellence* and all other systems of communication are derived from it and presume its existence', and secondly that 'any human communication of non-verbal messages presupposes a circuit of verbal messages without a reverse implication'.[1] This recognition is founded on previous research which demonstrated that verbal signifiers are present in, and have a structuring effect on, the very formation of images (camera angles, the figuration of characters and events in narrative films).[2] At the time, I used the term 'literalisms' to designate clear-cut instances of words marking specific figurations in films. However, the many different types of 'literalism' that could be detected suggested that the problem not only needed further investigation, but that the possibility of there being 'considerations of representability' at work in cinema raised issues which went far beyond the mere classification of different forms of literalisms. What follows constitutes a preliminary reconnaissance of the terrain opened up by the introduction into film theory of the concept of inner speech and considerations of representability and attempts to formulate a few theses which may help to focus the issues.

Some Theses
1. The Audiovisual Fantasy
Questions addressed to the relation between language and image tend to be posed as if these two terms corresponded to homogeneous units which can (or cannot) entertain specific, identifiable relations with each other. However, the first requirement when considering this question is to distinguish between the various dimensions or levels of language, from the phonemic system to the discursive, and between the various aspects of the imaged discourse, from the figurations within the image to their sequential arrangement.

The first distinction to be made is that between the verbal signifier, the word (or morpheme), and its corresponding signified. Although there is no signifier without a signified and vice versa, by now it has been established fairly conclusively that the two sides of the sign enjoy a relative autonomy in relation to each other: they do not operate in the same way nor are they structured in the same way. Their relation, in Jakobson's phrase, is one of coded contiguity. Lacan's rewriting of psychoanalysis insists that the coded contiguity addressed by linguists is in fact a special case of coding related to the domain of the conscious, whereas contiguity operates quite differently in signification in general, as can be deduced from the laws of unconscious signification. Consequently, the concept of the signifier in psychoanalysis has little or nothing in common with that of the signifier in linguistics. In psychoanalysis, any element of language, from the distinctive features of phonemes through phonemes themselves to morphemes and discursive units, from semantic features to concepts and their various forms of 'presentation', can function as a signifier.

Remaining within the domain of linguistics, verbal signifiers can be seen to be present in cinema in specific phenomenal forms either on the soundtrack[3] or as writing within the field of the image. By restricting language to its phenomenal forms, the currently dominant ideologies promote the notion of the audiovisual, asserting that the orders

28

of the figure and of the word are two homogeneous blocks that can only be juxtaposed, confronted or combined, but can never be merged in hybrid forms of signification, interpenetrating each other.

According to this audiovisual scenario, a film can be described as cinematic in inverse proportion to the quantity of verbal – crudely identified with the literary – signifiers empirically present in the text. In addition, positions which imply that cinema is a matter of showing rather than telling, of light patterns rather than signification, are also founded on this same scenario, reducing complex forms of heterogeneity to singular homogeneous essences. These views simply ignore the fact that meaning, an inevitable by-product of any 'mark' in whatever material of expression, is itself a verbal phenomenon; it is part of the domain of semantics. As Roland Barthes pointed out: 'To perceive what a substance signifies is inevitably to fall back on the individuation of a language: there is no meaning which is not designated, and the world of signifieds is none other than that of language.'[4]

By opposing or juxtaposing the 'audio' element to the 'visual' element, the ideology of the audiovisual engineers a psychodramatic confrontation of the figure and the word founded on the excision of meaning from the realm of language in order to maintain the gap between language and image. All relations between the two blocks become entirely external, formal, optional and ultimately dispensable or worse: naturalised and unproblematic.

2. The Presence of the Verbal Signified: Lexicalisation

Perhaps the most obvious examples of verbal language conditioning ostensibly non-verbal sign systems are instances where words or phrases directly model and determine the signs of a secondary system. Although the terms 'primary' and 'secondary modelling system' are somewhat misleading,[5] in this context they seem appropriate. The 'literalism' operative in the representation of 'looking up to' by a low-angle shot is one example. Another is the rendering of the verbal metaphor 'flame' for desire, love, passion, and so on, by some sort of fire in an image or scene containing a couple (usually young and of opposite sexes). A more elaborate example of symbolisation is described by Karel Brusak in his analysis of signs in Chinese theatre.[6] Brusak found that make-up constituted 'a self-contained artificial system. The scheme painted on the actor's face is, in fact, a chart of the moral qualities of the dramatis persona', a system not unlike the typing of heroes and villains in early silent cinema, where white equals good, and dark or black equals bad. Brusak lists an interesting scheme of colours corresponding to specific verbal meanings:

> Black means simplicity, sincerity, courage and steadfastness; red denotes loyalty, honesty and patriotism; crimson is used with old men as a sign for the calm of old age and prudence allied to these

qualities; blue expresses obstinacy, cruelty and pride; yellow indicates ruthlessness, slyness and wiliness; white stands for hypocrisy, irascibility, baseness and viciousness. The extent of the coloured area on the actor's face corresponds to the extent of the moral quality in the character of the dramatis persona. Green is reserved for spirits and devils, gold for gods.

Brusak also comments on other substitutes for verbal expressions:

> Movements of the facial muscles are conventionalised; binding stipulations govern which facial expression should be used to express a given emotion relative to character type and age and the nature, intensity and duration of the feeling.

Movements such as a particular sleeve gesture are 'a sign replacing the verbal wish that the other desist from his greetings', and Brusak stresses that Chinese classical theatre manifests 'a stock of several systems of lexicalised signs'. Although such conventions cannot be regarded as literalisms, they nevertheless constitute examples of the lexicalisation of visual signs, of a kind of verbal score being performed by means of non-verbal signs.

But lexicalisation appears to be only one aspect of the verbal presence in the visual. The other is its structuring function in the dynamic of the textual system as a whole. Brusak's examples of the latter, although they refer to theatre, are equally applicable to the cinema: all that is required to effect the transition is the filming of a performance. His examples are particularly interesting in that they constitute instances of condensation: the apparent absence of a code or 'language' produces deformations or exaggerations in other sign systems. Brusak noticed that on the one hand 'the use of scenic articles linked to costume comprehensibly delineates the character of the personage while obviating the necessity for explanatory passages in the dialogue'. But as the delineation of character is already coded by the make-up, the linked usage of scenic articles and costume presumably functions as a conventional instance of double coding or motivation.

This would suggest that the second aspect of the function is perhaps more important: the replacement of explanatory passages in the dialogue. In cinema such instances are often referred to as 'condensation' – for example, the need to condense a novel into a film. Brusak suggests that what disappears from the dialogue resurfaces in the combination of costume and scenic objects. This de-cathexis of one register accompanied by a hyper-cathexis of another is intensified by a further aspect of the use of costume: as 'Chinese classical theatre is without lighting effects, this gives rise to the magnificence of Chinese theatrical costume', since it must also perform the task of 'forming the scene', of structuring scenic space. The splendour of the costumes is thus the result of two separate but cumulative processes. In it we can trace the 'absence' of lighting and of dialogue. An extension of the argument that immediately suggests itself is that silent cinema can be understood as functioning with similar condensations: heightened stylisation as a result of the 'absence' of audible dialogue, noise and colour. The same applies to the prevalence of dramatic lighting and expressive styles of montage.

These things seem obvious and have been remarked on by many critics and theorists. But the implications of such remarks are seldom pursued. The question is whether the invention of sound cinema made it possible to absorb and accommodate on the soundtrack all possible manifestations of language that could not in some way be located in the image. Was audible speech really the only extra form of language that needed accommodation in the film text? The actualisation of audible speech via the soundtrack did profoundly affect the processes of filmic figuration. But a number of examples of the remaining structuring impact of the verbal can he disengaged fairly easily. In Monte Hellman's *Two-Lane Blacktop* (1971) the last image of the film-strip, representing the final 'burn out', looks as if the celluloid caught fire in the projector. But there are also examples where the presence of the word, or indeed of intersecting chains of verbal signifiers, structures aspects of films which cannot easily be accounted for as one-to-one substitutions of images for words. For instance, in Sam Fuller's *Pickup on South Street* (1953), there is a camera movement which starts with a close shot of Skip/Richard Widmark and Candy/Jean Peters, then the camera backs away and travels to the left while keeping the kissing couple in the centre of the frame. The camera stops moving when the two chains hooked together in the middle of the image vertically divide the frame. After a few seconds, the camera completes the shot by returning to its initial close shot of the couple, still kissing. This 'hook' appears to function in a number of different verbally determined ways: the two are getting hooked on each other, but Skip/Widmark and Candy/Peters are also each 'on the hook' in the film. Moreover, the hook also connects chains from which hang the McGuffin of the film. The apparently pointless camera movement thus hooks into a number of different semantic strands. Finally, Terence Fisher's *Frankenstein and the Monster from Hell* (1973) charts the tribulations of a creature which combines the mind of a scientist, the body of a murderer and the soul of an artist and is torn between these different forces. In the end, the creature is literally torn to pieces. This suggests that the presence of language in cinema cannot be confined to the soundtrack, nor even to the occurrence of specific literalisms.

Although the discourse of the 'hooks' or of the 'tearing apart' is not explicitly spoken, it is nevertheless an integral discourse of the text. In

The Interpretation of Dreams, Freud came across this form of presence of language with such frequency that he discounted the idea that some peculiar symbolising activity of the mind was in operation, and argued that all such 'images' were grounded in folklore, popular myths, legends, linguistic idioms, proverbial wisdom and current jokes – all of them, in fact, verbal activities.[7]

3. Verbal Discourse as Framework

Another type of verbal manifestation, already hinted at with the example of the code of make-up in Chinese classical theatre, is the production of semantic effects apparently unmotivated by any of the signifiers underpinning it. This phenomenon has been explored extensively in terms of sound or colour symbolisms and is brought about through a mapping of relations of resemblance (themselves culturally determined and possibly formed through the process of synaesthetic thinking that characterises early childhood) onto the relation of coded contiguity between signifier and signified. Such a process can be provoked by phonemes or even by component features of phonemes. Taking this type of functioning into account, it is impossible to conceive of any type of 'mark' which is radically a-signifying. As Jakobson wrote: 'Owing to neuro-psychological laws of synaesthesia, phonic oppositions can themselves evoke relations with musical, chromatic, olfactory, tactile etc. sensations.'[8]

This process can also work in the opposite direction. For instance, in view of the multitude of references to music as the a-semantic art *par excellence*, it is of some interest to note that the musicologist Jean Jacques Nattiez identified such a notion as a hangover from mid-nineteenth-century Romanticism.[9] Nattiez insists that it is the social discourses within which music is embedded that determine which sets of selections, of rhythmical patterns and so on, are identified as significant, as constituting the difference between one piece of music and another. Furthermore, all music is shot through with semantic values far exceeding notions of sound symbolism, as can be seen from the various types of musical 'quotes' studied by Zofia Lissa.[10] Jakobson also comments on the phonological, that is, cultural rootedness of musical systems'.[11] This is not to suggest that musical signifiers have stable signifieds and are therefore translatable into a continuous verbal discourse. The point is that it is not possible to abstract music from the discourses within which it functions and in terms of which it is produced. To isolate music from this verbal context and to define it as an autonomous object necessarily means transforming it into 'meaningless' noises or undifferentiated, unorganised sound effects.

Even in the case of music, then, allegedly the most ethereal of arts, verbal discourse is implicated from the outset in its production and perception. What semantisms illustrate is that there is no such thing as an essentially a-signifying practice and that all signifying practices, regardless of the matter of expression involved, are embedded in and subject to the social discourses that surround them. As Monique Plaza has argued:

> Nothing for human beings escapes the symbolic ordering of language. [E]ven if one postulates the inscription in the archaic Ucs level of a thing presentation (mother's body) [t]his becomes psychically meaningful through the inscription of a word presentation 'mother's body'. And, precisely, the fantasy about the mother's body can only appear as a psychic production at the point where the psychic apparatus assimilates the significance that another gives to the utterance 'mother's body'. All these psychic elaborations of the body of the mother rely necessarily on this signifying system limited by a language. When psychoanalysis refers, for example, the castration complex back to an anatomical observation, it is making a theoretical error since it postulates that a thing presentation could be inscribed by a look outside any signifying system.[12]

Meaning, that is, that language cannot be escaped or bracketed, although it can be repressed. Interestingly, and predictably, artistic practices that are claimed to be specific and materialist (in the sense of 'oriented towards their materials of expression') are always accompanied by verbal discourse, at times verging on logorrhoea. What is thrown out of the door returns, with a vengeance, through the window: verbal language has never fared so well as in the so-called civilisation of the image. It is instructive to read the writings of painters such as Mondrian to discover the way in which the discursive 'programme' determines the figurations produced. It emerges that the painterly practices are closely dependent on the definition of which 'painterly' discourses to reject, transform or develop. In this sense, verbal discourse frames a given painting in the very moment of its production. Paintings must be understood simultaneously – and in a hierarchical order to be determined in each case – in terms of the function and place certain painterly practices have in 'painting', and on the other hand, the function and place they have within a discursive formation that includes and locates 'painting' as an art form. The issue to be analysed in each specific instance is the interaction between those three terms. Furthermore, due consideration must be given to the fact that such a complex dialectic is itself always embedded in, and determined by, the encompassing dialectic at work between the three instances that make up the social formation: the ideological, the economic and the political, with the latter providing the articulation of the two others.

In view of this extreme complexity, it is necessary, if only for methodological reasons, also to chart the trajectories of specific component elements or partial sets of interrelating elements. And in this respect, formalist analyses have been and still can be very productive, as semiology has demonstrated. The point at issue there is the place and function of 'formalisms' in any given situation: which discourses or methods of analysis they displace or oppose. It is a question of avoiding the hypothesis of formalisms as scientific, non-ideological, and so on, and of always thinking of an analytical practice as a social, historical production of meaning.

4. Language and Cinema

The most systematic account of the location of language in cinema within a semiological model has been formulated by Christian Metz in his book *Language and Cinema*.[13] For Metz, language is present in cinema as recorded phonetic sound and as writing in the image. As such it covers two of the five matters of expression whose combination constitutes the specificity of cinematic language, the other three being recorded noise, recorded musical sound and the moving photographic image. Metz also gives due consideration to the semantic aspect of language, but confines it to the codes of content which, although an integral part of any film, are not specific to cinema. His conception of cinema is complex and involves both a recognition of languages as techno-sensoral unities and as analytical constructs, that is, as codes or collections of codes at work within these units.

Nevertheless, there is no place within Metz's semiology for hybrid forms of signification, nor for a consideration of signification as a discursive process in terms of subject productions and positions. That such processes need to be addressed is signalled by Metz's introduction of the concept of filmic writing to account for the displacements, transformations, substitutions and overlaps affecting the play of codes in any given signifying network and any particular text. But such displacements are not simply products of random interactions between autonomous and homogeneous codes or homogeneous techno-sensoral unities. As Metz's notion of filmic reading suggests, there is something at work in signification which exceeds the interaction of semiologically defined sets of codes. Metz goes so far as to speak of the destruction of codes in signification, referring to the work of Julia Kristeva as a possible source for an understanding of that process. Presumably, when he cursorily inserts Kristeva's name into the space between cinematic language and filmic writing, he is seeking to invoke her concern with the function of Ucs processes and with questions of subject production in processes of representation. In his more recent writing, Metz concentrates on precisely the shifts and transformations effected in the domain of semiology as a result of the encounter with psychoanalysis. The problem of language re-emerges, significantly, as the question of the very possibility of an articulation between semiology and psychoanalysis.

34

This issue is posed rather interestingly in the collection of essays by Metz entitled *Le Signifiant imaginaire*.[14] At one point, in an essay first published in 1977, Metz states that the maintenance of a rigorous dividing line between the orders of discourse and of figuration in effect prevents any possible articulation of semiology and psychoanalysis. Nevertheless, in another essay included in the book, this time a piece first published in 1975, he approves of that very separation, stating that 'the Ucs doesn't think, doesn't produce a discourse, but is figured in images'. In this opposition, images pertain to the domain of the Ucs, while language belongs exclusively to the secondary processes, themselves identified with the Pcs/Cs system. The possibility of an agency or instance operating on both sides of the divide between the Ucs and the Pcs/Cs systems receives no mention. The implicit recognition that the crucial problem here is exactly the way in which the Ucs works through into the Pcs/Cs systems is presented by Metz in the form of questions: how to understand censorship?[15] or in terms less likely to reactivate the idea of an absolute barrier: how to understand resistance? This question radically shifts the whole problematic set up by the concepts of cinematic language and filmic writing. No longer is the relation between them analogous to that between language system (*langue*) and speech. Now the absolute insistence on the homogeneity of the matters of expression inevitably becomes a little less absolute, and the cinematic codes begin to occupy the place of the symbolic in psychoanalysis. The question of how to think of resistance can also be reformulated as how to think of the articulation between heterogeneous orders, each of which is itself far from homogeneous, in that the symbolic and imaginary always coexist in a necessary simultaneity without any clearly demarcated dividing lines. The question of resistance is also that of the join between the Ucs and Pcs/Cs systems, that of a discourse which articulates, in its very texture, thing- and word-presentations. The fact that the rest of Metz's book can be read as a systematic skirting of that question in no way diminishes the merit of having posed it in the first place.

The problem appears to be that Metz continues to think of cinematic language in terms of techno-sensoral unities. Whenever he addresses the status of verbal language and its relation to the Ucs, he discusses the matter in terms of equations between thing-presentations, film images, the Ucs and the imaginary; word-presentations are equated with the spoken and written appearance of words, without any transitional discourse being considered as articulating both orders. Equally, the possibility of phonemes or phrases having a structuring impact on the formation and sequencing of images is held in suspense or reduced to the viewer's socially determined ability to identify iconic figures as objects, that is, the code of iconic naming.

Although he repeatedly refers to the work of Lacan, certain fundamental aspects of that work appear to be left out of the picture. The first is the basic notion of the repressed signifier, with the subsequent point that an image, part of an image or even a series of images can be produced by the repression of a verbal signifier. Such an idea cannot be accommodated in a semiological framework, where a signifier is always manifested in one and only one matter of expression, ruling out hybrid formations.

The notion that the repressed signifier 'can only give itself up under the cover of images',[16] when applied to cinematic discourse, infringes the absolute distinction between language and the moving photographic image. Secondly, the idea that 'a symbol is only an operator in a structure, a means of effecting the distinctive oppositions necessary to the existence of a significant structure'[17] abolishes the definition of the signifier in terms of material specificity, making it into any 'mark' of difference, into the support of the process of differing. This allows for the thinking of signification as operating with heterogeneous signifiers. It also renders it impossible to equate verbal language as such with the symbolic: it is the system of language, imprinted, true enough, by the encounter with the word, which defines the symbolic, but the presence of verbal language is not an automatic indicator of the symbolic, nor is its absence necessarily equatable with the register of the imaginary. What is at stake here is precisely the possibility of a discourse which, although structured 'like' a language, nevertheless works with the widest variety of signifiers, and thus can be sited at the join of the Ucs and Pcs/Cs systems, the site of the processes of resistance.

The materiality of the signifier does not become irrelevant, but merely becomes a second order factor affecting the movement of signification. The materiality of the 'defiles of the signifier', to use Lacan's phrase, affects the resistance encountered by drives and thus inflects the signifying process. But as signifiers are products of overdetermination, what is resistance in relation to one component drive may be facilitation in relation to another. In this way, the question of censorship that Metz posed as crucial for any theory of signification is reactivated along a different route: this time, what is at issue is the resistance of the discourse as opposed to the intra-psychic resistance of the subject. Both types of resistance have to do with transportation (*Entstellung*) of signifiers, that is to say, with the movement of signification.

5. Inner Speech and the Ego
What emerges from these considerations is that it is necessary to think of the articulation of textual systems both with social discourses and with Ucs signification in terms of a discursive form grounded in verbal language but able to operate with a heterogeneous signifying chain.

The function of linguistic processes in the articulation of the Ucs and the social has been addressed by means of concepts such as discourse and the notion of subject production, with the discourse of the Other (the symbolic) producing inescapable subject positions. This conceptual apparatus has been deployed primarily to suggest a unilateral determination by 'the' signifier of 'the' signifying chain pinning subjects in specific positions. In this fundamentally idealist view, subjects are abstracted entities adrift on a sea of discursiveness, helplessly buffeted between discourses whose effectiveness operates via the Ucs and is thus by definition removed from any possible area of social struggle. A more nuanced theoretical position insists that the processes of subject production are always already in the social and thus avoids conflating social determination with determination by the Ucs. But although this position recognises that it is necessary to think of the articulation between heterogeneous orders (the inextricable co-presence of real, symbolic and imaginary in any discursive process), it nevertheless stops short of addressing the terms of that 'embedding' in the social in a way which would open up the possibility of concerted action, that is, struggle against specific forms of social organisation.

A third position argues that it is necessary to start from the need for struggle, rather than from the effectiveness of the signifier. Ideologies are seen as contradictory unities which, via the effectiveness of institutions, try to hold subjects in/to determinate positions. But it is also specified that this process of subject production is determined by extra-discursive factors as well as discursive ones.[18] Although such a model comes closer to an understanding of subjectivity in history which does not automatically block any possible concept of struggle, it is nevertheless unsatisfactory in that it still relies exclusively on a model of psychic functioning reduced to a simple opposition between the Ucs and the Pcs/Cs systems. As such, it drastically devalues or even discounts Freud's second topography of instances (Ego, Id, Superego) which must be superimposed on the first one. Laplanche has pointed out that:

> what is currently known as ego psychology is, in fact, a conception which makes of the ego an agency of the total person, differentiated [e]ssentially as a function of problems of adaptation. [But] ego psychology has the merit – or at least the ambition – of wanting to re-establish the bridge between psychoanalysis and the investigations and discoveries of non-psychoanalytic psychology.[19]

That ego psychology has proved incapable of providing the means to think about the articulation between the subject and the social, substituting instead a notion of adaptation, has unfortunately also discredited the ambition. Opposition to ego psychology has, in the area of the theory of ideological practices, facilitated and legitimised the formulation of an equally crude position: ideologism, using terms such as 'concept', 'discourse' and 'subject' as fetishes to exorcise any possibility of ideological struggle. In its place is posed the total autonomy of the discursive (the signifying chain pinning subjects in determinate positions). In fact, any argument suggesting that the effect of the social on the subject is restricted to the impact on the Ucs of the language into which a child is born, overlooks the specific function of the ego as a psychic instance, formed and intervening in its own right at a later stage. Even if the social is re-invoked in a second movement as determining the constraints within which discourses are formulated and subjects put into place, the relay of thought processes and their specific function and mode of operation finds no space in that model of discourse production. In this sense, the necessary attack on ego psychology would seem to have resulted in a repression or bracketing of the ego as an active instance in the construction of subjectivity.

The ego is a concept relating to that aspect of the dialectic between 'I' and 'other' which, via complex processes of identification (that is, displacements), installs a force field, a reservoir of libidinal energy, a field that binds the free flow of sexual energy and as such can come to be regarded as an active agency. As Laplanche puts it, the ego is a:

> specific formation [that] enters into conflicts as a participant by virtue of its double function: an inhibiting function or a function of binding [a]nd a defensive function, [t]hrough the dual modes of pathological and normal defence. [It is] a kind of relay object, capable of passing itself off, in a more or less deceptive and usurpatory manner, as a desiring and wishing subject.[21]

Furthermore:

> If it is not forgotten that what is at stake here are chains of ideas, the ego turns out to be what introduces into the circulation of fantasy a certain ballast, a process of binding which retains a certain energy and causes it to stagnate in the fantasmatic system, preventing it from circulating in an absolutely free and mad manner. Such is the appearance of the secondary process.[22]

But Laplanche immediately goes on to warn that there is no identity between the secondary process and the ego properly speaking (if we keep in mind the Ucs aspect of the ego). This leads to a distinction concerning the ego between a 'permanent portion' and a 'changing one'. A related distinction that will be important later in this chapter is L. Vygotsky's differentiation between meaning as a relatively stable core and sense as its shifting, mobile periphery.

The 'permanent portion' of the ego concerns that part of the structure which has to do with the Cs system, while the changing part (Freud invoked the image of the mobile contours of an amoeba, contracting and expanding) relates to the Pcs but also to the Ucs. The functions allotted to the ego include 'not only the control of mobility and perception, reality testing, anticipation, the temporal ordering of the mental processes, rational thought, and so on, but also refusal to recognise the facts, rationalisation and compulsive defence against instinctual demands'.[23] This suggests that the ego functions as the site where heterogeneous systems separated by the bar of repression and contradictions are articulated, or that the ego is a 'frontier creature', in Freud's phrase.

In *The Interpretation of Dreams*, Freud's account of the functioning of the mental apparatus stresses the topographical distinction between the Ucs and the Pcs/Cs systems: the former working with thing-presentations, the latter with word-presentations. In between the two is located that particular effect of resistance Freud called censorship. In the light of the second topography, involving the notion of the ego, such a rigorous demarcation begins to appear less absolute. Not that the barrier is removed or weakened, but a force field is instituted at the join of these systems, a field that extends – unequally – on either side of the barrier. The crossing of, and the consequent deformations operated by, this barrier of repression have been described in terms of a movement from a given medium to another one with a different refraction index.[24] This site where resistance works over the join between thing- and word-presentations, where ideational representatives can encounter 'their' predicates according to the transformational laws imposed by the necessity of articulating contradictions and heterogeneity, is precisely the site of the ego. Laplanche describes the passage from one side to the other in these terms:

> The transition of an Ucs idea to the Pcs/Cs level: the verbal representatives are superimposed through a kind of addition, on the Ucs representative. [T]his does not mean that a Cs sentence duplicates an Ucs sentence as its translation, but rather that isolated representatives individually cathected, induce locally around each of them an energy field accounting for the phenomenon of attention.[25]

In this context, attention itself is a mobile process in that it allows for various degrees of intensity, from day-dreaming to focused concentration, from discursive registers on the periphery of the Ucs to different processes of thought and inner speech, and to consciously articulated, logical, grammatical, verbal discourse. It is in this space that the repressed signifier that gave itself up in the Ucs under the guise of an image, re-finds a verbal signifier. This movement may pass through indeterminate stages, and the signifier(s) re-found will not be the same as the signifier(s) repressed, because of the intervention of resistance and refraction. Suffice it to say that the re-found signifier(s) will bear the mark of that transit, which is the process of signification itself. This means that the registers of discourse that operate in the site of the ego may be unequally or incompletely secondarised. The degree of the mix between word- and thing-presentations will depend on various factors (real or desired proximity to the Ucs, the nature of the discourses in play and the degrees of resistance they activate, degrees of 'attention', possible resistance to word-presentations *per se*, and so forth), but both will always be co-present, like the often cited recto and verso of a piece of paper. It is also important to realise that such registers of discourse operating at the join of Ucs and Pcs/Cs systems must always be structures in dominance working with different types of signifiers, otherwise no transition process would be thinkable. Just as the Ucs persists in all discursive practices, so does verbal language, even when repressed.

The discourse of attention, thought, has been conceptualised as inner speech (intra-psychic speech, in Jakobson's terminology). Inner speech, like the ego, is a frontier creature. But without its function of binding subject and text in sociality, no signification would be possible other than delirium. The secondarising work of inner speech, providing the initial stabilisation of the signifying process according to those contradictory demands the ego is there to bind, constitutes thought. Thus inner speech constitutes the activity associated with an agency which holds sets of contradictions in socially as well as unconsciously determined balances of forces. In this light, the most perceptive characterisation of inner speech was provided by C. S. Peirce: 'a dialogue between different phases of the ego'.[26] This formulation also has the merit of reinforcing the notion that the ego is produced as an imaginary, or rather a contradictory, unity in the dialectic of 'I' and 'other'.

6. *Theories of Inner Speech*
It should be stressed that inner speech is not to be regarded as speech by the ego. The ego is not the subject of inner speech, nor of any other discourse for that matter. As Peirce made clear, the subject of inner speech is split; it is sustained in that split as the tension between 'I' and 'other'. This suggests that it may be misleading to call inner speech a discourse. It might more accurately be described as a process of signification providing the conditions of existence for any social discourse. Consequently, the production of subject positions via discourses is necessarily always doubled by this particular process. Inner speech lines (as the lining of a jacket helps prevent it coming apart at the seams) any process of meaning production, both at the stage of text manufacturing and of reading.

This lining accounts to some extent for the difference between the subject-image produced by a text and the historical, biological subject which presided over its manufacture. Neither is more 'authentic' than the other. If the (self-)image constructed through discourse never coincides with the subject's sense of identity, this is not solely because that identity is the image of an other, but also because it is split in itself, caught up in an unceasing dialogic process. Perhaps it would be possible to consider the production of a (self-)image through discursive practices as an attempt to halt that oscillatory dialogue, to freeze it, to produce a signifier that marks the gap within the structure of the 'differential subject' of inner speech. Nevertheless, inner speech remains a fairly enigmatic concept. Jakobson wrote that:

> Besides the more palpable, interpersonal face of communication, its intra-personal aspect is equally pertinent. Thus, for instance, inner speech, astutely conceived by Peirce as an 'internal dialogue' and until recently rather disregarded in linguistic literature, is a cardinal factor in the network of language and serves as one's connection with the self's past and future.[27]

Some of these terms are questionable, but the thrust of the remark is clear enough.

The importance of the concept of inner speech for cinema was first raised by Boris Eikhenbaum in an essay called 'Problems of Film Stylistics'[28] published in 1927. Eikhenbaum was concerned to account for the way in which filmic writing – film texts – can be understood. He argued that the sequential arrangement of images produced meaning only in relation to a verbal discourse functioning as a constant ground against which the filmic was marked off or profiled. Thus the verbal in a sense becomes the screen upon which the film is projected, a mapping of the two producing the particular regime of signification. Eikhenbaum called the verbal discourse a doubling, a lining of the film, with inner speech or thought being opposed to manifested spoken or written language which is the stuff of social speech and literature. He suggested that a film viewer must:

> perform the complex mental labour of coupling the frames (construction of film phrases and film periods) [o]r else he will not understand anything. [P]erception and understanding of a motion picture is inextricably bound up with the development of inner speech which makes the connections between separate shots.

The main function of inner speech would thus reside in language's capacity to construct superordinate structures rather than in its lexical aspect. Eikhenbaum is less concerned with the code of iconic

41

naming, with the lexicalisation of the image, than with its ability to construct a network of relations.

In contrast, Metz addressed himself to the problem of un-enunciated speech in an essay entitled, significantly, 'The Perceived and the Named'.[29] He concentrated exclusively on what psycholinguists would call 'labelling', concluding that 'the perceptual object is a constructed unit, socially constructed, and also (partly) a linguistic unit' in that language (*langue*) permanently accompanies vision, ceaselessly glossing it, either 'aloud or simply by calling the phonetic signifier to mind'. Such a notion of inner speech reduces it to the unspoken but formally identical replica of phonetically enunciated speech. This, as Vygotsky noted,[30] is to come close to a behaviourism which considers thought a reflex inhibited in its motor part. Although Metz is too perceptive a phenomenologist to allow himself to get bogged down in the morass of reflexology, his code of iconic labelling appears to be haunted by the mythical opposition between thinkers and doers that helped install behaviourism as an ideology in certain social formations. This ghost in Metz's discourse (in the sense that one talks of a ghost image in a faulty television transmission) is perhaps produced by the temporary convergence of the positivist discursive current shared by semiology and behaviourism.

For his part, Eikhenbaum avoids this trap and never reduces inner speech to endophony, the soundless enunciation of words. In his discussion of film metaphor, he specifies that:

> Film metaphor is entirely dependent on verbal metaphor. The viewer can understand it only when he possesses a corresponding metaphoric expression in his own verbal baggage [but] the film metaphor is not realised in the consciousness of the viewer to the point of a complete verbal statement.[31]

Inner speech becomes the cement between text, subject and the social. As such, this concept of inner speech inserts an extra discourse into the dialectic of text and subject, opening up a different way of thinking about subject production. The subject production effected by the text, defined as a set of chains of signifiers in determinate relations with clusters of semantic features, will have to pass through inner speech, itself a discursive process determined by the social and the psychoanalytic histories that combined to produce that particular 'individual' in that place at that time. In this respect, inner speech indeed becomes, in Eikhenbaum's words, 'one of the most important problems in cinematic theory'.

Eikhenbaum's intimation that inner speech differs functionally from manifested language was reformulated two years later, in 1929, in the *Theses* published by the Prague linguistic circle. The *Theses* corrected Eikhenbaum's assumption that 'external' speech predominates in everyday life, pointing out that for most speakers manifested speech is far less frequent than the use of linguistic forms in thought processes. Nevertheless, the *Theses* tended to reintroduce the notion that inner speech was formally equivalent to manifested speech in spite of Eikhenbaum's rejection of this notion. For Eikhenbaum:

> the very act of thinking consists in the organisation of our inner speech along specific modalities and conditions, [t]o the extent that we sometimes find it hard to translate an internal discourse into an external one, as if the difference between the respective codes raised the kind of problems and difficulties of translation analogous to the ones encountered in translation proper.[32]

Although endophony, the calling to mind of the phonetic signifier, can occur in inner speech, the latter cannot be reduced to the former. It also works with images, phonemes, fragments of images, fragments or blocks of writing, schemata, mathematical symbols, and so on; in short, it works with all the things that can work as ideational representatives in the psychoanalytic sense, as well as with word-presentations in their phonetic and graphic forms. Some of these functional differences between the two 'languages' become clearer when we relate them to Jakobson's representation of social communication, involving an addresser who can exchange messages with an addressee given that they are in contact, if they share a code and are aware of the context within which the whole operation takes place. In inner speech, addresser and addressee are the same or at least intra-personal, which means firstly that the context need not be taken into account, that there is no need for redundancies and repetitions, elaborate syntagmatic arrangements and so on; secondly, that there is no necessity for metalinguistic verifications of the code or even to maintain the process within a given code; and thirdly, that the phatic function, ascertaining contact, can be dispensed with. Of course, this does not mean that none of these things occurs in inner speech: merely that they are not indispensable to it.

Such modifications prompted Vygotsky to concur with the Prague linguists in stressing that 'Inner speech must be regarded, not as speech minus sound, but as an entirely separate speech function',[33] and Jakobson went so far as to speak of a different grammar being involved. Vygotsky continued to point out that: 'Inner speech appears disconnected and incomplete. [I]t shows a tendency towards an altogether specific form of abbreviation: namely, omitting the subject of a sentence and all words connected with it, while preserving the predicate.' Vygotsky is overstating the case here a little, because words connected with the subject (for example shifters) do in fact persist in inner speech. But this dominant tendency towards predication and condensation does explain to some extent why inner speech can so freely integrate thing-presentations in its chain of signifiers, a facility it shares with cinema. This convergence also favours the production of the prevalent misconception that verbal discourse is absent from imaged discourse because some of their signifying configurations appear to overlap.

In his discussion of the relations between thought and language, Vygotsky makes some interesting observations. Firstly, he distinguishes between thought, word meaning (that is, signifieds) and speech (the phonetic or graphic practice of linguistic signs). This tripartite order calls to mind Hjelmslev's triad of matter, substance and form, although there are some crucial and productive divergences. Metz summarised and clarified Hjelmslev's triad in the following terms:

> The material [r]epresents the originally amorphous something in which the form is inscribed [a]nd the substance is that which appears when one projects the form onto the material as a stretched string projects its shadow onto an uninterrupted surface.[34]

For Vygotsky the synaesthetic registration of perceptions (translated in the American version as 'heaps') appears to function as the semantic matter, 'word meanings' or 'concepts' operate as the semantic form, while thought becomes analogous to substance, the locus of the organising and structuring impact/imprint of language on what Freud calls memory traces. Vygotsky's placing of 'speech' in relation to 'word meanings' and thought emphasises the coded contiguity between signifier and signified, thus articulating thought with the phonemic system, that is, with the spoken discourse, the Word into which we are born.

Jakobson's phrase of coded contiguity is a particularly happy one for two reasons. In the first place, it evokes the possibility of variations in coding or even of radically different codes obtaining between signifier(s) and signified(s), while at the same time it allows the possibility of the coding established in verbal language to operate in relation to 'non-verbal' or mixed signifying systems. In this way, 'literalisms', the use of non-verbal stand-ins for verbal signifiers, a result of repression, can be understood as straightforward substitutions of signifiers while the coding of the contiguity is maintained. The change in signifier does however make the sign available for discursive practice in a different manner, allowing it to circulate according to the rules of a different signifying regime and thus satisfying the requirements of resistance. Secondly, Jakobson's phrase is a useful reminder that the relation between signifier and signified is by no means arbitrary, but is firmly grounded in the social.

The most productive aspect of the difference between Hjelmslev and Vygotsky, at least in this context, relates to the way in which they conceive of the 'matter' onto which form is projected. For Hjelmslev, matter is an amorphous but nevertheless homogeneous entity, while for Vygotsky it is a-signifying but by no means necessarily amorphous or homogeneous. In this way, the material can be regarded as being constituted by the free interplay of sensory registration with Ucs drives, the *chora* in Kristeva's usage (a term she borrows, ironically, from Plato). The form is then provided by the language into which a child is born, and the substance by the imprint of that language on the *chora*. The production of this imprint is itself to be understood in two phases, logically distinct but continuous in practice: firstly, the registration of difference and secondly, the organisation of differences into a symbolic system, the 'becoming meaningful' of the process of differentiation.

The gradual nature of this process through which language as a symbolic system is anchored in the *chora* not only produces the ground of signification, it also accounts for the slack in the system, the lack of fit between the code of language and that which it organises. This lack of fit, this being out of true, is reinforced by the fact that the material, the *chora*, is itself not amorphous but constitutes an interplay of perception and drives, a protean mass traversed by libidinal currents setting up energy fields, force lines which both resist and facilitate the structuring impact of language, the join of signifiers and memory traces. In this movement towards coded contiguity, the constituent features of both signifiers and signifieds (distinctive features and phonemes in the former, semantic features or 'atoms of meaning' in the latter) still enjoy a relative autonomy and operate in a dispersed form. Entry into the symbolic then becomes the recognition of a social relation *vis-à-vis* the code of language, an ability to place 'I' in language, an ability that will always operate in the face of and against the pressure of the process of Kristeva's notion of *signifiance*, the pressure of the *chora*. In other words, the practice of coded contiguity in language will always retain the traces of that movement towards/ into the symbolic. In the semantic structure of a language such traces produce an unstable field around signifieds, a floating periphery of sense around meaning, the cathexis of which makes the chains of signifiers veer off, activating new semantic clusters, and so on. Such a dialectic between signifier and signified determines the production of ideational representatives at the intersection of multiple strands of signification. This process of veering off, of limited drift, has been theorised in terms of the work of the primary processes which, according to Lacan and Metz, are none other than the laws of signification itself.

Vygotsky's second major distinction, that between sense and meaning, can thus be seen to foreshadow the discoveries of structural semantics. Meaning is defined as the lexically fixed core(s) of a signified, its most stable aspect(s), while sense encompasses all the possible semantic features clustering around such a core. In social speech the meaning functions as the dominant element, while in inner speech – the frontier creature – words are saturated with sense:

> Inner speech works with semantics, not phonetics. The specific semantic structure of inner speech also contributes to abbreviation. The syntax of meanings in inner speech is no less original than its grammatical syntax. [There is a] preponderance of the sense of a word over its meaning. [T]he sense of a word [is] the sum of all the psychological events aroused in our consciousness [and Ucs – *PW*] by the word. It is a dynamic, fluid, complex whole, which has several zones of unequal stability. Meaning is only one of the zones of sense, the most stable and precise zone.[35]

'Inner speech is to a large extent thinking in pure meanings. It is a dynamic, shifting, unstable thing, fluttering between word and thought.'[36] Although Vygotsky dismisses psychoanalysis as mystic idealism, his conception of inner speech is perfectly compatible with Freud's description of the way chains of thought (that is, isotopies) can function in dream processes. Furthermore, the projection of Vygotsky onto Hjelmslev, the notion that thought represents the imprint of language on the a-signifying *chora*, helps to resolve some ambiguities relating to Freud's notion of memory traces, which are at times defined as mere registration, at other times as registration structured under the impact of signifiers (in the psychoanalytic sense of the term). Vygotsky also mentions that 'thought itself is engendered by motivation, i.e. by our desires and needs, our interests and emotions'.[37] In psychoanalytic terms, this can be theorised in terms of the drives determining the pattern of the criss-crossing networks of isotopies traced by the movement of ideational representatives in 'unconscious' thought. However, it must be pointed out that Vygotsky's theory has no concept of resistance other than that offered by the 'adult language' into which the child is born and to which it must submit, a process represented as a linear development of maturation culminating in the fantasy of a language of pure reason. Repression does not appear to exist within his conceptual apparatus, although he does allow for the survival of 'infantile' modes of thought in 'adult' usages of language. Another major point is that for Freud it is the process of signification itself that matters, and not the contents involved as such. The dream work, not the dream thoughts, constitutes the essence of the dream.

7. Avant-garde Cinema and Language

Vygotsky's collaborator and disciple, A. R. Luria, continued the investigation of the connections between language and thought, concentrating on the empirical verification of the structuring function of language. In his book *The Mind of a Mnemonist*,[38] he reports on a study, conducted over a number of years, of a man who was able to perform the most astonishing feats of memory. It emerged that the man, referred to as '5', transcoded all verbal information into visual figures with due regard for the 'considerations of representability'. Nonsense words or foreign words he would transform through a system of lines and colours corresponding to the phonemic structure of the word in question, producing images akin to 'abstract' paintings. '5' also reported that he remembered his childhood in terms of vague synaesthetic sensations. Proto-linguistic (that is, pre-oedipal) childhood was dominated by splashes of colour corresponding to the perception of phonetic sounds.

Later, with the acquisition of language, figurative images would form as distinct, delineated units, but any imprecision in, or interference with, his perception of phonetic sounds, such as unclear pronunciation, overlapping voices or an extraneous noise blotting out a sound, would produce blurs, splashes or puffs of smoke in his ideational representatives. Also, the ideational representatives evoked would set off their own chain of thought and, along the lines of specific isotopies, lead back to scenes from his childhood. The coincidence of this production of clearly delineated images with the acquisition of language is worth noting. But the most important element here is the impact that phonemes are seen to have on the figuration of images, demonstrating that language is present in images not just in the form of repressed/transformed words or as the concatenations of semantic features into isotopies, but also as transformed phonemes.[39]

A second study, this time of a soldier who had been shot in the head, proves equally illuminating. Luria writes that:

> He referred to his major disability as a loss of speech memory. [E]ach word was part of a vital world to which it was linked by thousands of associations; each aroused a flood of vivid and graphic recollections. To be in command of a word meant he was able to evoke almost any impression of the past, to understand relationships between things, conceive ideas and be in command of his life. And now all this had been obliterated.[40]

Eventually, the soldier recovered enough to be able to write sentences. He informed Luria that he was:

> in a kind of fog all the time, like a heavy half-sleep. My memory is a blank. I can't think of a single word. All that flashes through my head are some images, hazy visions that suddenly appear and just as suddenly disappear giving way to fresh images. [W]hatever I do

remember is scattered, broken down into disconnected bits and pieces.[41]

Luria also noted that for the soldier, space made no sense and lacked stability. The similarity of such a loss of language to some experimental films is striking, to say the least.

What emerges from Luria's work, among other things, is that any firm distinction between the orders of discourse and figuration must be discarded as a fantasy conveying the wish for an Edenic state of 'signification' unsullied by the requirements of the symbolic, a world where difference doesn't exist: in short, a desire to repress language. Luria accounts for the imbrication of language and images in terms of the neuro-physiological structure of the brain, and his comments are of considerable interest, even though Freud explicitly located the production of ideational representatives on 'another scene', adding: 'We may, I think, discount the possibility of giving the phrase an anatomical interpretation and supposing it to refer to physiological cerebral localisation or even to the histological layer of the cerebral cortex.'[42]

However, consideration of the neuro-physiological development of the brain is not entirely irrelevant in this context. It seems reasonable to assume that processes associated with various aspects of the brain do leave memory traces which are available for reactivation (on 'another scene') under certain circumstances. The brain functions appear to fall into three main stages:

The primary visual cortex [b]reaks down images of the external world into millions of constituent parts. The secondary visual cortex converts the individual features of objects perceived into complete, manifold structures ... [d]ynamic patterns. The function of the tertiary cognitive part of the cortex is to combine the visual, tactile-motor and auditory-vestibular sections of the brain. These sections are not even fully developed in the human infant but mature gradually and become effective by age four to seven.[43]

As the ideational activity associated with these different functions must leave memory traces, it follows that, for instance, the repression of language, which is associated with the tertiary regions, may reactivate 'thought' problems. In this way, the symptoms manifested by the brain-damaged soldier (trouble with spatial relations, fragmentation, blurring, images flickering meaninglessly, reduction to blank memory-screens, and so on) can be represented by anyone who, although not in the least brain-damaged, feels compelled to reactivate pre-linguistic processes of signification.[44]

Some Problems

1. The Image as Secondary Elaboration

Because of the connection between inner speech and the ego, one could say that one of inner speech's functions is also to resist the pressure of the Ucs. As Roland Barthes noted in relation to the captions of photographs, verbal language is there to resist the unlimited polysemy of images: 'The primary function of speech is to immobilise perception at a certain level of intelligibility [f]ixing its level of reading.'[45] From a somewhat different perspective, Laplanche suggested that: 'The ego, if it is the instrument of reality, does not bring a privileged access to the real ... [i]ts function is essentially inhibitive: to prevent hallucination, to cut off that "excess of reality" coming from internal excitation.'[46]

But it should be stressed that the images or hallucinations resisted and limited by language were engendered through their encounter with language in the first place. As Monique Plaza insisted, no thing-presentation can be inscribed by a look outside any signifying system. So it emerges that images are constrained by language at both ends of the psychic apparatus, so to speak, and this draws into question the firmly established view of the image as a continuous field, a plenitude. It is well known that images always exceed verbal language. Even though each aspect of an image is in itself 'speakable', the sum of its parts is not, being implicated in that excess Laplanche mentions. In this sense, the plenitude of an image can be understood as a product of secondarisation, a filling-in operation reconstituting the fantasy of pre-oedipal plenitude, a fantasy always marked by the symbolic incision of the frame. For instance, it would be interesting to know what produced the change from isolated graphic figures towards continuous fields contained within a frame.

Another aspect of this excess can be related to the fact that images, although involved in displacement, are primarily to be understood in terms of condensation. Freud, and Metz after him, describes the translation of the verbal into an image as a process of displacement from one register of signs to another. But this only refers to forms of literalisms. On the other hand, Freud also stresses that each element of a dream text, of a thing-presentation, is rooted in a whole series of chains and can thus be seen as a nodal point, an intersection of significations 'bound to branch out in every direction into the intricate network of our world of thought'.[47] In the same way, the 'infinite polysemy' of images has no ending: there will always be unanalysed material, although no unanalysable material.

So it could be argued that it is the condensation process presiding over image production which guarantees the image as a proliferating nexus of meanings and sense, with some aspects referring to Cs or Pcs material, and others providing the space for Ucs chains of signifiers to affix themselves to the figurations involved. Moreover, as paradigmatised blocks of discourses massively overdetermined in all aspects, the image is also always 'lined' by two distinct instances of inner speech: one at the time of production, binding image, subject and sense in sociality; the other repeating the process at the time of reading, a change that guarantees the insertion of the image into an entirely different set of discourses.

Yet one more process must be taken into consideration in this proliferation of sense provoked/produced by the image: the materiality of the signs/marks in images, their matter(s) of expression and the codes at work in them, these also affect the trajectory of meaning production. The cumulative effects of these considerations make for an extremely high degree of indeterminacy, even in the most figurative of figurations. The signifying practices having recourse to images can thus be described, in Mukarovsky's words, as 'designed to render things imprecise', as a movement towards indeterminacy. Mukarovsky saw this movement as indicating a decrease in the communicative function of the discourse and foregrounding the aesthetic (poetic) function. Jakobson echoed this view, specifying that 'the supremacy of the poetic function over the referential function does not obliterate reference [b]ut renders it ambiguous'.[48] This notion – that a recourse to images connotes a move towards imprecision and the poetic function of discourse – can be counterposed to the common-sense position that the prime virtue of images is that they 'refer' more accurately. Many of the more assiduous documentary film-makers have become aware of this contradiction, complaining that it is impossible to shoot slums and misery without somehow aestheticising them – a paradox generated by the widely held but nevertheless false premise that images represent more 'accurately' than other forms of representation, and that the choice is between imprecise (poetic) 'pictorialism' and precise, referential 'photography of record'.[49] Whereas captions and titles fix levels of reading, images move backwards through language, in an attempt to elude the strictures of resistance, reinforcing the misconception that while 'verbal discourse' is oppressive and authoritarian, images 'speak for themselves' and are more democratic, thus less socially and ideologically determined. Such a belief ignores the full extent of the role of language in helping to determine firstly, what image shall be produced; secondly, the material(s) organised in/by it; thirdly, the social function and placing of imaged discourse in a given discursive formation; and fourthly, the readings produced in relation to it.

2. Ideology and Politics
The idea that verbal language is an important determinant in relation to the formation, function and placing of imaged discourse in a given discursive conjuncture, and thus also in the way it is read, requires a few explanatory remarks, particularly because it opens up in terms of

ideology and politics the question of verbal discourse in relation to imaged discourse. If we consider a discursive formation (the ideological instance of the social formation) as composed of bundles of discourses in struggle, organised into unities via institutions,[50] it becomes possible to address the problem of the interrelation of discourses, their mutually determining dynamic. As suggested earlier with regard to the 'false' premise of the 'accuracy' of photographic representation, the definition of a discursive practice (produced through verbal discourses) to a large extent – but never totally – governs the discourses produced to oppose or reinforce it. For instance, just as an oppositional ideology which defines verbal discourse itself as somehow suspect, rather than analysing which particular discourses are 'suspect' and how and why they are so, will automatically have recourse to configuration changes (partly as a result of the oppositional practices, or for entirely different, even extra-discursive reasons), so too will the oppositional value/function of the practices in question, and the process will therefore start over again. Such would be a (somewhat overly) schematic representation of the mechanical aspects of the dialectic at work.

However, in view of the function of inner speech discussed above, an extra process must be inserted into this dialectic – a process that engages the status of the subject, the binding of text, subject and sense into sociality. This process, which doubles/lines every signifying practice, operates to articulate the laws of Ucs signification (the subject's psychoanalytic history) into the social. What I am proposing here is that inner speech is the discourse that binds the psychoanalytic subject and the subject in history, functioning as a locus of condensation, a site where the two overlap so that the 'mechanical' dialectic must always be read as a function of the productivity of Ucs processes. This is not the same as subscribing to any notion of determination by the Ucs – quite the contrary.

Finally, it should be stressed that any consideration of the problems of signification in relation to subjects in history will be at best inhibiting, at worst reactionary, if the discourse that attends to those issues is itself not theorised as 'in history'. In other words, theoretical discourses on film must be seen in terms of the same dialectical relations that govern the production of all texts. Such theories of discourse are 'produced' in specific places of the discursive formations, with specific functions in relation to other discourses, the whole caught up in the struggle that constitutes 'the motor of history'. It may be that the moment has come to take distance from a number of discourses which in the not too distant past performed a progressive function in ideological struggles with regard to the cinematic institution. One prime candidate for such a critical distance would be any discourse that essentialises and hypothesises notions of subject production/positioning, autonomises the discursive and invokes the Ucs whenever the question of politics and the real is mentioned. The problem is no longer just the thinking of signification in history, it is one of thinking signification so as to promote an understanding of how social formations can be changed, since changing them is the point.

Postscript

In the discussion that followed the presentation of the paper on which this chapter is based, two points were made which engage directly with the issues and theses put forward. Firstly it was noted by Stephen Heath that the very term 'inner speech' was likely to evoke the binary opposition inner/outer, carrying in its wake the dangers of psychologism, with inner speech being on the side of the individual psyche, while manifested, external speech would be on the side of the social. This connotation is indeed present in the way Eikhenbaum, Vygotsky and Jakobson use the terms involved. The fact that inner speech is not phonetically manifested, nor indeed manifested at all except in the traces it imprints in acts of social (that is, manifested) enunciation, may tend to suggest that it is an extremely 'individual' discursive activity, located 'within' and thus highly idiosyncratic. However, inner speech is located under the sign of the ego, which participates of the Ucs. Insofar as the Ucs impinges upon the formation of inner speech, the latter is trans-individual, that is to say, profoundly social. The Ucs, if it is to be defined topologically, is a *locus communis* where locutions are indeed 'in common' – something clinical practice constantly attests and which led C. G. Jung to try to extrapolate the Ucs from history altogether through his invention of the collective Ucs with its archetypes and universal symbols. In this respect, Freud's reply that the Ucs is by definition 'collective', and that consequently any attempt to differentiate a special agency called 'the collective Ucs' is a tautology, also means that what conventional psychology designates as the most 'private' is also and simultaneously the most social. At which point the distinction between inner and outer collapses.

The second comment the paper provoked relates to this same issue. Stephen Heath remarked that 'literalisms' in cinema appeared always to take the form of heavily coded, ritualised and stereotyped formulas and phrases. In other words, the traces of inner speech in the visual, in the figuration of a narrative or a tableau, take the form of, precisely, *loci communes*, of the socially and linguistically commonplace. This is one more argument why 'images' should be considered as products of secondary elaboration, that is to say, displaced enunciations invested by/with Ucs discursive processes, giving the lie to, and locating the function of, any ideology that insists on maintaining a rigorous separation between the orders of discourse and of the figure. In this way, inner speech, the concatenation of literalisms subjected to specific processes of 'thought work' (in an analogy with the concept of 'dream work'), should then indeed be considered as the site where the subjective and the social are articulated, with the 'subjective' being traced in that very process of articulation. In the same sense that the image can be seen as a specific formation sandwiched between two moments of language, so too the subjective can be seen as an articulation between two moments of the social. Film images would thus be closely related, although not for the reasons usually invoked, to dream images: both can be regarded as 'grounded in folklore, popular myths, legends, linguistic idioms, proverbial wisdom and current jokes'.[51]

Notes

1. Roman Jakobson, *Main Trends in the Science of Language* (London: Allen & Unwin, 1973), p. 32.
2. Paul Willemen, 'Reflections on Eikhenbaum's Concept of Internal Speech in the Cinema', in *Screen*, vol. 15 no. 4, Winter 1974/75, pp. 59–70.
3. It is worth signalling in this context that Metz also argued that sound is, in fact, never 'off': 'Claiming to speak about sound one in fact thinks of the visual image of the sound's source', ('Le perçu et le nommé', in *Vers une esthétique sans entrave: Mélanges offerts à Michel Dufrenne*, Paris: Union Générale d'Éditions, 1975, pp. 373–5). Also Claude Bailbé in 'Programmation de l'écoute', in *Cahiers du cinéma*, n. 292, September 1978, pp. 53–9, makes the point that by virtue of the placing of the speaker behind the screen, sound is located in the image itself. He makes the interesting observation, contradicting Metz' suggestion, that sounds are constructed according to the rules of an aural perspective analogous to monocular perspective. This last remark has significant implications in relation to the recently formulated arguments that hearing is less patriarchally invested than seeing; see, for example Luce Irigaray's remarks quoted in Stephen Heath, 'Difference', in *Screen*, vol. 19 no. 3, Autumn 1978, p. 84.
4. Roland Barthes, *Elements of Semiology* (New York: Hill & Wang, 1968), pp. 10–11.
5. Yuri Lotman introduced these terms to suggest that 'since man's consciousness is a linguistic consciousness, all the varieties of models constructed on the basis of consciousness – and art is among them – can be defined as secondary modelling systems', in *Die Struktur des kunstlerischen Textes* [1973], quoted in Ben Brewster, 'Notes on the Text "John Ford's *Young Mr. Lincoln*"', in *Screen*, vol. 14 no. 3, Autumn 1973, p. 42.
6. Karel Brusak, 'Signs in the Chinese Theatre' [1939], in Ladislaw Matejka and Irwin R. Titunik (eds.), *Semiotics of Art : Prague School Contributions* (Cambridge: MIT Press, 1976), pp. 59–73.
7. Sigmund Freud, *The Interpretation of Dreams* (Harmondsworth: Penguin Books, 1976), p. 468.
8. Roman Jakobson, *Six Lectures on Sound and Meaning* (Brighton: Harvester Press, 1978), p. 113.
9. Jacques Nattiez, *Fondements d'une sémiologie de la musique* (Paris: Union Générale d'Éditions, 1975).
10. Zofia Lissa, 'Aesthetische Funktionen des musikalischen Zitats', in Roman Jakobson, Algiridas Julien Greimas *et al.* (eds.), *Sign, Language, Culture* (The Hague–Paris: Mouton, 1970), pp. 674–89.
11. Roman Jakobson, 'Musikwissenschaft und Linguistik', in *Selected Writings*, Vol. II (The Hague–Paris: Mouton, 1971), pp. 551–3.

12. Monique Plaza, 'Phallomorphic Power and the Psychology of "Woman"', in *Ideology and Consciousness*, no. 4, 1978, p. 12.
13. Christian Metz, *Language and Cinema* (The Hague–Paris: Mouton, 1974), pp. 153, 280.
14. Christian Metz, *Le Signifiant imaginaire* (Paris: Union Générale d'Éditions, 1977).
15. Ibid., p. 281.
16. Anika Lemaire, *Jacques Lacan* (London: Routledge & Kegan Paul, 1977), p. 46.
17. Ibid., p. 281.
18. Paul Willemen, 'Notes on Subjectivity', in *Screen* vol. 19 no. 1, Spring 1978.
19. Jean Laplanche, *Life and Death in Psychoanalysis* (Baltimore: Johns Hopkins University Press, 1976), p. 51.
20. Ideologism proclaims the autonomy of the discursive *vis-à-vis* the political and the economic; it abolishes the need to think of politics in any terms other than those of rhetoric, opportunism and accommodation to institutional requirements combined with self-promotion. More recently (since the middle of the 80s), this trend has mutated into a variety of 'postmodernism' celebrating or at least legitimating the kind of cultural practices required or desired by advertisers and other advocates of 'deregulation' in the media.
21. Laplanche, *Life and Death in Psychoanalysis*, p. 66.
22. Ibid., p. 63.
23. Jean Laplanche and J.-B. Pontalis, *The Language of Psychoanalysis* (London: Hogarth Press, 1973), p. 139.
24. Ibid., p. 63.
25. Laplanche, *Life and Death in Psychoanalysis*, p. 126.
26. Quoted in Jakobson, *Main Trends in the Science of Language*, p. 33.
27. Ibid.
28. Boris Eikhenbaum, 'Problems of Film Stylistics' [1927], in *Screen* vol. 15 no. 4, Winter 1974/5, pp. 7–34. See also Ron Levaco, 'Eikhenbaum, Inner Speech and Film Stylistics', ibid., pp. 47–58.
29. Metz, 'Le perçu et le nommé', pp. 345–77.
30. Lev S. Vygotsky, *Thought and Language* [1936] (Cambridge: MIT Press, 1962), p. 2.
31. Eikhenbaum, 'Problems of Film Stylistics' [1927].
32. Emilio Garroni, 'Langage verbal et éléments non-verbaux dans le message filmico-télévisuel', in Dominique Noguez (ed.), *Cinéma: théorie, lectures* (Paris: Klincksieck, 1973), p. 116.
33. Vygotsky, pp. 145–6.
34. Metz, *Language and Cinema*, p. 209.
35. Vygotsky, *Thought and Language*, pp. 145–6.
36. Ibid., p. 149.
37. Ibid., p. 150.
38. Aleksandr R. Luria, *The Mind of a Mnemonist* (Harmondsworth: Penguin Books, 1975).
39. The translation of the phonetic elements of a word into ideational representatives is illustrated by Eisenstein's 'Mary-variations': he produced a set of images, each corresponding to a version of the name Mary (Maria, Maryushka, Masha, and so on) and each image would be determined by the phonemic structure of the name. Luria added that: 'Eisenstein, in testing students to select those he would train as film directors, asked them to describe their impressions of the variations on the name Mariya. He found this an infallible way to single out those who were keenly sensitive to the expressive force of words'. A. R. Luria, *The Mind of a Mnemonist* (Harmondsworth: Penguin Books, 1975), p. 72.

40. A. R. Luria, *The Man with a Shattered World* (Harmondsworth: Penguin Books, 1975), p. 89.
41. Ibid., p. 60.
42. Freud, *The Interpretation of Dreams*, p. 113.
43. Luria, *The Man with a Shattered World*, pp. 35–40.
44. It is perhaps worthwhile to point out that such a regression is not necessarily to be equated with reaction in the political sense. That would be an essentialist procedure which ignores the fact that the political value of a given set of signifying practices depends on its location and function in a given intertextual field, that is, in a discursive (sub)formation.
45. Roland Barthes, *Système de la mode* (Paris: Le Seuil, 1967), p. 23.
46. Laplanche, *Life and Death in Psychoanalysis*, p. 62.
47. Freud, *The Interpretation of Dreams*, p. 672.
48. Roman Jakobson, 'Concluding Statement: Linguistics and Poetics', in T. Sebeok (ed.), *Style and Language* (Cambridge: MIT Press, 1960), p. 371.
49. Peter Wollen, 'Photography and Aesthetics', in *Screen* vol. 19 no. 4, Winter 1978/79, pp. 9–28.
50. See Chapter 2.
51. Freud, *The Interpretation of Dreams*, p. 468.

Chapter 2

Notes on Subjectivity

Within the debates triggered by reflections on the semiotics of narrative and the implications of the relevance of psychoanalytic concepts of subjectivity for film theory, a number of mainly American scholars have turned to detailed analyses of the way point of view is orchestrated in individual texts. Edward Branigan's comparative analysis of the structures of subjectivity in Fellini's *8½* and in Oshima's *The Story of a Man who Left his Will on Film* draws attention to some fundamental problems in film studies and raises an important issue in film theory. More specifically, it constitutes a contribution to the attempts to bring about a shift away from film studies to an engagement with signifying practices, considering film as a practice of production of meaning, rather than as an autonomous object of study.

I.1.

As Branigan states in the footnote to the title of his essay, his piece was produced in the context of a general study of point of view (POV) in the cinema. As such, it can be seen as part of the work on structures of POV produced at the University of Wisconsin, Madison, of which *Screen* has published some examples.[1] These articles are important partly because they all signal to some extent the above-mentioned shift within the confines of an institutionalised academic discourse on the cinema. By attending to the problem of enunciation and subjectivity, they help mark a possible site of exit from formal semiotics and mechanical structuralism, both of which tend to locate films as messages circulating between inscribed or abstractly conceived addressers and addressees, the ahistorical persons put into place by conventional information theory.

The analysis of the two films questions to some extent the model produced by information theory in so far as it contrasts rather than compares the notions of subjectivity implied by each of them. Fellini's film is seen as working 'near the limits of classical representation', but as retaining the classic notion of character as the central point of coherence for the narrative's spatial and temporal co-ordinates. On the whole, the film remains 'committed to assumptions of traditional subjective narration, finding its centre in the consciousness of a character', while Oshima's film challenges this and poses the concept of the subject in radically new terms, 'seeing character as existing only in the interstices of social practice' with a 'potential for ceaseless self-criticism, a doubling back onto oneself in contradiction'. In this respect, Oshima's film is said to be modernist and to change the role of the viewer 'who must confront new conditions of meaning' because the film 'presents two distinct ideologies, side by side, which articulate [t]wo different forms of the same character, existing side by side and in contradiction', generating 'impossible characters' and 'impossible events'. This clash between 'two opposing ideologies produces in the text gaps, fissures, contradictions and impossibilities which are neither hidden nor resolved as they are in *8½*.

Branigan argues this point via a formal analysis of POV structures and the construction of coherent fictional characters. By examining Fellini's and Oshima's films in relation to the formal inscription of character and POV, Oshima's film emerges as the negation, the reverse side of Fellini's film, rather than as a film opening up the possibility of an entirely different theorisation of subjectivity in cinema. The very formulation of the title of Branigan's essay ('from . . . to') suggests a linearity, a shared field, rather than a radical heterogeneity, a radically different approach to signifying practices. Instead, throughout the essay, the two films are constantly pulled into the same space, firstly by the reiteration of areas of overlap between them and secondly by the assertion that *8½* is not entirely within the coherence of traditional narration, while Oshima's film is not entirely outside it.

This pulling together is achieved, perhaps ironically in an essay addressing problems of subjectivity, by failing to address the question of the subject of the enunciation as constructed, located by the films themselves as discursive formations. Branigan analyses in detail how Guido is represented in *8½* as the full consciousness from which the 'film within the film' emanates. But when the framing narrative is itself shown to contain the same type of disturbances which in the *framed* narration are seen as motivated by Guido's artistic consciousness, Branigan omits the conclusion that the framed film relates to its subject in the same way as the framing narration is supposed to relate to its expressive source: Fellini. But this is the whole point of the construction of Guido as artist in relation to the inner film. It is in this context that the strategy of retrospective attribution, remarked on by Branigan, makes sense: we are presented with images and sounds which we are then invited to relate to Guido, who stands as their origin. In the same way, the film as a whole presents us with images and sounds which the audience can then attribute analogously to Fellini, who is thus retroactively constituted not only as another

Guido but as somehow greater than Guido, an artistic consciousness expressing and encompassing the represented artistry of Guido. Only by remaining within the confines of an immanent analysis can Branigan claim a certain degree of heterogeneity and openness for Fellini's film: the marks of the outside source of expression are left hanging in the air, reinvested in the film as impossible signs, as, precisely, marks of heterogeneity. But in so doing, what gets blocked is the possibility of thinking discursive practices as constructing subjectivity in social formations, in/for ideology. The essay thus sets in motion a series of confusions bearing primarily on the unthought differences between the subject of enunciation and the subject as constructed through discourses in ideology.

The question of the subject of an enunciation is examined through the analysis of POV only in relation to characters in the fiction, perhaps because to extend notions of POV to the subject of the enunciation of the film as discourse would inevitably raise the issue of the relation between texts and authors/readers, themselves embedded in history.

I.2.

It is the academic practice of close reading, the ghost of empiricism, which produces the demand that readings be constructed exclusively on the evidence provided by the phenomenal aspects of the text (including the form of the content – although this immediately begs the question of how semantic values are constructed, read and located in history). In this way, the cumbersome extra-textual, the outside of the text, is evacuated from the analysis: an outside consisting of discourses in struggle, discursive formations cohering into conjunctures of ideologies. But such an evacuation also makes it possible to demonstrate, rather than assert, the very conclusions Branigan seeks to propose. He writes:

> The Oshima film is a text of difficult spaces – 360-degree space, impossible camera positions – in which the spectator cannot fix a level of narration and so come to rest on a perfect, unseen observer [j]ust as it constructs inconsistent characters, the text constructs an inconsistent spectator.

Exactly how, on what grounds and with what implications this jump from character to spectator is to be thought, is left unexplained, perhaps because to think the articulation character-text-spectator would require thinking the already evacuated problem of the articulation character-text-author.

Furthermore, the problem of how to proceed from the definition of 'character' as inconsistent to the demonstration of the thesis (in itself probably quite plausible) that Oshima's film sees character as existing only in the interstices of social practice also remains unclear. It is unclear whether the social practice referred to is the practice represented in the text in relation to a set of characters or whether Branigan's statement suggests – as I think it should – that the very notion of character itself, including therefore its status as a critical concept, exists only in the interstices of social practice, that is, in the practice of meaning construction in ideology which is, in this instance, the practice of the critic.

However, Branigan's analysis certainly implies the former notion of social practice. Hence he goes on to say that the inconsistency he locates in the film is due to the simultaneous inscription of two contradictory ideologies *in relation to a character* (my emphasis). In fact, all so-called psychologically complex fictional characters are located at the intersection of contradictory ideologies and impossible POV shots – and 360° spaces – are commonplace to a great many classic narratives (*The Fall of the House of Usher* (Roger Corman, 1960), *The Appaloosa* (Sidney Furie, 1966), *North By North-West* (Alfred Hitchcock, 1959), *Le deuxième souffle* (Jean-Pierre Melville, 1966), and so on). Impossible camera positions always connote impossible POVs and always refer to a subject of an enunciation, whether retroactively attributed to a character or not. The absence of an attempted articulation of the inside and outside of an empirically given text collapses the argument onto the level of an immanent reading, thus blocking the theorisation of the construction of subjectivity in social practices.

Branigan's remark about the inscription of two ideologies probably means that there are two ideologies at work in Oshima's film: one that says that character X is the expressive subject, the author of the testament film; the other that says he isn't. However, according to the analysis proposed, this inconsistency is contained within the enounced (*énoncé*) of the film, which leaves the authorial subjects untouched: Fellini and Oshima stand outside the text, as full subjects constructing a text for a reader, or better, constructing readers through their texts. Secondly, to say that characters are inconsistent leaves the notion of character itself unquestioned, positing character as the source of motivations lending coherence to the narrated events. After suggesting that Oshima's film explodes the notion of character, and mentioning that the characters are logically speaking 'impossible', the essay nevertheless ends with the statement that Motoki is indeed a character, but one for whom the possibility of change consists in his potential for ceaseless self-criticism, a statement even Fellini would agree with.

The concept of character stems from a specific type of literary practice and its concomitant ideologies. By stating that Oshima's film forces upon us a redefinition of the coherence we have come to designate as character, one type of character-coherence is merely substituted for another. Instead of a character grounded in the notion of consciousness, we now have a character, as Branigan puts it at the end of his essay, doubling back on itself in critical self-examination. But the entire analysis of the relation of Motoki and Yasuko to the testament-film clearly shows that something quite different from critical self-examination is at stake: a questioning of the construction of subjectivity through discursive practices. In Oshima's film, the concept of character as it emerged from the nineteenth-century novel is not redefined, it is made irrelevant. And in a way, this is precisely what Branigan's analysis shows in the interstices of its own practice. It is not the inconsistency of the characters that produces 'gaps, fissures, contradictions' in Oshima's film: it is rather the attempt to mobilise the very concept of character in relation to this film which produces gaps, fissures and contradictions in Branigan's essay.

But perhaps the real crux of the question is to be found in the assertion that the text constructs an inconsistent spectator. One could object to the notion of inconsistency put forward on the grounds that it is perfectly possible to produce a consistent, that is to say, coherent and systematic reading of Oshima's text. To some extent, this is precisely what Branigan attempts in the course of his analysis. Obversely, to the extent that I argue here that Branigan's reading is inconsistent, Branigan may justifiably, although perhaps disingenuously, point out that his reading is indeed evidence of the power of Oshima's text to construct inconsistent spectators. However, the main point with which I want to take issue in this context is the suggestion that texts construct spectators, with all its implications of subjugation and unilateral determination, not to say terrorism. What is it exactly that texts do construct, if anything other than themselves?

II.1.
The articulation of inscribed authors and readers with subjects in history must pass through an engagement with notions of ideology. In the words of Stephen Heath:

> There is no subject outside of a social formation, outside of social processes which include and define positions of meaning, which specify ideological places. [I]t is not that there is first of all a construction of a subject for social/ideological formations and then the placing of that constructed subject-support in those formations, it is that the two processes are one, in a kind of necessary simultaneity – like the recto and the verso of a piece of paper.[2]

Likewise, texts do not construct subjects outside of social processes for them then to be placed in those formations – where that 'placing in' would constitute an object of study for sociology. But with texts too, there is a necessary simultaneity, a subject-construction always already in history. The distinction between aesthetic and sociological studies of literature, cinema, and so on, must be seen as a specific ideological operation, not a recognition of pre-existing divisions in the real. In fact, such distinctions and divisions block the thinking of signifying practices as fundamentally ideological, always embedded in, and deriving their significance from, the contradictory and hetero-geneous processes which constitute given social formations.

The introduction of ideology as a concept remains largely ineffec-tive within the formalism of textual POV analyses perhaps because of the imprecision and confusion surrounding its definition. The symp-tom of that confusion manifests itself in Branigan's analysis in the form of the presence, within a set of formal categories, of the term 'mind', itself a mask for what is elsewhere designated as ideology. The essay thus intertwines two heterogeneous, not to say mutually exclus-ive discourses: a dominant formalist idealism occasionally disturbed by signs of a wish for a materialist theory of the subject.

The coexistence of the terms 'ideology' and 'mind' as equally valid concepts illustrates this point most clearly. When Branigan writes that 'mind' is that condition of consciousness which is represented as the principle of coherence of the representation, while arguing that Oshima's film destroys the fiction of coherent characters by inscribing them within two different ideologies, ending with the claim that ideology is that practice which orders the significance of the world and places the individual as significant in the world, he has, in effect, and in spite of his denial, equated ideology and mind, even within his own terms of reference. In two ideologies becomes 'in two minds' and Oshima's film ends up being about a clinical case of schizophrenia: the coherence of the character is re-established in terms of psycho-pathology.[3]

Conflating representational system, text and film, ideology is at one point reduced to 'represented ideology' without clarifying its possible difference from non-represented ideology. It becomes merely one term in the triad: character/represented ideology/event, where rep-resented ideology appears to be something similar to Barthes's her-meneutic code: the formal organisation which poses, maintains and finally resolves the enigmatic relation between characters and events. That is to say, it is the principle of intelligibility of the narrative. At this point, we are back where we started: ideology equals mind.

But in the above-mentioned definition of ideology as the practice which orders the significance of the world, the introduction of the term 'practice' offers a way out of the impasse, because it implies that signifying practices articulate subjectivity and social processes. As such, the process of meaning production can no longer be thought as the effectiveness of a system of representation, but rather as a produc-tion of and by subjects already in social practices; a production not dependent on any single system of representation, but instead determined by the relations of force, the conjuncture of discursive, economic and political practices which produces subjects-in-history. As to the dialectical relations between these sets of practices, each of them a terrain of struggle, this currently constitutes a major issue in dialectical materialism which I will return to, rather obliquely, later.

Oshima's film, then, is supposed to destroy the notion of the coherent character by simultaneously inscribing two different principles of intelligibility in relation to its fictional personages. By embedding the character in two mutually exclusive structures of understanding, the coherence of the narrative is destroyed, is rendered unintelligible. In this way, the film supposedly forces the reader to draw his or her conclusions regarding the possibility of change and revolution.

This introduces the concept of the reader as the locus of truth. In effect, it is the mind of the reader which is supposed to provide the terms of the coherence of the text, its intelligibility. The reader is thus presented as the point at which the productivity of the text stops. This is as it should be according to the precepts of communication theory. But Oshima's film is simultaneously supposed to invalidate this theory by questioning the status of its two poles, its two boundaries: addresser and addressee. The centre of coherence which Fellini's film poses, via Guido, as being in the mind of the author, is merely relocated at the other end of the chain of communication: the reader. However, the reader is seen as determined by the text, which itself relates to an outside agency, unquestioned and unproblematic, the author. Via the text, the reader is thus supposed to be subjected to the intentionality of the author. The ideal, the 'correct' reading is then one where reader and author coincide, with the reader functioning as the point of coherence, more or less accurately reconstructing, that is, reading, the intentionality of the author, a process verifiable through interviews with the author and biographies, which are themselves 'read' to produce an authorial intentionality backing up and filling out the image of the author as read from the texts.

This procedure places the text outside ideology, outside social formations and outside history, a once and for all given stability, an empirical given, the Truth of which resides in the 'mind' of the author. As the text inscribes a reader, this reader is therefore also posed outside ideology and history: the text, if read correctly, is supposed to have determinate and inevitable effects on the reader.

II.2.
The notion of POV, with its potential (and at present dominant) implication of full subjects having a POV and even imposing it on others, is one more element deriving from the traditional model of communication, perhaps best formulated by Boris Uspensky:

In terms of communication theory, we may treat the literary [here the film] work as a message, the author as the sender and the reader as the receiver – correspondingly, we can distinguish the point of view of the author (the sender) and the point of view of the reader (the receiver); we can also distinguish the point of view of a person whom the message describes (a character in the narrative).[4]

Further distinctions, such as author/narrator and reader/narratee, allow the bringing into play of a complex battery of relations between subjects and/or their representatives within the (in this type of analysis usually narrative) message. But there remains an unbridgeable gap between 'real' readers and authors and inscribed ones, constructed or marked in and by the text. Real readers are subjects in history, living in given social formations, rather than mere subjects of a single text. The two types of subject are not commensurate, but for the purposes of formalism, real readers are supposed to coincide with the constructed readers. Should they have the temerity to consider the text as a profoundly unstable economy of discourses, whose coherence will vary according to their location in historico-ideological configurations (thus becoming a potential locus of struggle), then these readers will be accused of running the risk of distorting or simply failing to recognise the aesthetic structure as a self-regulating system that makes sense only from a particular vantage point.

Thus, text and reader freeze each other into immobility. This inscribed vantage point is always outside the text, in a position symmetrical to that of the author. It is given once and for all by the disposition of the chain of signifiers which constitutes the text. It is the point at which the productivity of the text ceases, its point of coherence, the moment when contradictions are lifted and things make sense. By projecting this point into the text – to rediscover it via a formal analysis – as a virtual image, the process of communication, or rather of signification, becomes once more a closed circuit, cut off from subjects living in the social sphere and therefore always 'in process'. As Geoffrey Nowell-Smith says of formalism: 'The subject was outside the system – on the one hand as an irrelevance to objective study, but on the other hand also as foundation, negligible because taken for granted.'[5] This allowed readers to be conceived of as blanks, mere functions supporting the text and therefore passive – to be constructed and put into place according to the whim of the texts ... and their authors.

The existence of authors was never in doubt. Even if the author had to be considered as a structure, by some coincidence there were always as many authorial structures objectively describable as there were names of directors, writers, and so on. The same never seemed to apply to readers, who remained subordinate to the effectiveness of the text. In so far as they were not, in so far as their productions diverged from the inscribed structure, this was attributed to realms beyond the boundaries of aesthetics (society, the psychopathology of individuals, and so forth).

II.3.
Although the introduction of the critical category of POV constitutes an attempt to locate the text in relations of subjectivity, it is still complicit with the ideology of centrality and identity, with the model of communication theory which the development of a theory of the subject seeks to displace. In the analysis of processes of linguistic signification, POV operates within the same framework that governs the perspectival organisation of space. In relation to the novel, it arose as a concept produced by and for the type of literary practice exemplified by the nineteenth-century novel, a practice still massively dominant today in literature, television and cinema. However, there are differences between, for example, European monocular perspective, Japanese systems of perspective and Byzantine lack of perspective; between different framing procedures and the imbrication of spatial layers and/or ornamental planes in different historico-ideological formations. These differences should stand as sufficient warning against the use of POV as a universally valid scientific concept for the discussion of problems of subjectivity in signifying practices. Our present tradition has a POV of the author and of the narrator, a POV of the narratee and of the reader. The text is the space of their encounter, with the narrator in the name of the author seeking to impose a POV on the narratee taken for the reader. The latter retaliates via his/her socially sanctioned (not to say imposed) substitutes (critics, teachers, journalists), who seek to produce, by claiming to 'find', the POV of the author-to-be-consumed. The author inscribes readers at the point of reception; readers produce authors as the point of origin. Each claims to find what they laboriously produced.

The formalist solution to this paranoid game (authors claiming critics are failed or frustrated artists in order to protect themselves against the possibility of the critics returning to them the image of an author they have no wish to recognise as their own) is to enclose this process of exchange into a self-contained unit, circumscribed by unified, formally identified images of authors and readers. Equality has been restored: both have become images and neither need have any relation to the people actually involved in the production of meaning. The rest is history and/or psychopathology. As Pierre Macherey concluded in his lecture, *Problems of Reflection*, 'We rediscover the author with his initiatory potential, no longer, admittedly, in the warm intimacy of his creativity, but opposite it, in an external relationship which is nonetheless closely related to it.'[6]

The ideological-political implications of the model of communication described by Uspensky were clearly spelled out by Umberto Eco:

The page (or the book) is the communication of an absolute – and therefore something unalterable – between two universals: a man on one side and a man on the other. To read is to penetrate into this intangible and unique universe which the man on the other side transfused into form. The form is what it is: from the moment it is born, it does not adapt itself to the world, to history, to society, to space and time, but the world, society, history, space and time adapt themselves to it and form themselves in its image. To read is to accomplish this act of identification and unification, to penetrate into this knot of eternity where everything has but one definition, where all change is licence and where all the possible is resolved in the obedience to the higher laws of form.[7]

Eco continued that in fact:

Each sign of a message corresponds to a precise signification only if signifieds, signifiers and code are taken on the abstract and statistical level of a theoretical communication; in fact, in the mind of the one who receives it, each signifier opens onto a rather large semantic field, [a] message always constitutes a bet on the way it will be received.

Although it would be more accurate to say that each signifier always opens onto a rather large field of other signifiers, and in spite of the ghost of formalism haunting Eco's remarks, he nevertheless clearly outlines both the ideology presiding over communication theory and, if artistic production is to be seen as a form of gambling (why not?), the need to rethink the rules of the game.

III.1.

The problems besetting the concepts of formal POV analyses such as character, ideology and the twinning of reader/author, stem from the attempt to yoke together elements from both communication theory and the theory of the subject as elaborated in psychoanalysis. In other words, they arise from the lack of a theory of discursive practice, and of the attendant concepts of the construction and positioning of subjects in the social.

Formalism in all its various modalities has been dogged by this problem for a number of years. The most sophisticated and at the same time the most revealing attempt to solve the problem within the terms of a structural poetics has been formulated by Tzvetan Todorov. In his essay 'Les Catégories du récit littéraire' (1966), he elaborated the concepts of the inscribed reader and author of a text: 'The narrator is the subject of the enunciation represented by a book [or a film]. [B]ut [his/her] fugitive image cannot be pinned down and assumes contradictory masks, ranging from that of a flesh and blood author to that of some character. There is nevertheless a place where it would seem we can come near enough to that image: we can call it the level of appreciation' which can be recognised through recourse to 'a code of psychological reactions and principles which the narrator postulates as being common to the reader and himself.' The images of narrator and reader/narrator 'are closely dependent on each other, and as soon as the image of the *imaginary* [my emphasis] narrator becomes clearer, so does the outline of the imaginary reader become more precise'.[8]

Here we still have the model of communication theory, but narrator/sender and narratee/receiver have now been split into: (a) functions of the text, that is, the 'I' and the 'You' always posed by an enunciation, whether the source of that enunciation is represented as present (as in discourse) or as absent (as in history),[9] and: (b) real authors and readers embedded in social reality but outside the system of the text. This split makes texts into autonomous, self-enclosed and self-regulating systems available for appropriation by 'objective' structural analyses. Although the reader is not immune to the impact of other sets of discourses, Todorov suggests at least the possibility of stripping away these extraneous interferences, this socially produced 'noise', in order to read the text as it was, and always will be, supposed to be read.

III.2.
Todorov returns to the problem in a more recent essay entitled, significantly, 'La Lecture comme construction' (1975).[10] Here he specifies that in between the flesh and blood reader and the image of the reader, there is a third

> as yet unexplored domain: that of the logic of the reading, not represented in the text and yet anterior to individual variation. [T]he question of reading can thus be formulated in a more restricted manner: how does a text lead us to the construction of an imaginary universe? Which aspects of the text determine the construction we produce when reading, and in what manner?

In the course of his investigation of these questions, Todorov establishes a series of distinctions not accounted for in his previous essay. Firstly, he distinguishes between signification and symbolisation:

> Signified facts are understood: all that is required is to understand the language in which the text is written. Symbolised facts are interpreted; and interpretations vary from subject to subject. [H]aving constructed the events constituting a story, we engage in a work of reinterpretation enabling us to construct, on the one hand, the characters, and on the other hand, the system of ideas

and values underlying the text [that is, something like Branigan's represented ideology]. This reinterpretation is not arbitrary, but it is controlled by two sets of constraints. The first set is contained within the text itself: all that is required is that the author teaches us for a certain amount of time to interpret the events evoked [through the use of repetitions and other forms of redundancy]. The second series of constraints comes from the cultural context: if we read that someone has cut up his wife into little pieces, we do not need any indications in the text that he is cruel [or in *8½*, we don't need to be told that Guido is a great imaginative artist]. These cultural constraints, which are nothing but the common-places of a society (its verisimilitude), change with time.

In this way, Todorov makes provision for the insertion of texts into history via the manner in which they are read: symbolisation, an essential aspect of reading, is subject to existing models of reading, sets of expectations, automatisms, and so on. Readings are subject to doxa, defined by Roland Barthes as: 'Public Opinion, the mind of the majority, petty-bourgeois Consensus, the Voice of Nature, the Violence of Prejudice. We can call [a] *doxology* any way of speaking adapted to appearance, to opinion, or to practice.'[11] In short, symbolisation is an ideological operation. Todorov then goes on to make a further distinction:

> characters, ideas: these types of elements are symbolised through actions; but they can also be signified. [T]he character thus consti-tuted must be distinguished from the person: all persons do not have a character. The person is a segment of the spatio-temporal universe represented, nothing more; there is a person from the moment a referencing linguistic form (a name, certain nominal syntagms, personal pronouns) appears in the text in relation to an anthropomorphous being: someone is identified without being de-scribed. [B]ut as soon as psychological determination emerges, the person is transformed into a character. [C]haracter then can also be an effect of reading: there is a psychologising reading to which every text can be submitted.

This appears to be what happens in Branigan's essay: Oshima's film is subjected to a psychologising reading. The only difference between Branigan's reading and traditional psychologising readings is that, while most critics condemn inconsistency in character construc-tion, Branigan values it.

The person, also sometimes called an actant (for example, in the work of Greimas), corresponds to the subject of the enunciation, to that which is constructed and put into place by what Jakobson calls shifters (I/you, here/there, verbal tenses, and so on). It is through symbolisation that subject positions become meaningful, that 'I' is constructed and placed in relation to others, as different from others. This type of formal analysis opens the way to a thinking of the articulation between the subjects of enunciations and subjects in ideology, although Todorov sidesteps that issue, seeking refuge in the dubious realm of psycho-sociology and/or navel-gazing: 'One of the difficulties of the study of reading stems from the fact that it is not easy to scrutinise it: introspection is unreliable, psycho-sociological investigation is cumbersome.' Now, although a theory of the subject as constructed by/through the incidence of different discourses upon each other, some proffered by the text and others always braided through it, seems just around the corner, formalism re-establishes its dominance, again severing reading from social practice.

Having established that there is an element of historical determination in reading, Todorov once more lapses into a reliance on the model of communication theory, stating that texts force readings upon us and that these readings will be referentially coherent or indeterminate:

> The modern novel forces us into a different reading: the text is indeed referential, but construction [of a coherent fiction] doesn't take place, because in a way it is undecidable. [F]or instance, we saw that the identity of the person was founded on the identity and the univocality of the name. Let us now imagine that in a text the same person is successively evoked by means of different names at one time as 'the man with black hair' and at another as 'the man with blue eyes'. This would represent a shift from the mis-recognised to the unknowable. This modern literary practice has its counterpoint outside literature: in the schizophrenic discourse.[12]

The analogy with Branigan's analysis of Motoki and Yasuko in Oshima's film is evident, as is the echo of the schizophrenic discourse in Branigan's notion of critical self-examination, the character doubling back on itself. But this undecidability is not absolute. The construction of a coherent fiction with characters, firm and fixed identities, with the concomitant authorial characters as subjects of the fictional discourse, has become more than just impossible in the so-called modern text: it has become literally im-pertinent. The problem of discourse construction has itself been shifted onto another terrain, one where the sender/message/receiver model no longer operates as the criterion by which particular texts are judged to be conventional or transgressive. Oshima's text is not the other side, the simple transgression of the type of discourse represented by Fellini's banal and crude stereotype of artistic production: it partakes of a radically different ideological space, a space where coherent unities are evoked only to be exploded (rather than reconstituted in terms of a schizoid split of self-criticism, through the psychopathology of a given character), and where subjects are constructed and placed on the trace of a plurality in intersecting discourses.

There are two options: Oshima's text will be either impossible, the incomprehensible negative of Fellini, or it requires the activation of the extra-textual, that is to say the historically determined ideological configurations within which the textual signifiers are embedded and by which they are placed in history. Oshima's film thus poses the question of the construction of subjectivity through practice in history. Or better, it allows this question to be posed more readily than others.

Branigan's construction of Oshima's film is such a practice in history and therefore derives its significance, its specific difference, from its relation to other critical discourses, from the type of reading it attacks, displaces, reinforces, and so on. It is in this context that one must assess both the comparison/contrast between Oshima's film and Fellini's and the method of analysis deployed. What is at stake in Branigan's article is an attempt to break out of the confines of a formal(ist) type of analysis currently threatening to become dominant in certain academic institutions (hence the necessity to contrast Fellini and Oshima), while remaining within the terms of reference, within the theoretical problematic, of that very type of analysis.

Although recognising that Oshima's film cannot be thought in the same terms as Fellini's, Branigan nevertheless proceeds to do precisely that, with the consequence that the terms of the argument are constantly undermined. Acknowledging that the notion of character is exploded in Oshima's film, Branigan still talks of 'two different forms of the same character'. Assertions of difference rely on unthought operations of reading equally relevant to both texts, thus undermining that very assertion: 'A more complete analysis of Yasuko's position would reveal the ideology which locates women in society.' In fact, a feminist reading, that is, a historically and politically determined reading of the position of any woman or man in any film, including 8½, will reveal this ideology. There is also the statement that both films 'portray the making of a film within a system of production', as if a Marxist collective not designed for film production and a Cinecittà studio are both to be regarded as alternative 'systems' of film production. Guido is inserted in a system of production with a studio, producers, and so on, while Motoki, or at any rate the subject of the testament film, operates as a home movie-maker. The trouble being that there appears to be no connection between the private home movie and the politico-ideological work of the Marxist collective to which he is said to belong.

Oshima's film can be seen as addressing itself to the articulation of individual discursive practices with politico-ideological practices and as doing this through the activation and problematisation of the processes of cinematic enunciation and of the dramatisation of vision.[13] Fellini's film merely regurgitates the problem of being a great artist in an industrialised country. The two films have nothing in common other than that both are part of the cinema as an institution.

To locate Oshima on the same terrain as Fellini and to refer their differences to the same set of criteria is indeed to highlight a specific and crucial problem of the social practice of cinema: films are read unpredictably, they can be pulled into more or less any ideological space, and can be mobilised for diverse and even contradictory critical projects. All that textual strategies can achieve by themselves is at best to activate forgotten or problematic areas of that space, activating dormant, repressed contradictions within it. This also means that the activity of the text must be thought in terms of which set of discourses it encounters in any particular set of circumstances. One must consider how this encounter may restructure both the productivity of the text and the discourses with which it combines to form an intertextual field which is always in ideology, in history. Some texts can be recalcitrant if pulled into a particular field, while others can be fitted into it comfortably. Descriptive analyses tabulating formal devices and procedures (for instance, the construction of space in Ozu's films, the tracing of POVs in Oshima's films) and conclusions drawn from such descriptions regarding for example modes of address, modes of representation, and conventions, are a necessary though limited and preparatory task in an attempt to locate readings and texts in history. This can be seen most clearly in the work of Branigan's colleagues, Kristin Thompson and David Bordwell, when they argue that Ozu's films in some sense represent a modernist practice. Their description of spatial structures in Ozu's films is perceptive and detailed, clearly demonstrating that there are other forms of spatio-temporal narrative construction than the ones we have got used to seeing in Hollywood cinema. But to use this descriptive account as a basis for claiming Ozu's cinema for modernism is reminiscent of the cubist and surrealist claims that African tribal sculpture was modernist. As J. L. Anderson has pointed out, Ozu's films

> partake of the style of the Shochiku studio of the period. Shimazu, a contemporary of Ozu at Shochiku, used a similar spatial style. While this studio style seems to the westerners to create space outside the narrative, it relates to a long Japanese tradition of spatial techniques which, once again, coincides with techniques employed by contemporary western artists. Both aesthetics consider space as an element separate from the narrative space inhabited by characters. Inagaki and Ozu are dissimilar directors whose work converges only in regard to this use of space. This

technique can be seen not only in the work of film-makers but also in scroll paintings, kabuki theatre and even music.[14]

Anderson also makes the point that the notion of the well-made plot 'has little relevance in Japan. There, the emphasis is primarily on separate units and their juxtaposition.' Kristin Thompson argues the claim of Ozu's alleged modernism 'on the basis of *his* [my emphasis] creation of a spatial system that challenges the supremacy of narrative without completely rejecting narrative itself' and argues that 'Ozu side-steps the classical continuity style; the unique system *he* [my emphasis] created presents an alternative to, not a critique of the pervasive Hollywood approach'.[15] However, if this is the case, Ozu's films cannot be claimed as modernist, since modernism is precisely a critique of, not a neutral alternative to, dominant aesthetic practices. If Mitchell Leisen or Henry King had made a film with spatial structures similar to Ozu's, then, perhaps, those aspects of their films might be called modernist. That Kurosawa adopted some elements of John Ford's cinema might give some credibility to the argument that he is a Japanese modernist, if it weren't for the fact that these elements were read, in Japan, as crude western imports.

The point is that nearly all Japanese films can be said to be modernist in some way or other if tested against the Hollywood norm (itself the result of a specific critical production): acting styles in Japanese films are radically different due to the existence of different relationships between the body and the sign, themselves founded on the way various Japanese practices structure the inside/outside opposition in the context of the plurality of codes that have regulated inter- and intra-class relations throughout Japanese history. Moreover, these different levels of signifying practices, encompassing for example the elements of Hollywood cinema introduced into Japanese cinema and television, stand in a dialectical relation to each other. All the extra-filmic discourses current in a given time and place help to mark Ozu's films as precisely Japanese classics. Japanese readings have always recognised the set of systematic differences pointed out by Thompson and Bordwell, but have located them as a form of traditionalism. This is not to say that the structural codes isolated and described in the conscientious formalist studies of these authors do not exist or do not produce effects, but that codes always operate within ideological configurations which not only assign them a large part of their signified but also determine their location in ideological practice. In this sense, the claim that Ozu is a modernist merely and exclusively on the basis of a set of systematic differences from the Hollywood norm produces, among other things, the signified 'cultural imperialism'. Branigan's troubled formalism at any rate opens up contradictions within academic formalism, which has taken the impetus of semiology, challenging impressionist subjectivism and other sets of discourses blocking film criticism and theory for decades, and defused and reintegrated it into the dominant educational doxa. As such, his article constitutes an advance on previous formalist studies published in *Screen*.

Peter Wollen's remark that the effectiveness of works of art is a function of the mode of reading, not of the text itself, perhaps needs some amplification: a progressive reading is not one that attributes progressive meanings to a given text, but a reading that attacks or displaces other readings which function as blockages in the struggle to bring about changes in the social formation. In this sense, the accuracy and precision of a reading is always conditional upon a recognition of its place and effects within a given (fragment of the) socio-historical conjuncture. The production of readings, and hence of criticism and theory, is always a more or less well calculated intervention in the battle of ideas on the terrain constituted by an ideological formation.

IV.1.

As individuals are born into a reality which not only pre-exists them, but which is also already made up of existing representations (the difference between reality and the real), it is by working on and in representation, in and on signification, that subjects come to be generated, produced and assigned a place. It is the consideration of this work of production that requires communication to be thought of as a signifying practice, that is, the articulation of subjectivity and symbolisation. Rosalind Coward has noted: 'Identifications are necessary for the subject to represent him or her-self in a system of difference which is learned language' and she stressed the necessity of 'positionality in language, a constituted subjectivity which will determine the production of an articulation in a signifying practice'.[16]

The way in which a subject finds itself a place in symbolisation constitutes the construction of the ego. This construction takes place by way of identifications, it is 'the transformation that takes place in the subject when he assumes an image'.[17] In this way, the mirror phase, which occurs before the child has found its place in symbolic relations, inaugurates the setting into place of, firstly, 'an ideal ego, another self which characterises all later identifications, [a] projection in which apparent unity the subject mis-recognises itself', and, secondly, 'the ego-ideal, a function by which that image of ideal unity is restored to the subject after the entry into language'.[18] In other words, communication is not a matter of some individual using signs to send messages to a receiver. A signifying practice involves two necessarily complementary and simultaneous moments: a subject can intend meaning only in so far as it produces itself as its support. To extend the metaphoric language of mirrors and images, the author constructs his/her subjectivity and its position, his/her ego-ideal via

72

the text, as does the reader, with the difference that the reader's productivity is subject to a further set of constraints of which the finished text is one.

The author, by definition, cannot be embedded in an intertextual space which already contains the set of discourses constituting the finished work. What the text produces is a set of signifiers installing a subject for it, that is, the subject of the enunciation which is always put into place and thus produced by any utterance. Moreover, partly as a result of the work of Russian and Czech formalists, it has been established that each statement, each text, is in fact a network of intersecting and overlapping statements: quotations, references, derivations, inversions, and so on. A text, any text, consists of a bundle of discourses, each discourse installing its subject of enunciation. This also means that it is misleading to describe a text as a signifying chain, as one discursive operation corresponding to one subject-production. As texts are imbrications of discourses, they must necessarily produce series of subject positions. But these subjects can be (and are) mapped onto each other, pulled into place, firstly by a unifying identificatory projection: the production of an ego-ideal, the text allowing – and to some extent being designed for – the production of a subject-image; and, secondly, by the unifying work of ideologies which fix images and places of viewing in sociality, grounding subjects in imaginary unities from which purposeful and directed action becomes possible.

IV.2.

The above allows the reformulation of the traditional model of communication, which is no longer a transmission of A's message to B under determinate conditions, but rather a discourse putting into place, simultaneously and as necessary correlates of each other, an 'I' and a 'You'. Both poles thus constructed by, and included in, the process of signification are actants according to the definition Julia Kristeva borrowed from A. J. Greimas: 'An actant is nothing but the discourse it assumes and through which it is designated.'[19] This is merely an abstract theoretical model. In fact, signifying practices always work with a plurality of discourses, and a given practice always includes at least one (but usually more than one) discourse about the interrelation of discourses, about the way in which various subjects of enunciations are supposed to relate to each other: overlap, identity, contradiction, and so forth.

Authors as producers of discourses thus anchor in the very act of elaborating a text, of working in signification, two sets of signifiers, one which Todorov called the image of the author and the other that of the reader, on the understanding that each image, each stand-in, is already an amalgam of different subject positions. But the (self-) image thus constructed never coincides with the subject's sense of identity, because, in the words of Lacan, the subject:

ends up by recognising that this being has never been anything more than his construct in the imaginary and that this construct disappoints all his certainties. For in this labour which he undertakes to reconstruct *for another*, he rediscovers the fundamental alienation that makes him construct it *like another*, and which has always destined it to be taken from him *by another*.[20]

An apt formulation of one discursive problematic underpinning Oshima's film (others being its location in history and its articulation of these problematics via the cinematic institution).

So there is always a discrepancy, or more accurately, a disphasure, an oscillation of presence/absence, recognition/difference, between the author as historical subject and the image of the author as inscribed subject. A triple alienation, in fact, because the ego-ideal with which the authorial image is supposed to overlap – always unsuccessfully – is itself the image of an other, and also because the authorial image returned by readers is a function in *their* process of subject construction and *their* circulation of projections and identifications. This in spite of the strategies deployed in texts to pin down the reader in places he or she is supposed to occupy. Readers are never there where the author imagines them: Eco's gamble is a sucker's game. This perpetual being out of phase is no doubt one reason why authors are subjected to a compulsion to repeat the work of text-construction, in pursuit of more satisfactory mirages, more adequate convergences of images constituting them as authors, until finally the totality of the body of work produces, by superimposing many partial images, a 'full' image, an imaginary body of the author.

V.1.

The social formation that puts into place the circuit producer–product–consumer privileges the producer, defining consumers as those who do not produce at all. The unequal competition between buyers and sellers (where sellers are the producers or their agents) which results in marketable value also determines the privileging of producers of saleable items. The sums such producers/sellers are paid for their products can in themselves be no mean stimulus for repeating the work of text-production. But in the conjunction of the two stimuli, one economic, the other narcissistic, there is room for the emergence of a new animal: the successful artist, the author as commodity. Such an author is produced via the mediation of journalists and critics committed to, and embedded in, the traditional ideologies of production and consumption: they too must privilege, or at least pay lipservice to, the production of authors. In the same way that the subject of the text is already a unified image of the subjects of the discourses organised in the text, this unified authorial image can be reinforced by overlapping and superimposing authorial images into a larger unity:

74

the author of a body of work as a palimpsest of authorial images. This is precisely the object auteur theory took over from the literary ideologies and to which structural author analyses addressed themselves, although from within a different set of discourses than journalistic celebrations of personalities. But the production of such an author/artist, it must be stressed, requires at least the active complicity of journalists and/or critics who set out to find and to identify the organisers of the text, instituting them as the well-spring, the source of value. In the cinema, this has not always been the director. On the contrary, studios and stars have tended to occupy this place, necessitating a struggle within dominant ideologies for the recognition of cinema as a signifying practice and opening up problems of how to read texts. Hence the progressive value of auteurism in some circumstances.

It is the conjunction of subjects constructed in/through discourse and capitalist relations of production which results in the notion of the author as we have come to know it. A whole series of texts have been (and still are) produced emphasising in various ways the construction of an authorial image. This has been achieved mainly but not exclusively via the emphatic inscription of signifiers marking subject positions, for example, by the emphatic inscription of infringements of an alleged norm, stylistic supplements, and so on: in short, the whole panoply of devices which characterise art cinema. The one condition is that such descriptions must be attributable to a single outside source, a unifying origin: the author.

A particularly blatant example of such a practice can be seen in Fellini's $8\frac{1}{2}$, as Branigan's analysis clearly shows. Not only does $8\frac{1}{2}$ set up a particularly authorial relation between Guido and the film-within-the-film, producing Guido as artist according to the most banal clichés of Neo-Romanticism, it further sets up a series of marks around Guido referring to an organising subject anterior to the film as a whole, whose relation to the film is thus produced as one analogous to that of Guido to the internal film. This constitutes a double production of Fellini as artist, if $8\frac{1}{2}$ is read through the currently dominant models of reading. And indeed, $8\frac{1}{2}$ fits these models so well that it would become a seriously recalcitrant text if pulled into any other ideological field.

Similar strategies of self-production as artist dominate the texts signed by Ken Russell, Robert Altman and others. Their films differ from $8\frac{1}{2}$ only in so far as they are embedded in, and determined by, different sets of discourses, different historico-ideological formations, but the unifying strategy underpinning them is identical. However, regardless of the wish particular individuals may have to constitute themselves as artistic values, that is, as saleable items, guaranteed sources of a creativity that could be quoted on a stock-market dealing in creativity-shares, it is the mode of reading which consecrates the author. It is here that we must locate the activity of the journalist-critic supplying a consumer's guide and peddling notions of individual creativity in the process.

This is not merely a matter of blind servility: it is also a matter of self-interest, for journalist-critics work in the same social formations as the artists, only in a different place. They too depend for their livelihood on an over-inscription of themselves as witty, cultured, intelligent, ordinary stars. In the art business and in the institutions upon which it impinges (universities, government departments) individuality, that is, personality, is a saleable item. That directors, critics, novelists, television presenters and academics should attempt overwhelmingly and repetitiously to reproduce the marks of their individuality, while never in any way threatening the security and fixity of readers' positions in relation to the texts produced, constitutes a sound commercial strategy. It is thus no accident, nor stupidity, nor machiavellian cunning, that reviewers should consecrate Fellini or Altman as artists. Indeed, in this respect it matters little what reviewers say or write: all that needs to be achieved is the general, overall legitimisation of strategies of self-promotion by acclaiming this to be the true hallmark of a strong individual personality.

I would like to emphasise that this excludes any shadow of conspiracy theories as to the relation between artists, journalist-critics, critics, academics and so on. They all attempt to satisfy narcissistic and economic needs while upholding the currently dominant mode of production which engendered the possibility of that particular mode of multiple gratification in the first place. Robert Altman, in a recent interview in *Time Out* (no. 334, August 1976), clearly recognised the mechanism, although obviously unaware of its implications:

> The critics give us an importance; although what they write doesn't really mean much, their presence does. Without them I wouldn't be sitting here because, on the basis of my track record, I'm a failure. But these guys who put up the money remain impressed! So, paradoxically, I have been sustained by the critics. I think it's phenomenal.

The only paradox being that in the Hollywood in which Altman works, the guys who put up the money appear to allow ideological interests to dominate over economic ones, at least in the short term. Of course, the complicity between those who stand to gain, narcissistically and materially, from the privilege accorded to the producer can break down: there are contradictions and squabbles regarding the authorial images which subjects wish or think were produced in their textual practice. But such diversions needn't detain us. The main point here is that the mode of reading determines the construction of the art cinema as a genre. As different readings are produced, so artists change, or, hopefully, disappear altogether. Similarly, as the currently dominant discourses are displaced, so will art cinema change and disappear, together with the type of films betting on being read as art.

V.2.

The place in the text where subject production is determined is that of the reader, on the understanding that authors also produce themselves as they read the traces, the signifiers of their presence in the text. The reader constructs the author as the other of the image he or she recognises or accepts as his or hers in relation to the text. As the inscribed reader, like the inscribed author, is already an imaginary unity,[21] a mapping onto each other of different 'You's' produced by the plurality of discourses that constitutes the text, the construction of that unity will differ according to the discourses (knowledges, prejudices, resistances) brought to bear by given readers on that place.

It is in this sense that inscribed subject positions are never hermetically sealed into a text, but are always positions in ideologies. Texts can restrict readings (offer resistances), but they can't determine them. They can hinder the productivity of the plurality of discourses at play in them, they can emphasise certain discourses as opposed to others (through repetition or other foregrounding devices). But each of the participants in a textual practice may construct a reader and an author (an action which is itself part of a specific ideological project: the construction of individuality) on the basis of a unification of actants and their amplification, their psychologisation into a fully constituted reader/author. It is the play of permutations, cross-identifications, projections and splits between the positions of author and reader outlined above, where each is also the producer of the other across the text in two separate productions of and within the same set of signifiers – the text – which institutes as its point of unity the subject of the film. This subject is then its impersonal and anonymous point of origin, the place where everything coheres, in turn ejecting both reader and author out of that place, and allowing them to become 'objective' witnesses and commentators on it.

This is one option for those who search for points of coherence while rejecting the traditional Romantic view of artistic subjectivity. One thus objectively recognises his/her mirror image as author and the other accepts or rejects his/her mirror image, according to the degree of recognition involved. At this point, the paranoid game of attributing to the other what the I is unwilling to assume starts all over again.[22]

But even this subject, at its most abstract and impersonal, is itself in history: the discourses regulating the paranoid game, determining the terms of its play, change according to the relation of forces of competing discourses intersecting in the place of the subject-in-history, that is, the individual's location in ideology at a particular moment and place in the social formation. As Stephen Heath pointed out in a text quoted earlier:

> It is not that there is first of all the construction of the subject for social/ideological formations and then the placing of that constructed subject-support in those formations, it is that the two processes are one, in a kind of necessary simultaneity like the recto and verso of a piece of paper. The individual is always entering, emerging, as subject in language at the point of individual/social articulation (the process *together* in which 'a sign represents something for someone' and 'a signifier represents a subject for another signifier').[23]

VI.1.

Any given enunciation always comprises a multiplicity of discourses and, therefore, a multiplicity of subjects, a multiplicity of I's and You's. The pulling together of these diverse subjects into a unified subject is brought about firstly by strategies such as the production of characters, the hierarchisation of discourses,[24] or the affixing of a signature, and, secondly, by the reader's production of subjectivity via the text. As the subjectivity of real readers, their mode of apprehending reality, is also a production involving a plurality of discourses (from the production of the subject in infancy, its emergence in language, up to the multiple sets of discourses encountered passively and actively throughout its life), the place of the inscribed reader is always the terrain where the subject as a discursive figure meets and interacts with the plural discourses of the text. Readers, like texts (and for that matter characters within texts), are always sites where pluralities intersect. The point is to figure out in each particular case which pluralities are dominant enough to determine and regulate the specific forcefields constituted by these intersections.

Eco's bet on the way a text will be read is a bet on the way intended/imagined readers have been constructed as subjects. The range of discourses at their disposal are precisely those discourses which produced them, except perhaps those whose effectiveness has been repressed, but which still work across the conscious and/or preconscious ones. This proviso is made only because it is not quite accurate to say that unconscious discourses are at the disposal of subjects.

These remarks carry some implications for the theory of ideology. An increasingly accepted definition of ideology is that it is a system of representations. However, in so far as systems of representations involve the production of subjects in determinate places, they are always manifested in terms of signifying practices. Moreover, as such practices occur within institutions (the family, educational institutions, sports organisations, unions, the media, and so on), one can say that ideology insists in discursive formations and that its mode of existence is institutional. The single discourse, the single signifying chain producing a subject is a theoretical fiction.

Discursive formations are imaginary unities, sites where disparate discourses cohere to produce a subject held to the coherence thus produced. The mode of coherence of the discursive formation, the way its subjects are pulled into a coherence, mapped onto each other, is then an ideology. The production of coherences is the function of institutions. It follows that ideologies organise contradictions, oppositions, and the like, through institutions. In short, they organise heterogeneity into an imaginary homogeneity, instituting subjects as the field holding together this heterogeneity, cementing it. One example of this is the legal ideology: on the one hand, law, and the legal ideology, addresses individuals, refusing to recognise classes, while on the other hand it operates in the name of the public against individuals. In other words, it sets up individuals in order to act against them. It simultaneously atomises and produces the fiction of unity which is the public. A second contradiction in the legal ideology is that its very exclusion of class struggle serves the class struggle of the bourgeoisie. Legal ideology is then the specific set of discourses produced by and in determinate institutions which holds subjects to the contradictory unity producing the legal subject.

Another example is Griersonism. Griersonism is a set of discourses, organised under the dominance of a realist ideology (itself organising separation/identity, reflection/transparency), which pulls together a notion of technicist neutrality – the apparatus as neutral recording instrument, relating to cinema as a neutral educational technology – and cinematic specificity, that is, the production of specifically cinematic texts, films as art. Obviously, Griersonism also organises a wide variety of other discourses, as shown in Jim Hillier and Alan Lovell's book *Studies in Documentary*.[25]

Ideologies then exist on many different levels, from the ideology specific to an individual (the organisation of ideologies with a specific coherence characteristic of an individual) via the ideology represented by a book (or a film or a painting) as a specific object to the – in our social formation – highest level of integration: bourgeois ideology. At this point, the level of integration is so tenuously abstract that it loses all its force, all ability to mark differences, and thus operates as a term blocking knowledge of ideologies, becoming part of dogmatism and anti-intellectualism. This latter point indicates also that given discourses can, and almost always do, form part of various different ideologies, that is to say, a given discourse can combine with diverse sets of discourses to produce different ideologies.

Institutions (social groupings whose coherence is determined by rituals, procedures, legal or journalistic definitions, constitutions, and so on – that is to say, by other discursive formations) function as machines freezing or producing specific unequal relations of force between ideologies, organising them into determinate balances of force. But although they organise domination and repression, the very plurality of discourses to be organised, and the plurality of institutions impinging upon each other, guarantee that institutions change or disappear. For instance, a change in personnel and/or alteration in the precariously held balance of forces between sets of discourses or between institutions (themselves held in encompassing institutions) can decisively affect the operation of that institution, generating the point where it may cease functioning or where it may have to be replaced by another institution.

It is worth emphasising that in its history the individual subject encounters ideologies at various levels and in various ways. When encountering a specific ideology one does not necessarily encounter its full range of discourses, nor does one encounter all of its discourses with equal force. According to the balance of forces within the institution where a subject encounters, say, academicism, that subject may never encounter the Todorovian formalist component discourses of that ideology on the terrain of the human sciences. Moreover, in certain ideological formations, the actualisation or the strengthening of, for example, formalist ideologies may well produce shifts in balances of power conducive to the type of change one seeks to accomplish in a given set of discourses and thus, in the longer term, in the social formation. The effectiveness of such changes and the direction(s) in which the balance of forces is altered will depend on the specific configuration of discourses within which interventions are made. Decisions regarding such interventions need to be made on the basis of an analysis of the given ideological formation (or sub-formation), the state of the balance of forces in the area of intervention, the identification of weaknesses in the cohesion of these contradictory unities, and so on. The reference above to auteurism is a good example of such an ideological intervention: although deeply implicated in individualism and theology, auteurism was – and in some cases still is – able to help displace or discredit the particularly stultifying ideologies of individual taste and the entire subjective impressionist edifice.

VI.2.

The next, rather vexed questions are: what organises the distribution of ideologies; which forces determine the production of ideological formations and how? Clearly, ideologies do not require particular classes (however defined) as their expressive subjects. On the contrary, the production of a class as an expressive subject is a variety of a particular idealist ideology. Individuals do have different relations to sets of discourses, in that their position in the social formation, their positioning in the real, will determine which sets of discourses a given subject is likely to encounter and in which ways it will do so. In other words, this position will determine which discursive formations are likely to combine and produce given individuals as subjects in ideology. For example, the function of the educational apparatus and its manifold institutions is not merely to train certain people for, or keep others from, specific jobs. It also has a more elaborate function: the control of the discourses through which subjects are to be constituted. This control is never total since unpredictable discourses always threaten that control and are therefore censored with various degrees of severity. Subjects produced by the intersection or overlap of undesirable or otherwise obstructive discourses can even be relegated to special institutions: correction centres, prisons, asylums, doss houses, schools.

Educational institutions, like broadcast organisations, journals, newspapers and so forth, can thus be seen as making sure not that a specific set of discourses is activated in relation to students or consumers, but that specific sets of discourses are marginalised or declared out of bounds. The exclusion of particular explanatory frameworks and theoretical discourses is more important and significant in the sense of being more productive over a longer term than what is included in an educational programme, a television programme or a newspaper. In this light, such institutions can be assessed according to their ability to anchor subjects in restricted discursive formations without having to be too dogmatic about contents. It is more important to be dogmatic about what shall not be provided, thus ensuring that even the subject-production of those who rebel against what is on offer also sets the boundaries within which that rebellion will be played out, together with the specific forms such rebellion may take: whether it is likely to affect the basic structures of a social formation, or whether it will dissipate its energy in censured but tolerated marginalities. What has to be withheld from the rebel is 'dangerous knowledge'. Provided politically and analytically effective means of understanding are not available to the rebels or more generally, to consumers, they can rebel to their heart's content ... and be dealt with via the criminal law, asylums or other appropriate institutions.

In this way, the concrete experience of the individual, determined by his or her place in the relations of production, his or her place in the real, will determine in its turn to a large extent which institutions, which discursive regimes, and so on, he/she will encounter and in what order. Obviously, such a mode of control is not foolproof. A given subject can be produced within, say, the family in such a way that it will engage with other sets of discourses in apparently unpredictable ways. It is precisely to such instances of subject-production that psychoanalytic practice addresses itself. Also, in order for there to be a specific class ideology aiming towards maximum political effectiveness, this must be produced for/in a class struggle by an institution defining itself as a class (or as a party or institution acting in the name, and with the support of, a large group of people sharing certain positions in the relations of production) against specific institutions (other class institutions, the state, parties, and the like). Furthermore, subjects thus produced in class positions may well, at one and the same time, be involved in, and positioned by, other ideologies, including some forged in the struggle against them by their opponents. It is very difficult, even at the best of times, to acquire an understanding of social processes if the intellectual means for constructing such an understanding have been systematically withheld from you and if even the very desire for understanding is constantly and pervasively denigrated in favour of 'emotional' and 'common sense' ways of knowing.

Having recognised the determining power of the real, it is equally necessary to recognise that the real is never in its place, to borrow a phrase from Lacan, in that it is always and only grasped as reality through discourse. This means that there is a dialectic, a relation between these modes of determination: the real determines to a large extent the encounter of and with discourses, while these encounters structure and produce reality, and consequently in their turn affect the subject's trajectory through the real. It is in this area that the answer to Althusser's notoriously vague formulation of the relative autonomy of the ideological may be specified in terms of the articulation through history between subjects in the real and subjects in ideology.

VI.3.

Ideological struggle would then involve two necessarily simultaneous moments: 1) the undermining and displacing of specific ideological configurations and/or discourses within them, in order to change determinate discursive regimes, to change the balance of forces within institutions and within ideologies; and 2) the production or the support of other sets of discourses, other subject productions in ideology, other imaginary unities which will allow or contribute to the political project (itself an imaginary unity) presiding over the struggle. Indeed, unified subject positions and institutions holding subjects to specific sets of discourses in determinate hierarchies, as with parties and party programmes, are a fundamental prerequisite for the production of social change.

The dangers of not conducting both operations at the same time, in a dialectical movement, are all too familiar. Starting from a position of intervention against discourses which dominate particular institutions and which need to be attacked and displaced through ideological struggle, it sometimes becomes all too tempting to adopt, as an essentialist dogma, a strategy of attack against all forms of imaginary unity, thus condemning oneself to a romantic-anarchist project of eternal and universal subversion/transgression. At the same time, such a radical project opens wide the door to the most suspect practices within the academy as within critical journalism: the perpetual dispersal and subversion of other discourses being precisely an extremely useful and widely practised strategy for the establishing of reputations which in no way hinder careerist tendencies.

The second major danger, connected with the privileging of the second moment of the dialectic, is perhaps more familiar in Ukania (to use Tom Nairn's apt label for the UK). The construction of imaginary unities, founded on a programmatically organised set of discourses (slogans, editorials, policy statements, and so on), necessary as this may be for political struggle, constantly raises the possibility of forgetting that all institutions are riddled with contradictions: for instance, in the context of identity or of economist politics, the positing of gender, race or class 'subject positions' is necessarily accompanied by the notion that a class, a gender group or a racially defined group constitutes an expressive subject, sole source of a particular, specific and as it were organic ideology. Positionality in the real does indeed affect subject production in ideology, as I pointed out earlier. But positionality in discursive formations (that is, in reality) and in 'the real' are two different things which must be thought together in a dialectical movement of mutual determination.

Notes

1. The debates were initiated in numerous issues of *Screen* in parallel with the publications accompanying the Edinburgh International Film Festival's retrospectives between 1971 and 1976. The point-of-view analyses seeking to make a contribution to these debates are mainly Edward Branigan's 'Formal Permutations of the POV Shot', *Screen* vol. 16 no. 3, 1975; his analysis of 'The Space of *Equinox Flower*', *Screen*, vol. 17 no. 2, 1976; and Kristin Thompson and David Bordwell's 'Space and Narration in the Films of Ozu' in the same issue. Unattributed quotes in my essay here are from Edward Branigan's 'Subjectivity Under Siege – From Fellini's 8½ to Oshima's *The Story of a Man Who Left His Will on Film*' in *Screen*, vol. 19 no. 1, 1978.
2. Stephen Heath, 'Screen Images, Film Memory', in *Edinburgh '76 Magazine*, 1976, p. 40.
3. In this context, it may be of some interest to note Yukio Mishima's account of the inscription of a contradiction (two ideologies) in relation to a character, demonstrating that such a notion can be perfectly well accommodated in the most traditionally idealist and frankly reactionary political ideology. In *Sun and Steel* (translated by John Bester, New York: Grove Press, 1970), Mishima writes: 'My mind devised a system that by installing within the self two mutually antipathetic elements – two elements that flowed alternatively in opposite directions – gave the appearance of inducing an ever wider split

in the personality, yet in practice created at each moment a living balance that was constantly being destroyed and brought to life again. The embracing of a dual polarity within the self and the acceptance of contradiction and collision – such was my own blend of art and action.'

4. Boris Uspensky, 'Study of Point of View: Spatial and Temporal Form', *Working Papers and Pre-Publications*, no. 24, (Urbino, 1973).
5. Geoffrey Nowell-Smith, 'A Note on History/Discourse', in *Edinburgh '76 Magazine*, 1976, p. 26.
6. Pierre Macherey, 'Problems of Reflection', in *Literature, Society and the Sociology of Literature: Proceedings of the Conference held at the University of Essex*, July 1976, p. 48.
7. Umberto Eco, 'Le Problème de la réception', in *Critique Sociologique et Critique Psychanalytique* (Brussels: Éditions de l'Institut de Sociologie, Université Libre de Bruxelles, 1970), pp. 13–14.
8. *Communications*, no. 8, 1966, pp. 146–7.
9. G. Nowell-Smith, 'A Note on History/Discourse'.
10. *Poétique*, no. 24, 1975, p. 420ff.
11. *Roland Barthes by Roland Barthes* (New York: Hill & Wang, 1971), p. 47.
12. *Poétique*, no. 24, 1975. Todorov uses the term *indécidable*, literally: undecidable, referring to a theoretical concept introduced by Jacques Derrida.
13. Stephen Heath, 'Anata Mo', in *Screen*, vol. 17 no. 4, 1976/7. In this essay, Heath makes a number of points about Oshima's *Death by Hanging*, clearly suggesting that *The Story of a Man Who Left His Will on Film* can be seen as extending and re-focusing the strategies outlined in the earlier film, but more specifically so in terms of cinematic representation.
14. Joseph L. Anderson, 'The Space In Between: American Criticism and Japanese Films', in *Wide Angle*, vol. 1 no. 4.
15. Kristin Thompson, 'Notes on the Spatial System of Ozu's Early Films', in *Wide Angle*, vol. 1 no. 4.
16. Rosalind Coward, 'Lacan and Signification', in *Edinburgh '76 Magazine*, 1976, p. 9.
17. Jacques Lacan, *Écrits: A Selection*, New York: Norton, 1977, p. 2.
18. R. Coward, 'Lacan and Signification', p. l6.
19. Julia Kristeva, *Le Texte du roman* (The Hague: Mouton, 1970), p. 85.
20. J. Lacan, *Écrits: A Selection*, p. 42.
21. It may be necessary in this context to emphasise that no appeal is being made to the early Althusserian equation between ideology and the imaginary. In fact, there is no pure imaginary to be opposed to the symbolic (or in Althusserian terms: science). Both instances always necessarily coexist in a relation of mutual presupposition, in the same sense that language and speech coexist in a necessary simultaneity in each utterance. Discourse is a formation at the intersection of the symbolic and the imaginary, in that it marks the figure of their incidence on/in each other. In so far as discursive subject positions can be mapped onto each other to produce an imaginary unity analogous to the unification of the body in pieces in the specular ego, this means that an imaginary unity is contradictory to the extent that it is marked by the symbolic. As all ideologies are such contradictory unities, there is no question of opposing ideology to the symbolic. Quite the contrary.
22. Paul Willemen, '*Pursued*: The Fugitive Subject', in Phil Hardy (ed.), *Raoul Walsh* (Edinburgh Film Festival, 1974).
23. Stephen Heath, 'Screen Images, Film Memory', p. 40.
24. Colin MacCabe, 'Realism and the Cinema: Notes on some Brechtian Theses', in *Screen*, vol. 15 no. 2, 1974.
25. London: Secker & Warburg, 1972.

Part Two

Chapter 3

The Sirkian System

Thomas Elsaesser's study of Vincente Minnelli's melodramas in *The Brighton Film Review* and *Screen*'s 1971 special issue on Douglas Sirk, followed by a retrospective and two books about the Danish-German-American master of melodrama, stimulated a great deal of speculation about various aspects of the melodrama genre. But many of the more basic issues still await serious study, especially in the area of film studies. In literature, the parameters of such a study have now been sketched out by Michael McKeon in *The Origins of the English Novel*. In *Mechanic Accents*,[1] Michael Denning has given an account of the way the industrialisation of 'popular' culture in the US between 1880 and 1920 transformed areas of US working-class culture by appropriating working-class concerns and aspirations in order to return them to that class suitably censored by, and adapted to, the requirements of lower middle-class culture's representatives.

Much of the most productive work about Euro-American film melodrama has centred on discussions of Douglas Sirk's work. As Jon Halliday has pointed out,[2] Sirk has been praised either for his stylistic qualities or for being a master of the weepie. He is either praised for making extraordinary films in spite of the exigencies of the weepie as a genre, or it is the weepie genre itself which is validated and Sirk is put forward as one of its most accomplished practitioners. Indeed, there are genuine contradictions within the work of Douglas Sirk which to some extent invite both approaches. The status of such contradictions and what they seek to manage or regulate – at times ostentatiously failing to do so – has been the main point at issue in the debates surrounding his work.

In order to understand and to assess the function of such contradictions in the Sirkian system, it is helpful to turn to Sirk's theatrical experience in Germany in the 1920s. In 1929, Sirk staged Brecht's *Threepenny Opera* with immense success. As left-wing intellectuals in the German theatrical world, both Brecht and Sirk reacted against expressionism, although it is quite clear that both were also influenced by that movement. Brecht's early plays bear witness to this influence and so do some of Sirk's later Hollywood films, especially *Tarnished Angels* (1957). Moreover, Sirk makes a direct allusion to the old expressionist ideas in the phantasmagoria speech in his *Captain Lightfoot* (1955). Although it is not clear whether Brecht approved of Sirk's production of the *Threepenny Opera*,[3] during his career in Hollywood Sirk made frequent use of techniques Brecht had pioneered in the play and he achieved very similar, indeed equally ironic results. Bernard Dort has described Brecht's pre-epic technique as that of the boomerang image. According to Dort, Brecht presented the theatre-going public of the time with the image of life it wanted to see on the stage in order to denounce the unreality of that very image, to denounce its ideological character.[4] Brecht himself explained that the *Threepenny Opera* attacked bourgeois conceptions not only by choosing to present them on the stage, but also by the manner of presentation itself. The play shows a way of life which the spectator wishes to see portrayed in the theatre. It is a fantasy life with a strongly utopian aspect, giving a fairly free reign to the pleasure principle. At the same time, however, the spectator is forced to confront aspects of that life which he/she would rather not confront. He/she not only sees wishes fulfilled, but is made to realise the cost of that fulfilment. In that sense, the spectator sees his or her utopian fantasies criticised and is encouraged to elaborate more socially, as well as individually, gratifying fantasies. Spectators may thus begin to perceive themselves as object rather than as subject of the fantasies represented. Bernard Dort continued:

> The picturesque robbers of the *Threepenny Opera* are not bandits: they are robbers only as the bourgeoisie dreams them. In the final analysis we realise that they are in fact members of the bourgeoisie. Or, more precisely, it is through the disguise of robbers that the spectators will come to recognise themselves as being bourgeois. A subtly engineered set of displacements and discontinuities facilitates such a self-recognition. In this way, Brecht has attempted to sabotage the notion of the theatre as a mirror (for our fantasies). Brecht puts on the stage what seems to be the image of the kind of exotic society that the spectator wants to see. In fact, what the spectator discovers in the very unreality of such an image, is himself. The mirror of the stage does not reflect the world of the audience anymore, but the ideological disguises of the audience itself. Suddenly, at that point, the mirror refers us back to our own reality. It bounces the images of the spectacle back at us – like a boomerang.[5]

Sirk's films could be described as the opposite of a distorting mirror: the world the audience wants to see (an exotic world of crime, wealth, corruption, passion) is a distorted projection of the audience's own fantasies to which Sirk applies a correcting device, mirroring these very distortions. This conjunction of, or rather this contradiction between, distanciation and implication, between fascination and its critique, allows Sirk to thematise a great many contradictions inherent in the society in which he worked and the world he depicted.[6] It equally gives us the means to read Sirk's own contradictory position within that society and in relation to that world. Jon Halliday has indicated,[7] and has been supported on this point by Sirk himself,[8] that the society depicted in most of the films is characterised by a smugness and a complacency masking decay and disintegration from within, which lies just beneath the surface. Sirk also pointed to his own contradictory position within the society in which he found himself.[9] He attempted to mount a critique of a society which provided him with the money and the tools to make his films, but could not offend that same society to the point of it withdrawing its support for the films through, for instance, a lack of box office receipts. This primary contradiction generated further, secondary ones in his work.

Firstly, although the films were products of, for and about Eisenhower's America, they were misunderstood at that time. Sirk explained this in terms of the American audience's failure to recognise irony and the lack of a genuine film culture based on an informed notion of aesthetics.[10] Secondly, now that the complexities of these films are beginning to be understood, even in English-speaking countries, American society has undergone a process of social change and is producing quite different films. While this social and historical shift is partly responsible for allowing us to 'see' Sirk today, it also contributes to the tendency of contemporary critics to misread Sirk's films again, though in a different manner: critics now tend to judge Sirk's presentation of Eisenhower's America by the standards of contemporary critiques of ideology, thus once more mistaking or neglecting the real relevance of the films both for the situation within which they were produced and for us today.

On reading Sirk's essays and interviews, it is possible to deduce that Sirk was familiar with the major theories of representation formulated in the first two decades of the century, both in Russia and in Western Europe. Although his aesthetic position cannot be confused with either expressionism or symbolism, it is evident that he shares their complete rejection of the conventions of illusionism.

Without fully subscribing to any single aesthetic movement, Sirk was undoubtedly greatly affected by the theatrical revolution which immediately preceded his career as a stage director. When analysing his American films, it becomes apparent that many stylistic features which had been rehabilitated by expressionism, together with the symbolist concept of correspondences, were adapted by Sirk to suit his own purposes. In his American melodramas in particular, it is possible to discern the echoes of such expressionist prescriptions as: 'The melody of a great gesture says more than the highest consummation of what is called naturalness' (Paul Kornfeld); or, 'The dullness and stupidity of men are so enormous that only enormities can counteract them. Let the new drama be enormous' (Yvan Goll); or again, 'Man and things will be shown as naked as possible and always through a magnifying glass for better effect' (also Yvan Goll).

For Sirk such prescriptions represent a source of inspiration and become no more than echoes, detectable in his magnification of emotionality, his use of pathos, choreography and music, reverberating within the mirror-ridden walls of the Sirkian decor. The meaning of this kind of stylisation does not necessarily become clear on the first viewing of a Sirk film. In order to grasp its full significance, it is necessary to take into account the circumstances under which Sirk was required to work: the big Hollywood studio, itself an element in the consciousness industry that had grown up to adjust primarily rural populations to the requirements of industrial living and all that such a change implied in terms of the need to spread new kinds of 'common sense', family values, public/private morality alignments, and so on.

The subject-matter of his films, as well as the general narrative outline, was imposed upon him, as was the need to please a very large audience so that producers and middle men might reap maximum profits. This meant that Sirk had to make films for the 'average' American audience as defined by the industry, which was its main economic as well as ideological target. However, Sirk knew this audience to be immune to irony: 'In general this public is too simple and too naive – in the best sense of these terms - to be susceptible to irony. It requires clearly delineated positions, for and against.'[11] As a European intellectual, he surprisingly enough found these new circumstances very stimulating: he wholeheartedly embraced the rules of the American genres and especially those of the melodrama.

Sirk drew on his theatrical experience to intensify the generic conventions, rather than to break them. Such intensification he achieved in a number of ways:

- by the deliberate use of symbols as emotional stimuli, their most striking feature being their total unequivocalness. For instance, the association of Kirby/Hudson in *All That Heaven Allows* (1955) with a Christmas tree and a deer; Sara Jane/Kohner's mud-stained white dress in *Imitation of Life* (1959);

- by setting the action in an echo chamber reminiscent of a stage: *Imitation of Life* is predominantly filmed in long shot, emphasising both the spaciousness and the confinement of the decor;

– through the use of choreography as a direct expression of excessive emotion in a character: for instance Sara Jane/Kohner's dance in *Imitation of Life* and Mary Lee/Malone's dance in *Written on the Wind* (1956);

– through the use of baroque colour schemes as in *Written on the Wind* and violent shadow contrasts in *Tarnished Angels* or in *There's Always Tomorrow* (1956).

The subject-matter of these melodramas is like that of other run-of-the-mill products. In fact, Sirk made a number of remakes. However, by stylising his treatment of a given narrative, he succeeded in introducing in a quite unique manner a distance between the film and its narrative pretext. The most striking example of this 'through a glass darkly' technique is the credit sequence of *Imitation of Life*. As the titles begin to appear on the screen, a large number of glass 'diamonds' slowly drift down as if poured by an invisible hand until they finally fill the screen by the time the director's credit appears. In an interview he gave to *Cahiers du Cinéma*,[12] Sirk explained the importance he attached to stylisation and stressed the importance of establishing a distance between the audience and the depicted action. In lectures at the National Film Theatre in London (1971) he also stressed the need for actors to have distance from the characters they portray.

Nevertheless, in general his melodramas mercilessly bind the audience into the narration. Ample proof of this can be found in the near hysterical audience reactions generated by his films: abundant tears and/or self-protective laughter. Such reactions indicate that the distance Sirk is referring to is not necessarily perceived by the commercially targeted audience. However, this does not mean that the distance does not exist in the text's construction, in the filmic system. It merely means that there appears to be a discrepancy between the two audiences Sirk has in mind while making the films: the audience which he knows will come to see his films; and the audience he hopes will 'see' his films by occupying a different intellectual, political or historical vantage point to that occupied by the audience as constructed by the consciousness industry.

When he has more directorial control, the techniques Sirk employs differ somewhat from those he uses in the straight studio products. He takes great care to ensure that the audience(s) experience(s) a sense of distanciation, for instance by making use of an epilogue, as in *Tarnished Angels*, or the drama-within-a-drama at the end of *Take Me to Town* (1953). Moreover, when we compare Sirk's films with other melodramas, such as the films of Frank Borzage, Leo McCarey or Vincente Minnelli, it becomes evident that Sirk's rhetoric does not refer to some facile dichotomy between fantasy and reality. Instead, Sirk informs the surface reality of the plot and of his characterisations with a secondary reality that may consist of a different story altogether, as in *Sign of the Pagan* (1954), where he grafted undercurrents of Marlowe's *Tamburlaine the Great* onto the main narrative. Alternatively, his secondary narrative may criticise the surface reality of the main story, as in *Written on the Wind, All I Desire* (1953) or *Imitation of Life*, through techniques of stylisation which refer the viewer to aesthetic concepts developed in the theatre (for instance, the intensification of generic conventions) and which bring about an anti-illusionist style of representation.

Yuri Tynianov, in a study of Dostoevsky and Gogol,[13] points out that stylisation and parody are closely linked to each other: 'Both live a double life. Beyond the work, there is a second level, stylised or prosodised. When stylisation is strongly marked it becomes parody.' To be clear about this, it must be stated that the term parody as used by Tynianov does not necessarily mean 'comic'. He defines parody as 'the mechanisation of a particular procedure, a mechanism which, of course, will only be noticeable where the procedure to which it applies is known. Hence, if the parody's style is not sufficiently familiar to the audience, they will be unaware that something is being parodied.' Although the notion of parody may not apply to Sirk's entire œuvre, many of the films have strong parodic elements in them. This becomes most evident in his use of cliché: what was referred to earlier as the deliberate use of symbols for emotional effect could, in Sirk's case, also be read as a deliberate use of cliché. Sirk's melodramas abound with cliché images: for example, the deer and the Christmas tree as symbols for nature; the cabaret with red lights standing for depravity; a red dress and a fast car standing for irresponsibility and loose living.

Here we are confronted with a systematic stylistic feature, a mechanisation of a stylistic procedure which characterises stories in popular weeklies and tabloid newspapers. It is extremely difficult to make a precise distinction between stylisation and parody, but Tynianov's remark about Dostoevsky could easily be applied to Sirk: 'It may very well be that this delicate interweaving of stylisation and parody, covering the development of a tragic subject, constitutes the originality of the sense of the grotesque in Dostoevsky.'[14]

Irony is also at work in the function of the camera movements. Sirk's camera, as a rule, remains at some distance from the actors. The space in the diegesis, although rigorously circumscribed, is vast and solidly established. Long shots and mid-shots predominate. The camera, however, is almost continuously in motion. This mobility implicates the viewer emotionally, dragging or guiding him or her into and through the diegesis, withholding portions of the space which then suddenly flash into view or are doubled in mirrors. At the same time, the technique establishes some detachment *vis-à-vis* the characters.

This apparent paradox between an involving mobility which maintains some insecurity about the viewer's position and the distance which generates detachment and endows the diegesis with a solid space refers to a dialectic which is perhaps the most dynamic aspect of the Sirkian system. People put themselves on show but simultaneously cloak themselves in roles, they reveal themselves through the deployment of artifice and clichés (in this respect Sirk is remarkably like Max Ophuls). Mirrors are nearly always there in the background to remind them and us that there is no escape from representation, that there is no private space, that all is show. Since they are under scrutiny, the characters clumsily stage their own appearance and thus betray their own shallowness, since the deepest personal tragedies and the most intense emotions are enacted in a conventional, clichéd repertoire of roles. The persona thus adopted in fact ends up as the most eloquent statement about the characters and leaves them vulnerable, exposed in all their stunted superficiality as profoundly damaged people. At the same time, the audience, which can relate to this double strategy or take the characters at the same face value they have in other melodramas, sees what it paid to see: more or less glamorous people suffering extremes of anxiety, titillating imagery, wealth and tourist brochure existences.

For those who perceive the parodic dimension of all this, they are not unaware of the viewer's watchful presence in the cinematic world. For them, the characters and the spaces are clearly on show (like the audience of the melodrama staged at the end of *Take Me to Town* which sees both the enacted play and the equally conventional confrontation – literally at a different level – of the hero and the villain through the same theatrically framed space). The effect is that the audience which came to see its fantasies enacted ends up seeing the distortions and the constraints which it forced upon the spectacle in the first place. In this way, the audience's entertainment ideology is unmasked and made to rebound back onto the audience itself, either as redoubled pleasure (if the viewer relishes the narcissistic as well as intellectual gratification to be derived from recognising the way the consciousness industry has been outsmarted by an artist) or in the form of a sense of unease, possibly boredom or even energetic rejection as the viewer refuses to, or cannot, recognise that his or her predigested wishes and entertainment ideology are being criticised.

This rebounding image is, of course, represented in the diegesis as well: the mirrors send boomerang images to the characters too. The best illustration of this doubling effect is the television set in Cary Scott/Jane Wyman's living room in *All That Heaven Allows*, a particularly poignant image for film and television students and lecturers if we remember that the critical study of melodrama inaugurated by Sirk's work eventually degenerated into mindless celebrations of television soaps by intellectuals anxious to legitimate the consciousness industry's more stultifying products. A Sirk film does for the audience what the television set does for Cary Scott/Wyman, or what surgery does for Helen Phillips/Wyman in *Magnificent Obsession* (1954). But it is only an intensification, a parody: that is to say, a mechanisation of a style of representation practised very widely in Hollywood, then and still today.

Parody does not destroy or replace what it parodies. Therefore, both the views of Sirk as the implacable Marxist critic of Eisenhower's America or of Sirk as the greatest exponent of the bourgeois weepie are equally misguided. In fact, Sirk's position in the history of the cinema closely parallels that of Tolstoy in the history of Russian literature. Lenin considered Tolstoy to be a unique and extremely valuable artist because he dramatised the contradictions within Russian society at the turn of the century when Tsarism was not strong enough to prevent a revolution, while the revolution did not yet have enough strength to defeat Tsarism.[15] Sirk performed a similar function for America in the 1950s: he depicted a society that appeared to be strong and booming, but which was in fact exhausted and being torn apart internally.

Considering Sirk's films as parodies makes it possible to understand and explain the enormous success of many of his best films at the time of their release and the subsequent neglect or rejection of that work by the intelligentsia for over a decade. That phenomenon is analogous to the success of Brecht's *Threepenny Opera*, a success which endures to this very day. As Bernard Dort has pointed out, the technique of the boomerang image carries with it some ominous pitfalls. The sophistication of the process is too easily ignored, allowing the bourgeois audience to operate a recovery manoeuvre: either it recognises its own image as indeed bourgeois but enhanced with the exotic prestige of robbers, corrupt millionaires, actresses or stunt flyers; or, alternatively, it fails to recognise the doubleness of the process and simply rejects the image of the bourgeoisie presented, fancying itself to be more sophisticated than the shallow characters and clichéd lives presented in the diegesis. Hence the rejection or the wilful misreading – by turning it into camp – of Sirk's films by reviewers and the more myopic critics. In spite of these pitfalls, the fact remains that Sirk, taking into account the circumstances in which he worked, developed a most refined and complex filmic system to convey his critique while remaining employable, rather as Gramsci evolved a particular style that allowed him to smuggle Marxist theory past his Fascist gaolers. In this way, Sirk at least manifested and thematised in his very style the contradictions within the society that presided over the making and the circulation of his films. Perhaps

94

only Lubitsch and Wilder in American film history managed to equal that feat.

Postscript

Over the last twenty years or so, a great many books and essays of widely varying quality have been published on US film melodrama and British television soaps. Some of that work, such as Laura Mulvey's *Melodrama Inside and Outside the Home* and Ashish Rajadhyaksha's *Neo-Traditionalism – Film as Popular Art in India*,[16] opens up perspectives for further research. Much could be learned by placing melodrama within the context of long-term socio-economic shifts and by considering it more specifically as a cultural form tied to the rise of the bourgeoisie still in dialogue with feudal and absolutist cultural and political forms, and to problems of industrialisation and their reverberating impact on established, mostly rural or artisanal as well as aristocratic forms of kinship networks.

The intriguing question presents itself that perhaps post-World War II US melodrama has marked, within narrative and entertainment formulas inherited from the late 19th century, a new epochal shift. As after a 300-year struggle spearheaded by the industrial bourgeoisie the absolutist order finally crumbled in the two world wars which marked the first half of the 20th century, the early 1950s in the US witnessed the dawn of a new epoch: the era of capitalism triumphant. This era can be dated from the end of the Korean War. In this new, unprecedented environment, new forms of living based on rapid increases of mobility (paralleling the emergence of finance capitalism as the dominant force within the capitalist formations) put new strains upon family networks and revived old fantasies.

A second epochal shift, also with massive cultural implications, went along with the bourgeoisie's triumphant though long delayed accession to the status of unchallengable (at least on the domestic front) ruling class. melodrama thrived on representing, in Ross Gibson's words: 'notions and sentiments that cannot be contained within the strictures of taste and social decorum'.[17] The social decorum and tastes at stake in the pre-World War II melodrama were still predominantly those of the upper strata of the bourgeoisie. The political conflict between the rising industrial bourgeoisie and the feudal absolutist order it was displacing took different forms in different European countries, from the revolutionary episodes in France to the bargain struck in Britain allowing the bourgeoisie a significant measure of political and economic power in exchange for adopting and internalising large chunks of the aristocratic socio-cultural ideologies crystallised in 'taste and social decorum'. The melodrama staged the at times fraught process of the bourgeoisie's attempts to settle the terms of this bargain and to deal with the discrepancies and tensions involved in that long-term negotiation.

However, with the conquest of power and the affirmation of an aggressive self-confidence by the post-World War II bourgeoisie, there was no longer any need for the bourgeoisie to agonise over the difficulties presented by the cultural side of their bargain. Instead, the new challenge was the double task, firstly, of presenting the outcome of those protracted and difficult negotiations not as a cobbled together, inconsistent and incoherent compromise, but as a coherent, 'universally valid' and naturally self-evident set of moral and social values; and secondly, of getting the 'lower orders' to accept and incorporate these values as the norms for taste and social decorum. Now it was up to the lower echelons of the bourgeoisie and the upper strata of the working-class, that is to say, those aspiring to the status of respectable middle-class, to come to terms with and to incorporate the new norms of social decorum propagated by the new rulers. Discrepancies and excesses were now to be measured according to a new set of strictures on taste and social decorum, enforced by different social strata in new institutions (in Britain, television, the press and the Arts Council have been the main institutions carrying out this task since the 50s). Consequently, the social scene of melodrama shifted considerably down the social scale as confrontations between 'the people' and 'aristocracy' (however impoverished) were replaced by confrontations between 'the people' and 'the wealthy'. The social sites privileged by these melodramas were the sites of lower middle-class and working-class acculturation. In Britain, these would be schools, pubs, housing estates, package holidays, night clubs and the like. In the US, a variety of white collar milieus became the privileged site of melodrama: the suburbs, hospitals, the service industries with their semi-industrialised intelligentsia (advertisers, writers, the Hollywood milieu itself) and, of course, schools and their 'delinquents'. What was at stake was no longer the excess *vis-à-vis* a social decorum calibrated on what the bourgeoisie assumed to be the aristocratic cultural and moral codes, but an excess measured by the norms of what was presented as middle-class social decorum to be incorporated and emulated by those who strove towards upward mobility.

Similarly, when Indian or Egyptian melodramas are located within the long-term socio-economic rhythms of historical change in their own social formations, they can be seen to mobilise local ('traditional' as well as their own versions of 'modern') cultural resources and to reshape them in context of the local and national, as well as regional, consciousness industries, reworking 'the family problematic' within industrial cultural forms for populations caught in massively disruptive processes of social change managed by and for the benefit of the local bourgeoisies. The resulting types of narrative, often called melodramas or given some pejorative alternative label, bear a family resemblance to Hollywood's types of melodrama. It would be grossly ethnocentric to exclude such films from the genre merely because they do not conform in all respects to the alleged nature of Western melodramas and television soaps, or because their pedigree cannot be related directly to the French Revolutionary or to the Victorian plays. Instead, the lack of fit should spur us to recognise that current kinds of film and television studies in Euro-American contexts must be drastically revised if they are to come to grips with the two most important questions facing considerations of media melodrama: which socio-historical forces are the main determinants generating these types of discourses; and secondly, in which direction do these media discourses actually seek to move their consumers?

A speculative answer to these questions might well turn out to be: melodramas are dramas of modernisation, in which socio-historical forces are reduced to their impact on what particular power blocks choose to define as 'traditional' kinship relations (that is, those put into place by a pre-industrial social formation) and valued accordingly. The critical evaluation of individual melodramas would then assess to what extent a film succeeds in countering the domestic blinkers imposed upon the 'problem' by the genre's conventions, for instance, through irony as in the films of Sirk and Valeria Sarmiento, or by refusing to make a 'drama' of personal emotions as in Chantal Akerman's *Nuit et jour* (1991), or by any other strategy underlining the deficiencies of the genre's dominant forms.

Finally, in the light of melodrama's profound imbrication in the process of industrialisation, a particularly intriguing period for study would be the pre-revolutionary Russian cinema. That cinema is the only major example we have of a cinema made while the absolutist regime was still in power and the industrial bourgeoisie was not yet powerful enough to displace it.[18] In such a context, one may expect especially the temporal aspects of melodramatic narrative, including the subjective experience of psychological time and the presentation of prospects for change, to be orchestrated in a manner markedly different from the way this was done in Europe (where the bourgeoisie was an ascendent force) and in the US.[19] Here again, as demonstrated in Michael McKeon's study of the origins of the English novel, the way discourses of Truth and Virtue are mapped onto conceptualisations of historical time may yield insights into the workings and purposes of melodrama in different cultural and political environments.

Notes

1. Michael McKeon, *The Origins of the English Novel, 1600–1740* (Baltimore: Johns Hopkins University Press, 1987); Michael Denning, *Mechanic Accents – Dime Novels and Working-Class Culture in America* (London: Verso, 1987). The latter work tends to espouse the currently dominant positive valuation of mass-marketed 'popular' culture, but is so intellectually honest

and scrupulously researched that the footnotes provide material for demonstrating an opposite valuation. The extended note 5 on pp. 219–20 is especially revealing.

2. Jon Halliday and Laura Mulvey (eds), *Douglas Sirk* (Edinburgh Film Festival, 1972).
3. Jon Halliday, *Sirk on Sirk* (London: Secker & Warburg, 1971), p. 23.
4. Bernard Dort, *Lecture de Brecht – Seconde édition revue et augmentée de pédagogie et forme épique* (Paris: Le Seuil, 1960), p. 189.
5. Bernard Dort, *Lecture de Brecht*, pp. 190–1.
6. This neologism is used to suggest a direct transformation of the conditions of production into a thematic element of the text. Another example of thematisation in this sense would be the reference to US capitalism through a recourse to, or the systematic avoidance of, very expensive camera movements such as elaborate crane shots.
7. *Douglas Sirk*, pp. 59ff.
8. *Sirk on Sirk*, p. 89.
9. *Sirk on Sirk*, p. 86.
10. *Sirk on Sirk*, pp. 72–3.
11. *Sirk on Sirk*, p. 73.
12. *Cahiers du Cinéma*, no. 189, 1967.
13. 'Destruction, Parodie' [1921], in *Change*, no. 2, 1969.
14. Ibid.
15. 'Tolstoy and the Proletarian Struggle' [1910], *Collected Works* vol. 16 (Moscow: Progress Publishers, 1963), pp. 353–4.
16. Reprinted in Laura Mulvey, *Visual and other Pleasures* (London: Macmillan, 1989); Ashish Rajadhyaksha's essay was published in *Framework* no. 32/33, 1986.
17. Ross Gibson, *South of the West: Postcolonialism and the Narrative Construction of Australia* (Bloomington: Indiana University Press, 1992), p. 29.
18. Early silent Japanese, Korean and Chinese cinemas may also provide productive areas of research in this respect.
19. Yuri Tsivian's research published under the title *Silent Witnesses – Russian films 1908–1919* (London: BFI, 1989), together with Mary Ann Doane's essay on these films, 'Melodrama, Temporality, Recognition: American and Russian Silent Cinema', in *East-West Film Journal*, vol. 4 no. 2, 1990, provide a useful starting-point.

Chapter 4

The Fourth Look

Most definitions of cinematic specificity exclude from their consideration the complex interactions of looks at play in the filmic process. On the contrary, the object-ness of the film text is emphasised in its autonomous, self-enclosed separation from the viewer – thus relegating the problem of the look to the realm of individual subjectivity. Looking itself thus becomes an unproblematic activity irrevocably tied to subjective intentionality.

Christian Metz emphasised this particular approach by insisting that, although film functions in many ways like a mirror, it differs from the mirror in one crucial respect: it doesn't reflect an image of the spectator's own body: 'film is not exhibitionist. I look at it but it doesn't look at me looking at it [t]he visible is entirely on the side of the screen'.[1] The spectator is cast in the role of 'invisible subject', identifying itself to the camera as the punctual source of the look which constitutes the image along the lines of a monocular perspective. Having split the cinematic operation into two distinct realms, film studies can be separated into on the one hand semiological study of the text as an autonomous object, and on the other the psychology of the spectator. Such a separation opens wide the door towards the two main idealist traditions dominating film criticism (and filmmaking): the film text becomes either a Kantian Object For Itself, as in mechanical structuralism or the more primitive forms of semiology; or the text exists solely by grace of the individual consciousness of the viewer, whose subjective intentionality determines the way he/she sees the text. The latter form of idealism leads to statements that there are as many ways of appreciating a film as there are individual spectators.

In a short article in the *Times Higher Educational Supplement*, Stephen Heath wrote that since 'the encounter of Marxism and psychoanalysis on the terrain of semiotics', film can now be studied as

a specific signifying practice: 'signifying' indicates the recognition of as system or series of systems of meaning, film as articulation.

99

'Practice' stresses the process of this articulation, which it thus refuses to hold under the assumption of notions such as representation and expression; it takes film as a work of production of meanings and in doing so brings into the analysis the question of the positioning of the subject, what kind of 'reader' and 'author' it constructs. 'Specificity' is both codes particular to cinema and the heterogeneity of its particular effect, its particular inscriptions of subject and meaning in ideology. Directed in this way the study of film is neither 'contents' nor 'forms' but, breaking the deadlock of that opposition, of operations, of the process of film and the relations of subjectivity in that process.[2]

It is in this context of the study of the relations of subjectivity in the filmic process that the problem of the look and the modes of its inscription acquire their full significance.

The remarkably few studies of this problem of the look in the cinema have tended to concentrate either on the organisation of intra-diegetic looks within the Hollywood narrative cinema (30-degree and 180-degree rules, eye-line matches, and so on) and their implications of involvement (via identification) or separation (via suturing effects) for the spectator; or on more formalist studies of point-of-view structures without taking into account that the point of view of the camera is not identical with that of the spectator if indeed the spectator can be said to have a point of view. In fact, the viewing subject is itself caught in a complex interaction of different looks from different places.

In Hollywood cinema, as Metz points out, the spectator is inscribed as invisible, but that does not mean that he or she is not also subjected to a look, merely that the look at the viewing subject is effaced through a series of aesthetic strategies. The viewer of Hollywood cinema is allowed to imagine him or herself as invisible:

> Conventional films tend to suppress all marks of the subject, of the [filmic] uttering (enunciation), so that the spectator may have the impression of being that subject but as an empty and absent subject, reduced to the mere faculty of vision. [A]ll the seen is rejected towards the side of the pure object.

Metz describes this as

> A drastically split situation in which the double denial without which there would be no story [*histoire*] is maintained at all costs: the scene ignores that it is seen [a]nd that ignorance allows the viewer to ignore him/herself as voyeur.[3]

In another essay, I attempted to show that a film text is always
100

traversed by two sets of marks relating to the looks of two different subjects, one assigned to the place of the author, the other to the place of the viewer, with the viewing subject as an instance incorporating that irrevocable split and vacillating between the two terms.[4] What needs to be studied is the variety of the modalities of the inscription of the look in the filmic process. A good starting-point can be found in Laura Mulvey's remarkable essay, *Visual Pleasure and Narrative Cinema*,[5] in which she outlines an initial approach to the problem.

Mulvey distinguishes three different looks: firstly, the camera's look as it records the pro-filmic event; secondly, the audience's look at the image; and thirdly, the look the characters exchange within the diegesis. What Metz referred to as the inscription of the reader as an invisible, empty and absent subject, Mulvey explains in the following terms: 'The conventions of narrative film deny the first two [looks] and subordinate them to the third, the conscious aim being always to eliminate intrusive camera presence and prevent a distancing awareness in the audience.' Such a distancing awareness occurs precisely when the viewer is confronted with marks of the subject, which directly interpellate the viewer-addressee of a constructed message, forcing him or her to abandon the cloak of invisibility which allowed the viewer to fantasise him or herself as subject of the discourse. Here Mulvey appears to overstate the case against traditional Hollywood narrative. Camera movements have always, even in Hollywood films, been fairly obtrusive and have always drawn attention to themselves, as with, for example, Anthony Mann's crane shots, Corman's dolly shots and zooms, and so on. But it is true that even the look of the camera has consistently been subordinated to the logic of intra-diegetic looks.

As regards the look cast by the spectator, Mulvey divides it into two types: firstly, the spectator can be in direct scopophilic contact with an object of desire; or secondly, he or she can be fascinated with the image of his or her like, identifying with this ideal ego and thus, in a roundabout way, gaining control and possession of the desired object within the diegesis. In this manner, the spectator's look at the spectacle and the intra-diegetic looks can be articulated to each other via the spectator's narcissistic identification with his or her representative in the diegesis. This distinction between the two types of looks cast by the viewer is in some ways open to question. It is true that the traditional forms of cinema are dedicated to the legitimation and perpetuation of a patriarchal order, and that in such a context the object of the look is traditionally the female form displayed for the gaze and enjoyment of men as the active controllers of the look. However, the real basis for the distinction between direct scopophilic contact with the object of desire and mediated contact with, and possession of, that object, must be sought in the origins of the scopophilic drive itself.

In 'Instincts and Their Vicissitudes', Freud wrote that 'At the beginning of its activity, the scopophilic instinct is auto-erotic: it has indeed an object, but that object is the subject's own body.'[6] The identification of the woman as privileged object of the scopophilic drive is therefore already the product of a displacement, as I will argue later in relation to the work of Anthony Mann. Mulvey doesn't allow sufficient room for the fact that in patriarchy the direct object of scopophilic desire can also be male. If scopophilic pleasure relates primarily to the observation of one's sexual like, as Freud suggests, then the two looks distinguished by Mulvey are in fact varieties of one single mechanism: the repression of homosexuality. The narcissistic identification with an ideal ego in the diegesis therefore would not be a mere mediation in order to get at a desired woman, but the contemplation of the male hero would be in itself a substantial source of gratification for a male viewer – as is demonstrated repeatedly in the contemporary American cinema's celebration of male couples. In such films, the suggested homosexual gratification appears to be in direct proportion to the degree to which women are absent from the diegesis. Gratification of the scopophilic drive necessarily reactivates traces of primary narcissism, a fact not sufficiently stressed in Mulvey's account, and which undermines the rigour of her distinction between two types of viewer's looks.

The films of Anthony Mann, for instance, while at times operating with the regimes of looking described by Mulvey, show that even the classic American cinema can mobilise both the sadistic and the fetishistic modes of looking in relation to figures other than images of women. In one sense, Mann's stories are mere excuses to replace one image by another, pretexts for the renewal of visual pleasure. The best example is the credit sequence of *Man of the West* (1958), which opens with an image in colour and cinemascope of an arid wasteland with one isolated figure, a man on horseback, quietly doing nothing in particular. The image and the figure in it are there simply to be looked at while the credits roll, to be enjoyed as pure pictoriality. While the subsequent drama provides the rationale for changing the images, the image-track itself offers endless variations and elaboration of that initial picture. When it has run the entire gamut available in the genre, the film closes with a return to that first image, not to stop the flow but to reactivate it as in a loop. All Mann's amazing Westerns, with their justly celebrated 'breathing' camera movements, play first and foremost on the motif of vision. Not necessarily on a narrative level, as for instance in the films of Hitchcock, but always in the presentation of the narrative, providing examples galore of what Mulvey describes as fetishistic looking.

In addition, as in *Man of the West*, this fetishistic structure of looking revolves around the look at the male figure: at issue is always the male in differing contexts. The viewer's experience is predicated on the pleasure of seeing the male exist, walk, talk, ride, move through or in cityscapes, landscapes or, more abstractly, history. The castration anxiety evoked by Mulvey in relation to the look is present in Mann's work also, but in the form of the unquiet pleasure at seeing the male mutilated, hurt or damaged in some way, often very graphically depicted. This fundamentally (repressed) homosexual looking produces just as much anxiety as the look at the female, especially when it is presented as directly as in the killing scenes in *T Men* (1947) or in *Border Incident* (1949). The anxiety is not simply to be assumed, it is marked in the images themselves: the shadowy world of the film noir where Mann often relies exclusively on lateral, fragmented lighting and bizarre camera angles; or the contorted, neurotic landscapes, shacks and ghost towns of his Westerns, replaced in his later work by the stylised opulence and giganticism of the epics. The images always draw attention to themselves, arresting the look and being narratively focused on the pleasures of seeing the male body in motion, a pleasure paid for, in the diegesis, by the mutilation or damaging of that body. It is the anxious aspect of the look at the male which is echoed in the thematic structures of the films – and which probably accounts for the enthusiasm for Mann's films of the 60s auteurists, an all-male group obsessed with Man's relation to everything.

This aspect is most explicit in the war films and in the Westerns, where the heroes ceaselessly try to eradicate the memory of some real or imaginary 'hurt' experienced, predictably enough, in the familial past. Moreover, given that the look is an integral part of the process of male narcissistic identifications, the theme of the attainment of some 'true' manhood produces the hero as someone searching for his identity (as the saying went two decades ago and again in the 90s). In Mann, this searching journey involves damaging the male body, followed by the finding of identity or of death. Mann's films then elaborate that motif of the pleasure and the anxiety of the look at the male into further narrative motifs, such as the recurrent device of the hero pursued by a name: a father's name, or the name the hero wants to make for himself, or merely the name that makes you a target, as in the list of names in Robespierre's black book in *Reign of Terror* (1949). The importance of this knot between the name and the male figure as both active searcher and object of the look is signalled in the ironically anonymous titles of the Westerns: *Man of the West*, *The Man from Laramie* (1955). It culminates in *El Cid* (1961), whose honorific name wins the battle as he, a corpse tied into a saddle, rides out to meet the enemy. Mann's films inscribe the look resolutely within a regime of spectacle, an array of eye-catching devices organised around fear and desire for the male.

However, it remains true that in patriarchy the female form is a privileged object of scopophilic desire. Mulvey continues her argument by pointing out that the contemplation of the female form itself trails problems in its wake, as it cannot fail to evoke, in return, the anxiety it originally signified, that is, castration. She explains that the male unconscious has two avenues of escape from this evocation of castration anxiety: firstly, a preoccupation with the re-enactment of the original trauma in the form of the investigation of the woman, the perpetual recommencing of attempts to see her guilty secret, counter-balanced by the devaluation, punishment and/or saving of the object culpably provoking anxiety; and secondly, a complete disavowal of castration by substituting a fetish object, even to the point of turning the represented figure itself into a fetish, as with the star cult.

Finally, Mulvey underlines that the first escape route has close links with sadism, a drive which is also aimed at repressing castration anxieties provoked in the subject. She links this sadistic component of voyeurism to the need for a narrative, as sadism depends on making something happen to something or someone else, while fetishistic scopophilia can exist outside linear time, happily contemplating a frozen image. Here again, the distinction between the two ways of coping with castration fears appears a bit hasty. The former route, the recurrent investigation of the female form, is itself a form of fetish-ism: 'I know she is castrated, and yet ... let's look again.' This attitude reproduces the traditional fetishistic split between belief and knowledge. So, both escapes are equally implicated in fetishism but offer different strategies of coping. The sadistic aggression of the woman, evident in narrative films, is easily paralleled by the ag-gression of the fetish frame or the emulsion, as in some avant-garde films. In her desire to pinpoint the various scopophilic mechanisms at play in narrative films, Mulvey overlooks the fact that in so-called non-narrative films exactly the same mechanisms are at play: scopo-philia, fetishism and sadism. Mulvey's article ends with what appears to be an error prompted by her concern to relate a feminist politics to an avant-garde orthodoxy.

Undoubtedly, the kind of voyeuristic pleasure which involves sadis-tic and fetishistic pleasure at the expense of an objectification of the image of women is to be criticised. But this does not mean that it is possible, or indeed, desirable, to expel these drives from the filmic process altogether, since such a move would simply abolish cinema itself. It is essential if cinema is to continue to exist that the scopophi-lic drive be granted some satisfaction. What matters is not whether this pleasure is present or absent, but rather the positioning of the subject in relation to it. In Stephen Heath's terms, what is important is what kind of 'reader' or 'author' it constructs.

Having described the three looks at play in the filmic process, the two different looks of the viewer and the two escapes from castration anxiety, Mulvey finishes her essay with the statement: 'This complex interaction of looks is specific to film.' However, few films propose the inscription of the look in its different modalities as their central paradigm. Most of Stephen Dwoskin's work stands as an isolated example of an attempt to work through this particular problematic. The reasons why this should have gone largely unnoticed (or at least uncommented upon) are to be found in the nature of the debates at present shaping the landscape of avant-garde film-making.

Battle lines appear to have been drawn around the issue of cinematic specificity: in Metzian terms, specifically cinematic signifiers versus filmic signifiers. Such a division neatly sidesteps the fact that signifieds cannot be expelled, just as it is impossible to present a sheet of paper with only one side. What is a signifier or a signified depends entirely on the level at which the analysis operates: a signified on one level can become a signifier on another level. But even the more sophisticated participants in the debate ignore the central cinematic fact of the inscription of the look, as this object cannot be unambiguously located on either side of the division between signified and signifier.

Moreover, such a division borders on, and is often invaded by, the old and familiar form/content opposition. Dwoskin's films, by focusing on the look itself, break the deadlock of that opposition and simultaneously see themselves relegated to marginality, or even rejected outright, by anyone holding to the old binary opposition: proponents of classic narrative films object to Dwoskin's formal concerns (see the reactions at the Cannes Festival to the showing of *Dyn Amo*, 1971), while 'structural' film-makers object to Dwoskin's use of a narrative and the presence of diegetic signifiers. Dwoskin is not even mentioned in P. Adams Sitney's book *Visionary Film* nor in the *Structural Film Anthology*,[7] edited by P. Gidal – in spite of his insistent foregrounding of specifically cinematic codes relating to processing, developing and printing techniques, for example in *Dirty* (1971) and *Me Myself & I* (1967). Dave Curtis, in his *Experimental Cinema*,[8] simply dismisses Dwoskin as a maker of conventional documentaries, a view that would certainly not be shared by the producer of a current affairs television programme like *Panorama*.

A detailed study of Dwoskin's films would have to engage with a great many aspects not addressed in this essay: such as the importance of music, of verbal language, the play on the structural elements of cinema. However, for my purposes here it is sufficient to argue that the films deal with the crucial and specifically cinematic place and function of the look by way of some fairly randomly selected examples.

For there to be a look, there has to be a subject and an object demarcating it – in the same way as, for there to be a message, there has to be a sender and a receiver. As in the structure of fantasy, the object and the subject may change places, but the term of their articulation remains. In this instance that term is the look. However, as Laura Mulvey points out, there are – as a rule – three looks in the cinema: intra-diegetic, camera/pro-filmic event, viewer/film. In non-figurative cinema, the intra-diegetic look is absent, while the camera/pro-filmic event look is still present, but erased in that no identifiably recognisable object is being looked at. The third look is still present.

In conventional narrative cinema, attempts are made to make the viewer/film look coincide with the camera/pro-filmic event look, and a considerable panoply of strategies is deployed to erase the marks of the presence of the camera's look as distinct from the viewer's. This is not to say that the camera sees something different, just that the camera sees differently. *Me Myself & I* focuses precisely on this difference. By varying the processing of the exposed film, the different modalities of the camera's look at the pro-filmic event are foregrounded, while the viewer's look at the image necessarily remains constant. Entry into the diegesis by means of narcissistic identification – an ever-present danger when using a pro-filmic event involving human figures – is prevented largely by camera movements and the proximity of the camera to its pro-filmic scene. So, although there is a recognisable pro-filmic event, entry to it is barred and what remains are the two looks: the camera's and the viewer's.

The material independence of the camera's look is also explored in *Take Me* (1968). In *Experimental Cinema*, Dave Curtis describes the film in these terms: 'A girl directly tries to seduce the camera, giving a come-on to the audience and the camera responds.'[9] Already, it appears that Curtis confuses the look of the camera with that of the audience and fails to make the distinction demanded by the text: the relation between the girl and the camera is not the same as that between the girl and the audience, as becomes evident in the rest of Curtis's description: 'the relationship is peculiar, the girl retires from a kiss with her mouth smeared with paint. She persists, slowly becoming covered with paint. [I]t is as though both the audience and the girl are being punished for their (mutual) complicity in a vicarious sexual relationship.' Indeed, the mutually vicarious sexual relationship between girl and audience is one of voyeurism, with the camera inscribed as 'other' agency, source of a different look with different effects on both girl and viewer.

The role of the camera in this film is even more significant than Curtis's description suggests. In the voyeuristic relationship between viewer and girl, the camera also functions as signifier of desire – the desire which supports the voyeuristic relationship in the first place. The paint which gradually covers the body of the girl acquires the status of traces imprinted on the object of voyeurism, traces which are imprinted by the signifier of desire, betraying the tactile elements present in the desire for physical possession implied and denied by the

106

voyeuristic relation. A critical account of the film would have to denounce the fact that the sadistic components redoubling the voyeurism are not themselves redirected towards the viewer, thus leaving the viewer's sadism as an unquestioned – and therefore uncriticised – given.

In a later film, *Girl* (1975), Dwoskin explores the implications of the scopophilic drive more fully. The film consists of one long static take of a naked girl standing on a bath mat. As the take continues, we become aware that the girl is uncomfortable: she fidgets, tries to cover herself with her hands and arms. However, the take continues, in silence, until the film runs out. In 'Instincts and Their Vicissitudes' Freud observed that an instinct (a drive) may undergo a reversal into its opposite, or may turn round upon the subject. This is precisely what happens during the viewing of *Girl*: the act of sadistic viewing rebounds on the subject as the viewer becomes aware that the look upon the girl is having disagreeable effects on her. Instead of the 'innocent' pleasure of watching a naked girl, the viewer now has to confront the considerable sadistic components present in his or her act of looking and, by implication, confront the castration anxieties provoked by the investigation of the naked female form in the diegesis. The film also demonstrates that in the filmic process there are not just three looks, as described in Mulvey's article, but four: the look at the viewer must be added.

Jacques Lacan described this fourth look as being 'not a seen gaze, but a gaze imagined by me in the field of the Other'. It is this look which 'surprises [me] in the function of voyeur, disturbs [me] and reduces [me] to a feeling of shame'.[10] It is this look which, in Sartre's *Being and Nothingness*, constitutes me in relation to the Other. In the filmic process, this look can be represented as the look which constitutes the viewer as visible subject. A tangible signifier of the look (not to be confused with the look itself, which is imagined) could be found in the reflection of the projection beam's light from the screen back onto the faces of the viewers. This look begins to play an ever more important role in *Girl* as the film progresses: as the viewer has to confront his or her sadistic voyeurism, the presence of the imagined look in the field of the other makes itself increasingly felt, producing a sense of shame at being caught in the act of voyeurism. By this time, the viewing subject has become the exhibitionist.

Trixie (1970) offers an equally aggressive exploratory look at a female figure with the camera showing the effects of the look on the woman looked at. In both films, the scopic drive has been turned back onto the subject and the active aim has become a passive one, delegating the role of actively viewing sadist, in a displacing gesture, onto the camera – sometimes, wrongly, identified with the film-maker. The scopic drive has been turned back upon the subject (girl-viewer) and has been reversed into its opposite (looking at–being looked at). This can, quite understandably, be accompanied by a change from voyeuristic pleasure to unpleasure, combined with a refusal to acknowledge one's unstable position in the viewing process.

It must be stressed that the fourth look is not of the same order as the other three, precisely because the subject of the look is an imaginary other, but this does not make the presence of that look any less real. However, although it is continuously present in all filmic experiences, the overwhelming majority of films, as well as the other aspects of the cinematic institution, such as theatres, projection conditions and so on, conspire to minimise its effects, with the aim of trying to erase it altogether. It is perhaps this fourth look which prompted theatre managers to locate the most expensive seats at the back: there, one feels better protected against the danger of being over-looked in one's voyeuristic pleasure, a protection people appear to be willing to pay for. In fact, the presence of the fourth look has considerable implications regarding the social experience of film-going, and may offer an insight into the differences between the various subject/object/spectacle relations in cinema and theatre.

The same complex dialectic of looks – all four of them – occurs in *Dyn Amo*, this time involving a de-centring of the camera's look by the main actress's 'direct' appeal, across the barrier of the screen, to the viewer, summoning him or her to come to her assistance in the diegesis. In fact, the whole film could be regarded as a textbook demonstration of the entire complex of drives mentioned in Mulvey's essay. The film plays expertly upon the distinctions and gradual transitions between a spectacle especially designed for an audience (both within the diegesis and in the actual film theatre), involving conscious sexual provocation, and the voyeuristic spectacle in which the object is supposed to be unaware of the look directed at it, followed by a re-inscription of the look, this time however directed at the viewer. There are also many aspects of the film which problematise the sadistic and fetishistic components implicated in the act of pleasurable viewing, but these too are redirected at the viewer by means of the fourth look. In this sense, *Dyn Amo* is an advance on an earlier orchestration of looks engineered by Dwoskin, *Chinese Checkers* (1964), in which the fourth look is not explicitly inscribed in the text, thus making the text more unproblematically pleasurable and therefore more politically suspect, since the implicit sexism is not foregrounded as a specific difficulty.

In *Chinese Checkers* the camera's look is distinguished by its mobility and its ability to vary the distance between lens and pro-filmic object, while the intra-diegetic look is exchanged between two women who gradually appear to merge into one abstract entity: female eroticism, but still subjected to a controlling gaze which is itself not interpellated. As happens in almost all of Dwoskin's films, the libidinal energy involved in the act of watching a film is displaced and crystallised in the diegesis, and placed before us (*vorgestellt*) in the form of erotic activity. In a sense, it is the very vagueness of the generalised eroticism of the diegetic activities which teases out the questions raised by the fact that the subject hangs on to a fantasy which hinges on the look.

The strategies deployed in *Dyn Amo* can also be seen at work, in an embryonic form, in earlier works such as *Moment* (1969). *Moment* presents a continuous fixed gaze by the camera at a girl's face. As in *Girl*, the fixedness of the camera parallels the spectator's position, but is marked off as different because of its refusal to 'blink' and thus to alleviate the intensity of the look by way of cuts, invisible transitions and so on, devices used by 'classic' cinema to stitch our subjectivity into the filmic text. *Moment* enables us to distinguish between the look of the camera at the pro-filmic event and the look of the viewer at the image. The sadistic components inherent in the exercise of the unflinchingly controlling gaze are returned to the viewer as we, in deciphering what is going on out of frame by reading the effects of the out-of-frame action on her face and from the sounds she makes, gradually become aware that we may well be watching some very intimate auto-erotic experience. The sadistic component becomes the viewer's direct responsibility as he or she constructs the narrative, the drama of the film, from nothing more than a fixed but relentless look at a woman's face.

It would be possible to quote many more examples of Dwoskin's skilled *mise en scène* of the look. At one time, in *Behindert* (1974), he even plays on the distinction (that is, the possible confusion) between the look of the camera and that of the film-maker, as well as questioning the narcissistic relation which both viewer and film-maker (who is also a viewer, but in another place) entertain with a character in the diegesis. In *Central Bazaar* (1976), the emphasis has been shifted again. The film shares with the rest of Dwoskin's work this overwhelming sense of being in the field of vision: everyone who participates in a Dwoskin film, including the director and the viewers, is drawn into the complex web of exchanged looks, the staging of masquerades to lure or deceive the look of the other, and of fantasies, always exposed, of being unseen.

Central Bazaar focuses on the interpersonal, intra-diegetic looks and their interrelation with the camera's look. The film was shot over a period of five weeks. A group of people, most of whom had no previous acting experience and who didn't even know each other, were given a multitude of props with which to build their personal fantasy persona. Each character constructs a fantasy image, either the fantasy image they have of themselves or the image they think others have of them. The fiction thus becomes a kaleidoscope of converging, diverging, conflicting, changing fantasies directed simultaneously at the camera and at each other, each of these two axes constantly modifying the other. By focusing on specific moments and gestures while the soundtrack structures the images rhythmically rather than dramatically, the development of a sequence of events in time is constantly frozen into its component units, the images also relating to each other rhythmically, rather than according to a strictly narrative syntax. However, by continuously evoking the possibility of the development of a narrative, its eternal postponement comes to function as an anti-narrative strategy rather than a non-narrative one, with moments of fetishistic looking promising rather than stopping the flow of a fiction. *Central Bazaar* thus shows fetishistic looking to be a kind of precondition of narrative: not a moment where the narrative stops, but a moment when another narrative could emerge. Seen in this way, the film addresses itself to the basic question of the cinematic construction of the subject in fiction, in fantasy, where that fiction-fantasy consists entirely and exclusively of relations of looking and hearing.

However, the present series of examples may suffice to back up my original thesis that Dwoskin's films focus on an aspect of the filmic process which, in spite of its specificity to the cinema, has been consistently overlooked. Simultaneously and perhaps inevitably, Dwoskin's films explore the ramifications that this complex interaction of looks has for 'the process of films and the relations of subjectivity in that process', to quote Stephen Heath once more. Moreover, it is no accident that the more limited the scope of the films' exploration of the problem of the look, the more suspect the films become politically. Only Dwoskin's more complex films encourage the viewer to become aware of the kind of structure of subjectivity in which he or she is implicated when indulging his or her scopophilic drive in relation to projected images.

Notes

1. Christian Metz, 'Histoire/discours', in Julia Kristeva, Jean-Claude Milner and Nicolas Ruwet (eds), *Langue, discours, societé – Pour Émile Benveniste* (Paris: Le Seuil 1975), pp. 304ff.
2. *Times Higher Educational Supplement*, 26 March 1976.
3. C. Metz, 'Histoire/discours', p. 306.
4. Paul Willemen, 'Pursued: The Fugitive Subject', in Phil Hardy (ed.), *Raoul Walsh* (Edinburgh Film Festival, 1974).
5. Laura Mulvey, 'Visual Pleasure and Narrative Cinema', in *Screen* vol. 16 no. 3, 1975.
6. Sigmund Freud, 'Instincts and Their Vicissitudes', *Collected Papers* vol. 4 (London: Hogarth Press, 1971), p. 72.
7. P. Adams Sitney, *Visionary Film: The American Avant-Garde* (New York: Oxford University Press, 1974); Peter Gidal, *Structural Film Anthology* (London: BFI, 1976).
8. David Curtis, *Experimental Cinema* (London: Studio Vista, 1971), p. 139.
9. Ibid.
10. Jacques Lacan, *The Four Fundamental Concepts of Pasycho-Analysis* (London: Hogarth Press, 1977), p. 84.

Chapter 5

Letter to John

Dear John,

Reading your article 'On Pornography' in the last issue of *Screen* (vol. 21 no. 1), my initial admiration for the clarity of your analysis gradually turned to a sort of irritation. This disturbance of the equilibrium in my libidinal economy sparked off an intense process of inner speech urging me to clarify my disagreements and to put my own reflections on the subject into a semblance of order. I found our positions to be very similar – and in some cases where that was not so, your arguments convinced me that they should be – but there were also passages which I thought skidded off the track. In the end, you arrived at a perfectly respectable destination, although it is also a dead end.

What does it mean to require porn to address the questions: 'What is sexuality? What is desire?' Either it is the case that porn has solved those questions in its daily and durable practice because it trades on the exploitation of their answer, or these are questions only psychoanalysis can deal with at all adequately. To ask porn to deal with them strikes me as an evasion of the very issues you raised. By bracketing questions of specific social-historical signifying regimes defined as porn, and by redirecting attention to philosophical and psychoanalytical issues posed in such a general and abstract manner, the specific institution of porn, that is, the terms on which it functions and changes, has been lost from sight.

Of course I agree that we must try to go beyond the currently available positions and your essay provides some of the signposts for such a trajectory. All I hope to do in this letter is to pick up on those signposts and perhaps add a few more.

The focus of my irritation centred on your footnote number twelve, where you assert that 'a bright point of light concentrated on the eyes of an actor is a standard indicator of an intense gaze in a film'. That is a mistake. Such a bright light, whether a point or a beam of light on the eyes of an actor/character, if shown in close-up (a necessary extra specification) does not indicate an intense gaze in a film. True enough, it is the indicator of a look, that is to say, it functions as the signifier of a gaze, but not necessarily a signifier of a gaze in the film, nor necessarily of an intense gaze anywhere. It may indicate that the actor/character is gazing intently at something or somebody, or that he or she is being gazed at intently, but it also may mean – and quite often does, as I pointed out in an analysis of *Pursued*[1] – that something is going on behind the eyes of the character, in which case it functions as the signifier in a metonymic process substituting the container for the content. This metonymy is particularly common in noir films, where a horizontal band of light across the eyes, leaving the rest of the image in relative obscurity but still plainly visible, tells us that the character is a psychopath and/or has been traumatised. As often as not, such an image can have the character gazing at nothing in particular, signifying madness, blindness, or initiating a memory sequence. In other words, what is being shown as going on behind the eyes is not at all what is being gazed at. The look inscribed into such an image is by no means always a gaze contained within the diegesis between characters or from a character to an object.

On the contrary, I would argue that the primary function of such an image is to mark the look at the image, that is, the look of the viewer as distinct from that of the camera, two looks which in most films are mapped onto each other. While the look of the camera constitutes the frame, the beam of light on the eyes pinpoints a look which, although from the same position as the camera, is not coextensive with it, introducing negativity into the image, a mark of difference: a different look is being interpellated. If we can say that in classic cinema the frame is absented (it functions as a masking of a continuous, homogeneous plenitude: the diegetic world in which the characters continue to exist even when they are out of frame), and that the image as seen by the camera is thus naturalised, the beam or the point of light inscribes a different look which denaturalises the image by presenting it in its 'to be looked-at-ness'.

Of course, that presentation can be, and often is, reintegrated into the diegesis by articulating it to a diegetically motivated look or assigning it to a diegetic light source, suturing the momentary fissure and binding the viewer's position back into the network of looks that sustains the narrative movement of the text. But such a recovery manoeuvre does not eradicate the moment of oscillation, the moment of risk. To put it somewhat crudely, and therefore perhaps misleadingly, the type of image you specify signifies (as opposed to 'implies') that it is one pole of an axis of which the other end is the viewer's eye. The look of the viewer is the signifier of that axis including its three constituent terms: viewer, image and the specular relation between the two. In that sense, its explicit inscription into the image functions as a mark of what in literature would be described as direct address. The mischaracterisation of that type of image in the context of your discussion of fetishism (which is where the footnote occurs) is as significant as your selection of that particular example is revealing.

I think a comparison between the 'light on the eyes' image and other images which stress their perspectival or compositional features will clarify my point. Both looks are present in both types of images (the look of the camera at the pro-filmic event and the look of the viewer at the image), but whereas the 'eyes image' distinguishes the two, the others don't and thus correspond much more directly to the structure of fetishism and its regime of split belief. The emphatically composed image both indicates and denies simultaneously its 'to be looked-at-ness', while the 'eyes image' designates the difference and thus goes against the grain of the fetishistic position, dislocating to some extent its regime of split belief. And I add that qualification only because there are more effective ways of designating the image as there 'for my look', as Buñuel showed with a razor-blade. It is interesting to note that the more fetishised image, the one which both draws attention to its 'to be looked-at-ness' and effaces, naturalises it by covering it with the camera's look, is usually regarded as the more aesthetically satisfying one. Freud's textbook example of fetishism, which you quote (the glance at the nose), is also an example of two looks being mapped onto each other: the look at the vagina and the look at the nose, the latter cancelling out the anxiety generated by the former. In that sense, it is the frame which constitutes the cinematic equivalent of the 'shine on the nose' and not the 'light on the eyes' type of image which works in the opposite direction by dissociating the two looks. The two processes are radically different.

I want to return to the 'to be looked-at-ness' of the image, which goes together with the inscription of the look of the viewer, with the donation of the image to the looking eye/I. As I suggested earlier, the kinds of images that foreground compositional features such as strong perspectival arrangements or a double *mise en cadre* by having frames within frames, tend to play around, timidly, with the mapping of the camera's look onto that of the viewer and achieve an increased aesthetic effect. Such effects have come to be regarded as evidence of a strong authorial presence, as marks of the process of enunciation.

But the fact that the 'eye images' you mention are in close-up separates them from the conventional forms of arty compositions. Whereas images in classic narrative cinema (for example, in films by Budd Boetticher or Frank Capra) use the frame as a mask, arty compositions (using that phrase as a slightly pejorative shorthand, although I am by no means prepared to dismiss all such images at all times) emphasise the frame and, in so doing, also stress that the look of the viewer is coextensive with that of the camera, that the two looks are one. In that way, they achieve an increase in their 'to be looked-at-ness' in terms of an increase in aesthetic effectiveness, while at the same time retaining the naturalisation of frame as mask for a continuous and homogeneous diegetic world.

Such images, directly analogous to fetishes, stress the presence of an organising 'I' which uses – directs – the camera's look to circumscribe and organise the viewer's field of vision, thus denying the autonomy, while acknowledging the presence, of the viewer's look, making it present yet absent at the same time. However, the type of close-up you refer to puts no such stress on the addresser of the enunciation: it opens up a space for the emergence of the addressee's position. Obviously, when one of these two protagonists emerges, the other one tags along in its shadow. But what I am arguing is that the two different types of images, one extremely common and liable to fill an entire film, the other more of a punctuation image, each stress a different side of the process of enunciation.

It is interesting that you should have evoked the image of light in the eyes because, although it cannot do what you ask of it, it nevertheless provides a useful way of engaging with the process of enunciation characteristic of pornographic imagery, that is, direct address: 'This is for you to look at.' What is at stake here is the fourth look:[2] that is to say, any articulation of images and looks which brings into play the position and activity of the viewer as a distinctly separate factor also destabilises that position and puts it at risk.

All drives have active and passive facets and the scopic drive is no exception. When the scopic drive is brought into focus, the viewer also runs the risk of becoming the object of the look, of being overlooked in the act of looking. The fourth look is the possibility of that overlooking-look and is always present in the wings, so to speak. The fourth look is not of the same order as the other three (intra-diegetic looks, the camera's look at the pro-filmic event and the viewer's look at the image), but is rather a look imagined by me in the field of the other which surprises me in the act of voyeurism and causes a feeling of shame.[3]

When the look of the viewer is separated off from the look of the camera, the fourth look emerges particularly strongly if the viewer's scopic drive is being gratified in relation to an object or scene which heightens the sense of censorship inherent in any form of gratification. In simpler terms: the fourth look gains in force when the viewer is looking at something he or she is not supposed to look at, either according to an internalised censorship (superego) or an external, legal one (as in clandestine viewings) or, as in most cases, according to both censorships combined. In this way, the fourth look problematises the social dimension, the field of the other of the system of looking at work in the cinematic institution, as well as in the photographic and televisual ones.

Direct address imagery is offered explicitly 'for me to look at', stressing the addressee's look as opposed to the addresser's intervention, and is particularly liable to bring that fourth look into play in full force. When you suggest that the 'shine on the nose' image of Freud's example is produced as an avoidance of the woman's gaze back at the child, you correctly but perhaps inadvertently stress the presence of the fourth look in Freud's scenario. The child avoids the eyes of the woman whose nose allows him to disavow what he has (not) seen lower down, because to encounter that look would threaten the pleasurable and reassuring structure of fetishism he has just managed to install in order to avoid that very threat. Whether the woman was or was not actually looking back at the child is beside the point in this context.

Much has been written about the political importance of the activation of the viewer in relation to an imaged discourse, and people such as Stephen Heath have commented on the importance of the look in that process.[4] But what has rarely been addressed (it has often been affirmed or denied but rarely addressed) is the question: how exactly, through which hybrid processes and in which mechanisms, can the interweaving, the articulation of the textual and the social, be traced in relation to the viewer? To my knowledge, only two credible processes partaking simultaneously of the textual and of the social situation within which it arises (as production or as reading) present themselves: inner speech and the fourth look. Inner speech is a complex problem I approached a couple of years ago.[5] The fourth look and its direct implication in both the social and the psychic aspects of censorship, of the law, introduces the social into the very act of looking, while remaining an integral part of the textual relations.

The look at, say, a Wim Wenders film or an Altman film does not pose many problems. Firstly because the viewer's look is caught in the fetishistic process of disavowal through the play on framing and composition that simultaneously highlights and denies the incision effected by the frame. The looks of the camera and of the viewer are both inscribed, but as a unity, thus dimming the focus on the viewer's position and illuminating the marks of enunciation to be credited to the absent organiser of the discourse, that is to say, to the author who thus signals his desire to be recognised as artist. Secondly, because the mapping of these looks binds the viewer into the spectacle, the fourth look is diverted and left dormant. Thirdly, the problems inherent in the exercise of one's voyeurism having been contained (indeed, having been covered by the mantel of art), the decrease in the overtness of the look's sexual grounding facilitates displacement, sublimation, and a reversal of affect: instead of the risk of being caught looking, a positive valuation has now been bestowed upon the voyeur's activity. Some would even go so far as to want to be seen looking at an Altman film.

This process of reversal forms the basis of the arguments around so-called artistic merit, as distinct from the 'free speech' arguments that are made in defence of a genre such as porn cinema. The weakness of the artistic merit argument has to do with the need to identify marks of enunciation so that they can then be credited to, or projected upon, a mythic 'source' of the discourse: the artist. No matter that discourses such as porn cinema are riddled with emphases on the marks of enunciation, the argument is displaced from the text onto the 'quality', which invariably means the journalistic reputation of that mythic source. The circularity of that trajectory is evident: if the text bears the hallmarks of an expressive subjectivity, it must have been done by an artist, and if it emanates from an artist, it must be art, and art can be distinguished by its emphatic marks of enunciation, and so forth. This is the circle the liberal position on porn tries to break by extending the right of free speech to (some) non-artists.

Your reference to the 'eyes image' occurs when you are constructing a transition within a passage which is itself a transition. The example signals the shift from an account of Laura Mulvey's discussion of visual pleasure[6] to the proposition that female pleasure itself has become a fetish in porn representations. This passage is itself embedded in the shift from a partial but pertinent consideration of the institution of porn on the basis of the Williams Report[7] to an attempt 'to find a way of characterising the representations designated as porn so that they can be seen as contradictory and open to change', in the words of the essay.

This is perhaps not the place to argue that representations do not have to be contradictory to be open to change: no representation is so univocal and homogeneous that it must remain outside history. Being caught up in contradictions is not quite the same as being contradictory. However, this second transition eventually allows you to arrive at the conclusion that the questions at stake in porn are: what is sexuality; and what is desire? Interesting and important as these questions are, I would suggest that more relevant, less all-encompassing questions might be: What are the terms of the social circulation of representations of sex? What are the terms of their economic exploitation? Perhaps my two questions can be subsumed in the formulation you propose, again in a footnote: who do porn representations think you are?

I have no answers to these questions, but the issues they raise allow the discussion initiated in your essay to be put into a more productive framework. The mode of address of porn imagery is characterised by a strange anonymity, a kind of emphatic anonymity. Porn films and photographs are mostly unsigned or signed with pseudonyms. This is not really to avoid prosecution, since it is publishers, exhibitors and retailers who tend to carry most of the legal risk. Besides, even where porn is legal, pseudonyms are still the rule. At the same time, when compared to the smoothly flowing regime of mainstream cinema, porn is heavily marked by the process of enunciation. But there is no author to whom these marks can be credited and to whom can thus be delegated the responsibility for the fantasy articulated in and by the discourse. Moreover, the traditional strategies deployed by mainstream cinema to achieve an impersonal mode of narration which nevertheless binds the viewer into the diegesis are not open to the porn film.

The specificity of the genre requires a maximum number of sexually explicit images, which necessarily fragment the narrative, produce constant repetitions and render suspense or an elementary sense of verisimilitude virtually impossible. The images must bear the marks of realist verisimilitude, but the narrative cannot. Strategies to elicit identification with a character are necessarily rudimentary, because there is almost no time and no context within which to construct such a figure. Hence the massive use of stereotypes and stock situations. Narrative is reduced to a minimum and becomes a barely (*sic*) motivated procedure for the juxtaposition of fantasy scenes whose combinatory logic is more that of the catalogue than that of narration.

In addition, the very arrangement of the figures in the image re-enforces their status as specifically designed for 'my' look. Their 'to be looked-at-ness' is stressed by the absence of the taboo on the look into the lens, by the disposition of the body or bodies in the diegesis so as to grant direct access to the genital areas, even if this means that the protagonists have to engage in most uncomfortable contortions, by the relentless use of punctuating close-ups of genitalia and their interactions, and so on. In porn, there is no way the viewer can fade into the diegesis or, alternatively, shove responsibility for the discourse onto the author. The viewer is left squarely facing the image without even the semblance of an alibi justifying his or her presence at the other end of the look. Porn imagery may well be the most blatant and uncompromising form of direct address short of physical contact.

Besides, the substitution of the look for physical contact is precisely the essential precondition for porn and the specific difference which distinguishes it from other scopophilic regimes such as looking at family snapshots or at Hollywood movies. Porn involves a direct form of address in which the look substitutes for physical (sexual) contact in a structure determined by conditions of production along with the emphatic presence of the fourth look. It is via that look, imagined by me in the field of the other, that porn imagery affects, and is affected by, the competing discourses and institutions that assign it its changing place within the register of signifying practices.

Crudely speaking, when mention is made of changes in the public presence and acceptability of porn, it is the institutionalisation of the fourth look within a social formation that we are talking about. Within that structure, there are different modes of looking. The dominant one is no doubt the fetishistic look, because images themselves, as objects, sustain the belief in a presence in the face of our knowledge of absence. This founding fetishism can be overlaid, doubled by a second-order and more specific fetishism when the depicted figure re-launches the need for some further disavowal. Obviously, the depiction of genitalia is a prime candidate for such a second-order disavowal. Hence the fact that in much, perhaps even in most porn imagery, the bodies depicted are shown as somehow contained, sheathed in paraphernalia such as boots, stockings, garter-belts or leather gear, making these bodies into representatives of the phallus according to the mechanisms lucidly described by Laura Mulvey in her article on the work of Allen Jones.[8] The disavowal operates by making the body into a phallus or by inscribing elsewhere in the image, often in multiplied form, what is looked for and seen to be missing.

However, porn also often plays on a second, more reassuring type of looking which can quite easily coexist with the fetishistic look, although it is in some sense its inverse. It is less a disavowal of 'her' castration than a confirmation of the viewer's phallic power. This specular relation is dependent on the emphatic direct address interpellating the viewer as possessor and donor of the phallus, the one who is required to complete the picture, as it were.

The representation of women experiencing pleasure is one variant on this theme. In most porn, women are the space onto (into) which male pleasure and phallic power is inscribed. This can take different forms: through the disposition of the body so as to grant maximum access to the look; through the imprinting on women of the traces of male pleasure (the come-shot, or money shot as it is called in the trade, usually disperses its seminal signifiers onto the body of the woman, while her orgasm either precedes it, is triggered by it or is left out of the picture altogether). Even when a woman is shown to be deriving pleasure from masturbation, her body is always arranged in 'display' poses maximising access of the look to her genital area, suggesting that the pleasure depicted is a narcissistic mirror for the viewer. Rare are the occasions when in such a scene the distinction between the look of the viewer and that of the camera is brought into play. The price the viewer pays for this guarantee of his or her phallic power is the price of porn itself: the radical separation from the object of desire required for the look to be able to function at all (as signifier of desire). The viewer's security depends on that separation: it is separation which guarantees phallic power.

If it is true, as you suggest, that there is a proliferation of vaginal imagery and of women-in-pleasure images, then this is the very opposite of 'an advance upon previous modes of represention of women', as you write. On the contrary, such a development constitutes an emphatic insistence on the centrality of phallic, male pleasure

118

and suggests that the male population in Western societies now requires to be reassured more often, more directly and more publicly than before. The increase in public visibility and availability of such imagery does address women: it tells them to stop threatening that centrality. The terms on which representations of sexuality appear to circulate at present seem to point to a severe crisis of male self-confidence. It would even be possible to confirm this by way of analyses of analogous developments in mainstream cinema: the proliferation of disaster movies about burning and collapsing sky-scrapers, crashing planes, suffocating and exploding ships, toppled presidents, and so on.

This address of women through the public display of porn operates indirectly through the fourth look: public visibility here means that the look imagined by me in the field of the other is that of a woman who sees the images which guarantee that female pleasure depends on a phallus. The more women object to this, the more effective the operation of the images is for men. Of course, to actually be caught looking, to be found out as needing reassurance, is quite a different matter. Nevertheless, that the proliferation of such images coincides with the growth of the women's movement, as well as with vocal demands for censorship, is not a coincidence.

I would also like to make a few points about the social inscription of porn images in relation to fantasy. Fantasy images, framed image-objects and what we see around us are three different things existing in different spaces. Each involves different relations between subject and look. The actualisation of fantasy scenarios into framed image-objects (still or moving) necessarily passes through 'the defiles of the signifier', as Lacan would say, as well as through the distortion processes unconscious signifiers are subjected to when passing into consciousness.

In relation to the imaged discourse, secondary elaboration and considerations of representability are extremely important. Figurative images, which is what porn images must be, require a social setting and an individuation which fantasy can do without. On the one hand, the surfeit of specific details due to the need for a frame to be filled produces an excess of signification. But this excess is also a loss: the lack of fit between the represented scenario and the fantasy transmuted into concrete images. In porn, this inevitable mismatch plays a particularly important role, because it is more acutely experienced. When a Western such as *Pursued* evokes the primal scene as a structuring fantasy, it does so in oblique and distorted ways.

Porn imagery, on the other hand, directly addresses the viewer with the fantasy itself. The fantasy no longer needs to be reconstructed. But now, it is the very incarnation of the fantasy that cannot but

119

produce a mismatch. The actors' bodies (pimples and all), the lighting, the sets, the noises on the soundtrack: everything is excessively concrete and never quite coincides with the selective vagueness of a fantasy image. A sexual fantasy can proceed very satisfactorily without having to specify the pattern on the wallpaper; a filmic fantasy cannot. In porn, and perhaps in all films, it is the loss generated by the friction between the fantasy looked for and the fantasy displayed which sustains the desire for ever-promised and never-found gratification.

Porn, as an institution, thrives on this repetition of loss, on the double separation between viewer and representation and between the fantasy looked for and the one on offer. It is perhaps in the tension between approximation and separation in relation to the representation of sex that the explanation can be found for the compensatory activity associated with porn: masturbation. And that pleasure in return re-launches the desire for the tensions provoked by porn in the first place. The close connection between porn and masturbation tends to generate defensiveness ... and further compensatory action. It is difficult to talk about porn without becoming too aggressive, too puritanical, too jokey, too excessive in one way or another. (Hence also the slightly excessive and scandalous aspects of a direct address in the form of a letter intended to be overlooked by *Screen*'s readers.)

The most common defensive strategy in relation to porn is the mobilisation of *double entendres*, sustained double meanings, witticisms, jokes, and so on. The verbal language that accompanies porn stresses this jokey aspect, insisting that it is not to be taken seriously. However, it is more than just a distancing device. Neither is the joke aspect of porn just a self-reflexive comment on the endlessly stereotyped and repetitive nature of the porn discourse itself. The way porn actualises unconscious significations is analogous to the way jokes do. Allowing for the differences between Freud's verbal jokes and cinematic porn, there is at least one striking similarity between their discursive mechanisms. It is a similarity relating not so much to the place of the fourth look in the process, but to its function as a space: perhaps even the only space, as far as the viewer is concerned, where the social and the textual mesh.

Tzvetan Todorov, in his book *Théories du symbole*,[9] schematises the process of enunciation involved in rude jokes: A (the man) addresses B (the woman), seeking to satisfy his sexual desire; the intervention of C (the rival) makes the satisfaction of desire impossible. Hence, a second situation develops: frustrated in his desire, A addresses aggressive remarks to B and appeals to C as an ally. A new transformation occurs, provoked by the absence of the woman, or by the need to observe a social code. Instead of addressing B, A addresses C by telling him a rude joke; B may well be absent, but instead of

120

being the addressee, she has become (implicitly) the object of what is said: C derives pleasure from A's joke. The only modification I would want to make to this scenario is that C, the rival addressed by the joke and the one who becomes the subject of its pleasure, does not have to be another person. Any censorship mechanism, whether internal or external to A, is equally effective in setting in motion the series of substitutions and displacements described.

Taking into account that the mode of address in visualised discourse operates through the organisation of a network of looks, the structure of address underpinning the joke process is very similar to that usually in play in porn: a man ends up showing a rude image of a woman to another man, who becomes the subject of its pleasure. The male addressee arrives in that place because the woman has been expelled from it. But as Poe demonstrated in his story of the purloined letter, messages always reach their destination. The initial demand of the man addressed to the woman was a demand for his gratification, that is to say, it was a demand for self-gratification through the detour of the woman. The rival is in fact this narcissistic double whose gratification is at stake, is the addresser in another place of the discursive process. His pleasure stands in for mine.

In that process, the woman has been eliminated and relegated to the field of the other, from where she, the repressed, returns as the subject of the fourth look. This allows the men to function as subjects and objects at the same time: one is the object of a look, the other is the subject of an enunciation. The representation of sexuality which men circulate substitutes for an address of a woman, who is thus relegated to a space below the barrier of repression, from where her look returns as the one that overlooks the male in his reassuringly defensive games of substitution.

This mechanism offers a way of understanding how a feminist politics can have effects within porn as a signifying practice. The historically changing content of porn imagery provides figurations of the contours, the imprint of women's struggles on the representations of male desire and its objects. The distance between the woman imagined as the subject of the fourth look and the woman (not) addressed in the first place measures the extent to which feminisms have impinged on male sexuality.

The porn industry addresses itself to women by representing back to them those changes in the form of the crisis provoked in male sexuality. But it does so obliquely: the images are not for women to look at, they are for women to overlook. To get annoyed by that mirror may be understandable, but it is a little beside the point. Which is not to say that one shouldn't oppose aspects of the porn industry: that business institutionalises and exploits both the crisis in male sexuality and the real women who are required to model for the images and the films. On the other hand, to oppose the representation of (sexual) fantasy merely modifies the regime of representation, not the fantasy.

Postscript

As regards changing the representation and not the fantasy, in Fleming's anaemic version of *Dr Jekyll and Mr Hyde* (1941), there is a strange sequence which appears to have been caused by just such censorship. But it is the way in which the fantasy has circumvented the censorship that is rather interesting in the context of a discussion about pornography. The passage occurs when Spencer Tracy/Hyde comes to visit Ingrid Bergman/Ivy in the secret apartment where Hyde keeps her to gratify his beastly desires. She is seen in a fairly distressed state when he enters. He starts by teasing her: 'What shall I ask you to do tonight, dear?' (or words to that effect), and then proceeds to build up the tension, suggesting a series of innocent-sounding activities which are immediately rejected. He gets more and more excited as he gets closer to voicing the awful thing he will require from her. Gradually, the full horror of what he is about to ask her to do dawns on her and she starts to whimper and moan in helpless despair: 'No, no ... not that!' Tracy replies: 'Yes ... Yes, my dear ... you shall ... SING to me.' And then we are treated at length to the anguished, tearful face of Bergman as she is forced to execute this filthy perversion. I think there are few scenes in the cinema which avoid showing sex in so blatant and graphic a manner. (Perhaps in Frank Tashlin's *Susan Slept Here* (1954), the middle-aged Dick Powell/Mr Chistopher and the seventeen-year-old Debbie Reynolds/Susan dancing throughout their wedding night, with dialogue lines about being able to keep it up all night, qualifies as another such sex scene.) This substitution of singing (and dancing) for sex may give a clue to the popularity of musicals.

Musicals do in fact share a marked structural similarity with porn films. In both cases, the importance of the generically obligatory sequences makes for a weak narrative. The story is simply there to link the graphic sex/musical numbers, with fairly predictably coded transitions from the narrative to its interruptions, the interruptions functioning as self-contained pieces. Moreover, the need to include such relatively autonomous segments as spectacles 'arresting' the look and thus, at least to a significant extent, suspending the narrative flow, makes for films that proceed with a halting rhythm. Also, in both genres such a structure makes it easier to add or to cut scenes without substantially altering the plot development. Finally, in both genres the interrupting segments consist of bodies displaying their physicality, either in isolation or in rhythmical unison.

All this makes the precise point at which the narrative tends to give way to a musical number rather interesting. It cannot be mere coincidence that moments of 'discovery' (when the lovers discover that they

122

are in love), or of 'union', tend to be the points where the rhythmical interactions are inserted. Other key moments are when one of the lead characters displays his or her body for seduction, for the look of the other: there too the narrative tends to swell into a musical number. Perhaps there is material here for a comparative study between Egyptian, Hindi and US musicals? A study of the look at the male body in the various types of musical interludes might prove especially instructive.

All the best.

PW

Notes

1. Paul Willemen, 'Pursued: The Fugitive Subject', in Phil Hardy (ed.), *Raoul Walsh* (Edinburgh Film Festival, 1974).
2. Paul Willemen, 'Voyeurism, the Look and Dwoskin', in *Afterimage*, no. 6, 1976. (A slightly rewritten and extended version of this essay is included in this collection as 'The Fourth Look'.)
3. Jacques Lacan, *The Four Fundamental Concepts of Psycho-Analysis* (London: Hogarth Press, 1977), p. 84.
4. Stephen Heath, 'Anata mo', in *Screen*, vol. 17 no. 4, 1976/77.
5. Paul Willemen, 'Cinematic Discourse: The Problem of Inner Speech', in Teresa de Lauretis and Stephen Heath (eds), *Cinema and Language* (Maryland: University Publications of America, 1981), included in this collection.
6. Laura Mulvey, 'Visual Pleasure and Narrative Cinema', in *Screen*, vol. 16 no. 3, 1975.
7. *Report of the Committee on Obscenity and Film Censorship* [The Williams Report], HMSO Cmnd 7772, November 1979.
8. Laura Mulvey, 'You don't know what you're doing, do you Mr Jones?', in *Spare Rib*, no. 8, 1973; reprinted in *Visual And Other Pleasures* (London: Macmillan, 1989).
9. Tzvetan Todorov, *Théories du symbole* (Paris: Le Seuil, 1978).

Chapter 6

Photogénie and Epstein

The reflections contained in these brief and somewhat unsystematic notes, prompted by a consideration of the uses of the term *photogénie* in the Epstein texts presented in this issue of *Afterimage*,[1] are intended to help identify and clarify some of the dynamics at work within 'impressionist' film theory, and by implication, to reflect on the reasons why such notions of cinema have by no means lost their actuality. Indeed, the formulations of the impressionists are sometimes mobilised today as a counter to film theory itself. Their insistence on a quasi-mystical concept of the cinematic experience as beyond verbal discourse resurfaces today as part of a campaign to censor film theory and film education in general, freeing film critics from the heavy burden of rationality.

In an informative description of the French 'impressionist' cinema that flourished between roughly 1918 and 1928, David Bordwell reviewed some of the ways in which the term *photogénie* – deployed by the cinematic impressionists as though it were their regimental banner – was used in the writings of Ricciotto Canudo, Louis Delluc, René Schwob, René Clair and Jean Epstein.[2] *Photogénie* was promoted as 'the law of cinema' (Delluc), and as 'the purest expression of cinema' (Epstein). Broadly speaking, it was said to be that mysterious, indefinable something present in the image which differentiated cinema from all other arts and therefore, according to the tenets of the modernism of the period later codified in the USA by Clement Greenberg, constituted the very foundation of cinematic art. As Bordwell puts it:

> The concept of *photogénie* grows out of an attempt to account for the mysteriously alienating quality of cinema's relation to reality. According to the impressionists, on viewing an image, even an image of a familiar object or event or locale, we experience a certain otherness about the content; the image's material seems to be revealed in a fresh way. [T]he idea that the screen somehow presents the 'soul' of a person or object was similarly common.

[A]ccording to René Clair, 'There is no detail of reality which is not immediately extended here [in cinema] into the domain of the wondrous'. [E]ven the most sophisticated theorists [that is to say, Epstein and Canudo] fall back too easily upon the assumption that *photogénie* is an impenetrable, quasi-supernatural enigma. This means that much written about *photogénie* is insupportable theoretically.[3]

Bordwell goes on to marvel at 'the astonishing variety of assumptions' underpinning the impressionists' writing:

> They constitute a bewildering compendium of variants of that broad position known as idealism. Delluc seems to opt for a reality which is stylised and idealised through artifice, though he remains mute on the ultimate nature of that reality. [S]chwob and Clair appeal to an unabashed mysticism. Epstein [a]t one moment [h]olds the Bergsonian position that art cuts through our cognitive constraints to reveal the flux of life; at another moment he is closer to a Beaudelairean theosophy which assumes that vast analogies interlace all phenomena; at yet another time he seems a Platonic Idealist, believing that a single image can become surrogate for a universal entity, the quintessence of the object.[4]

In the end, Bordwell cannot but acknowledge defeat: 'Such a contradiction illustrates the extent to which impressionist theory is an assemblage of various assumptions never raised to theoretical self-consciousness.' The suggestion here is that the discourse of impressionist theoreticians has not been organised and ordered sufficiently by subjection to the full force of secondary elaboration; that they are still too deeply marked by the assemblage of contradictions characteristic of pre-conscious modes of thought, in which displacement, condensation and considerations of representability have not as yet been fully bound into a rational coherence, cemented by the analytic rigours of logic. These assemblages instituting *photogénie* as the unfathomable mystery at the heart of cinema may well be theoretically insupportable and hopelessly idealist, but this is no reason to assume that they are devoid of logic, nor to abandon any attempt to discover which principle(s) of coherence, which socio-discursive dynamic can account for precisely these assemblages being elaborated at this particular time. Moreover, to dismiss their contradictions and confusions as simply variants of idealism allows no distinction to be made between the idealism of the impressionists and that of their opponents, predecessors and progeny. In fact, contradictions can never be bewildering in themselves: they only become so when put into an inadequate or inappropriate theoretical framework.

The term *photogénie* was not invented by Louis Delluc who, according to Epstein, launched it as a key concept for the cinematic impressionists some time around 1919. In an angry letter to Delluc's own magazine, *Cinéa*, Feuillade had protested against the impressionists' appropriation of a term that had appeared in the 1874 edition of the *Larousse* dictionary. Furthermore, as Epstein repeatedly points out, *photogénie* was presented as an indefinable concept and yet definitions were constantly attempted. The most common procedures adopted to define this 'impenetrable quasi-supernatural enigma' were a recourse to metaphors, to a process of negation (Epstein used the term 'amputation'), indicating what it was not, or to tautologies, giving examples of what was to be defined instead of the definition that would allow the reader to assess whether the example cited was appropriate or not.

In all these instances, *photogénie* invariably referred to something that had dropped away, something that ceaselessly falls through the net no matter how fine the mesh. Like all causes of desire, *photogénie* is by definition a lost object, something that has fallen into nothingness, outside all possible terms of reference. But, as Serge Leclaire writes in *Démasquer le réel*:[5] 'The difficulty then becomes the fact that it is no longer possible to get rid of it; nothing is more cumbersome than that detritus which does not fit into any order; [t]hat object is as lost and yet as present as a dead person is to his relatives, no matter how ceremoniously he has been buried.' Or as Epstein put it, 'the words are lacking. The words have not been found' which might fit *photogénie* into the order of things.

However, the question here is why *photogénie* should be 'impenetrable'. What contradictory functions are to be fulfilled in order for such a term to be needed at the very centre of a particular aesthetic discourse? A number of different points can be made about the way *photogénie* was mobilised and the weight it was required to bear.

As the 'law of cinema', it clearly sets in place a viewer's aesthetic. The defining characteristic of cinema is said to be something that pertains to the relationship between viewer and image, a momentary flash of recognition, or a moment when the look at ... something suddenly flares up with a particularly affective, emotional intensity. The founding aspect of cinematic quality, instead of its specificity, is located not in the recognition of an artistic sensibility or intentionality beyond the screen, as it were, but in the particular relationship supported or constituted by the spectatorial look, between projected image and viewer. As such, *photogénie* is a term mobilised to demarcate one set of viewers – those able to 'see' – from others. In this context it functions like a mark of distinction conferred by a special set of viewers upon film-makers, differentiating those who are qualified to make cinema and so are entitled to a position of cultural power from those who merely manufacture cinema, however professionally.

Moments of cinema, scenes and gestures are cited in which *photo-génie* is manifested for those viewers sufficiently sensitive to perceive it: 'Just as there are people insensitive to music, so there are those – in even greater number – insensitive to *photogénie*.' And Epstein immediately adds: 'For the moment, at least', implying that this sensitivity is learned rather than innate. But how are we to learn to recognise *photogénie* if not by patiently sitting at the feet of those gifted masters who can point out the relevant examples to us? And how did the masters acquire their sensitivity to this indefinable something in the first place? These questions are left unanswered, which suggests that they are not meant to be asked. *Photogénie* is presented as the distinguishing characteristic of cinema, but its effect is to institute demarcations between viewers by differentiating those who are 'sensitive' from those who are not.

That *photogénie* relates primarily to a viewers' aesthetic is important if seen in context of the movement that the French avant-garde directors of the 1920s helped to promote. This was the first institutionalised 'film culture' movement to be organised around exhibition priorities, through the film society movement initiated by Delluc and Canudo. Previous arguments for a 'cultural cinema' had been made in relation to the point of production, particularly in Italy, where the Film d'Arte movement used stage actors in famous roles and adaptations of classic literature for the cinema, a practice later taken over by Hollywood.

In fact, however, that social distinction between viewers, restricting the right to speak and write about cinema to those who are able to perceive, to see what others cannot (namely, the essence, the law of cinema), is founded upon an extremely unstable pivot. The line of demarcation is drawn according to whether one is able to see something which is supposed to be there, even if only intermittently (in isolated scenes and images), and the presence of which goes unnoticed by most viewers. This impossible object of infinite mystery, forever condemned to remain beyond words, unspoken, and which can only be referred to metaphorically, is meant to be manifested in the object of the look. Indeed, it functions as the magnetic pole of the look, in terms of which images are supposed to be organised and viewed. The metaphorical 'as if' discourse that ensues is then peppered with references to acts of substitution, appearances and disappearances. Epstein talks of the stripping away of plot, character and dramatic action as 'amputations', while Delluc and Canudo both insist on the necessity of substituting images for words.

As for what was desired, pure *photogénie* itself, Epstein provides two extraordinary and telling examples. Summarising a Sessue Hayakawa film, *The Honour of his House* (1918), as 'an improbable yarn: adultery and surgery', he goes on to isolate within this story of sex and cutting a scene where Hayakawa, his body erect but 'held at a slight angle', goes through a door, opening and closing it. Epstein describes this as '*photogénie*, pure *photogénie*, cadenced movement'.

The second example is even more explicit in its equation of *photogénie* with the mythical philosophers' stone of the alchemists:

> The cinema is essentially supernatural. Everything is transformed through the four *photogénie*s. Raymond Lulle never knew a finer powder for projection and emotion. All volumes are displaced and reach flashpoint. Life recruits atoms, molecular movement is as sensual as the hips of a woman or a young man. The hills harden like muscles. The universe is on edge. The philosophers' light. The atmosphere is heavy with love. I am looking.

That mysterious, indefinable thing sought as evidence of *photogénie*, that enigmatic entity which is like a stiffening muscle that fills the atmosphere with love, threatening to 'flash' and evoking images of women's and young men's hips, is defined elsewhere by Epstein as anything which 'moves and changes simultaneously in space and in time', as all erections should. The point, however, is that this evanescent condition, this little extra to be observed, intermittently, in cadenced movement, rears up at the sight of a female body: 'The mother whom we loved with naked eyes', a nice example of metathesis. In other words, *photogénie* emerges, flashes through the image, when a viewer finds figurations that trigger or rekindle the fantasy of the phallic mother. What is extraordinary in all this is not that Epstein should have stumbled on the fact that the cinematic gaze is caught in a fetishistic structure of looking and split belief, but rather the terms in which this fundamental aspect of cinema (truly one of its basic laws, as Delluc, perhaps unwittingly, stated) has simultaneously been hidden and shown, unspoken and writ large: the way, in short, that this fetishistic regime of split belief has been mimicked in the first theoretical writings about cinema.

Indeed it is arguable that these writings are 'theoretical' only in the sense that they refer, however obliquely, to a basic law of cinematic looking. On the other hand, the discovery that *photogénie* is a term marking the fetishistic aspect of cinematic looking is hardly worth dwelling upon any more. In so far as *photogénie* turns upon the look of the viewer, it could scarcely mark anything else and this look has been described and analysed far more pertinently in much theoretical work of the 70s.

What is more significant is the fact that *photogénie* is directly related to, and in large measure dependent on, the viewer in two specific ways. Firstly, because it is founded on the activation in, and recognition by, the viewer of phallic mother fantasies. What distinguishes viewers who are sensitive to *photogénie* from others is not that one group is caught in a structure of fetishistic looking while the others are not. The sensitive viewers must be willing to recognise the terms of that fantasy as fundamental to cinema, as the privileged moments where something of the foundation of the cinematic institution is at stake. Secondly, however, this recognition must remain unspoken. The price of this theoretical insight is that it must be relegated to the unspeakable (Epstein states: 'I wish there to be no words' to specify *photogénie*).

In this sense, *photogénie* designates a gap, a hole in cinematic-critical-theoretical discourse by covering it over in an operation of which the success is continually denied. This hole in the discourse is more like a black hole: it relentlessly attracts, like a magnet, discursive formulations, attempts at definition which spiral around a forever unreachable focal point – unreachable because it was never there in the first place and because its signifier has been expelled from discourse by decree. The point is not that *photogénie* is indefinable: it is rather that the impressionists decreed it to be so and then deployed an elaborate metaphoric discourse full of lyrical digressions and highly charged literary imagery in order to trace obsessively the contours of the absence which that discourse is designed to designate and contain. This is why every attempted definition must be accompanied by a denial of its adequacy and why a term such as 'amputation' can come to figure in the process.

Photogénie, then, refers to the unspeakable within the relation of looking and operates through the activation of a fantasy in the viewer which he or she refuses to verbalise. In this sense, it requires the viewer's complicity in refusing – as if refusal were sufficient to obliterate it – the fall into symbolic signification (language) and the corresponding privileging of a nostalgia for the pre-symbolic when 'communication' was possible without language in a process of symbiosis with the mother. A trace of this nostalgia for the psychotic existence of pre-oedipal childhood (that is, for utopia) can be read from the way in which the term 'soul' is mobilised in these writings: the souls of cinema and of the viewer are supposed to be able to 'fuse' in wordless interaction when divested of the inevitable material encumbrances inherent in any process of signification.

On the one hand, this wished-for refusal of the fall into language refers us back, paradoxically, to the structure of fetishism in its obsession to identify and isolate privileged moments which are both said to be beyond words and, at the same time, suggestive of specific, always deficient abstract terms. Note, for instance, Epstein's attempts to equate certain images with verbs such as 's'en aller'. In 1887, Alfred Binet had already identified this tendency towards abstraction in fetishism:

Amorous fetishism has a tendency towards complete detachment, towards isolation of the object of worship from everything that surrounds it and, when this object is part of a living person, the fetishist tries to make this part an independent whole. [See, for instance, Epstein's remarks on parts of the actors' bodies and his privileging of the close-up.] The necessity of fixing, by means of a word which serves as a sign, those fleeting little nuances leads us to adopt the term abstraction. Amorous fetishism has a tendency towards abstraction.[6]

On the other hand, the process of thought about the scopic relation underpinning cinematic signification and its narcissistic, mirroring implications, as initiated by Epstein and his contemporaries, refers us forward via the detour through post-war filmology and phenomenology to Christian Metz's essay, 'The Imaginary Signifier'.[7] Metz specifies in theoretical terms the kind of relationship Epstein is groping towards, but also refusing firstly by the refusal of psychoanalysis and secondly because a theory of the cinematic apparatus was simply not yet on the cards. When Epstein suggests that *photogénie* emerges with the clicking of the camera's shutter – that is, in the moment when the filmed is absented in favour of its replacement by an image frozen in an eternal present – he is initiating a movement of theoretical reflection that has culminated, at least for the time being, in Metz's discussion of cinematic specificity:

> I must perceive the photographed as absent, its photograph as present, and the presence of this absence as signifying [t]he absence of the object. [T]he codes of that absence are really produced in [cinema] by the physis of an equipment. The cinema is a body (a corpus for the semiologist), a fetish that can be loved.[8]

As for the elaboration of the viewers' aesthetic, Metz puts it thus in the same essay: 'The viewer identifies with himself as a pure act of perception.' The viewer identifies with his own look: '*Je regarde* – I am looking' – stands in splendid isolation as the clinching statement at the end of Epstein's *The Senses 1 (b)*.

Inverting the image in relation to the viewer's projections, it becomes a mirror for the spectator's illusory sense of unity. This is a double-edged mirroring: fantasies can be delegated to the image, leaving the viewer as an outside and thus blameless observer. In Epstein, the atmosphere 'swollen' with desire is presented as the magic of the cinema and not as the consequence of looking. But, as in the story of Dorian Gray, the mirror is also symbolically linked to the viewer, so that whatever happens to one refracts onto the other. The figure of the double, the narcissistic mirroring process, also refers us to the contradiction between stasis and process, between the moment and flux, and to the problem of time, that is to say, death. Therefore it is not surprising that Epstein's reflections on *photogénie* should also lead him to attempted definitions in terms of mobility ('cadenced movement') and time.

Other elements at work in Epstein's rehearsal of the problems provoked by his mobilisation of *photogénie* are related to more specifically cultural dimensions of repression. The refusal of psycho-analysis becomes both explicit and revealing when he talks of the bodies of actresses appearing to be transparent. The thinking of the relation between the image and the unspoken-unspeakable takes a distinctly Catholic turn when the image is made to 'confess', to reveal its hidden secrets. But again, this is done in the context of a refusal of language, while confession is part of an institution founded upon the injunction to tell all. The common misconception that cinema is founded upon an irretrievable and radical opposition between show-ing and telling, between image and word, is thus given a specifically Catholic, confessional inflection by Epstein. Speech is suppressed since images are supposed to tell us much more and to do so more directly, thus – ironically – more adequately fulfilling the injunction of the confessional to speak what elsewhere must remain unspoken, not to say unspeakable. For Epstein, the image of the actress is not an ideal metaphor for psychoanalysis: it is the fulfilment of the wish for an ideal confessional which absolves the desiring viewer through a process of direct semantic exchange which is one of the main path-ways towards mysticism. And as Bordwell remarks, mysticism was indeed the swamp in which most of the theoretical statements of the impressionists eventually drowned.

Finally, it is worth noting that, in spite of the serious shortcomings of their aesthetic position, the refusal of psychoanalysis by Epstein and his contemporaries of the French avant-garde at least preserved them from some of the surrealists' later mistakes. Throughout Epstein's writings, there are scattered a number of remarks referring not only to the double, but also to that type of recognition which Freud attempted to theorise in terms of the uncanny. Epstein's anec-dote about the impression made upon him by Léger's drawing is especially revealing in this context. There are many passages in which the 'mystery' of an inexplicable 'surplus' of familiarity, rendering the familiar uncanny, is invoked as an explanation for the specific emotional intensity produced by imaged discourses.

Paradoxically, again, surrealism (or, at least, André Breton) suc-ceeded in blunting the edge of the uncanny by the deliberate and strenuous efforts to provoke it through specific disciplines such as automatic writing, games, the cultivation of the oxymoron, and the use of drugs. Whereas Freud gave an equal reality status to psychic and material reality, Breton only admitted to the surreal what was conjured up and provoked in a never-ending attempt to manufacture facsimiles or analogues of the workings of the unconscious – as if the realm of the unconscious could be made conscious. Breton's position required not a psychic reality with its own rules and principles, but an unconscious reality beyond and separate from psychic reality, a separate object to be represented alongside or, preferably, instead of everyday psychic reality. In order to achieve such representations, facsimiles of the unconscious, he resorted to the use of fragments, or objects 'found' or extracted from their context and thus rendered autonomous like so many fetish traces, rearranging them in a ceaselessly repeated *bricolage*, with partial – and transitional – objects standing in for the irretrievably 'lost' object.

The endlessly pursued object, symbolised by the elusive ideal object of *amour fou*, is, of course, the maternal body. While Epstein deployed the term *photogénie* to mark the trace of his lost object, thus supporting the fantasy of restoring, reconstituting a lost plenitude, Breton managed to blunt the radical edge of the uncanny by domesticating its disquiet into an obsessional, perfectly regulated art of 'surprises'. In surrealism a rigorously coded set of procedures modified anxiety into surprise, thus naturalising precisely what was claimed to be the dynamo of their subversion.

Perhaps this difference goes some way towards accounting for the very different status of the surrealists and the 20s avant-garde in both film history and in conventional art history. Since Epstein did not even attempt to theorise the fetishism and the narcissism that underpins cinematic scopophilia (cinephilia), he managed to avoid reducing the radically disturbing dialectic of desire and death at work in his theory. By contrast, Breton's appeal to psychoanalysis for legitimation, and surrealism's drastic misappropriation of psychoanalysis, produced only a codified, domesticated version of that dialectic which, by definition, exceeds codification.

Epstein and his colleagues of the 'first' avant-garde paid a price for their refusal of psychoanalysis and for their consequent maintenance of the radical edge of the uncanny: a drift into mysticism and confusion, followed by a long period of total neglect and virtual oblivion. However, the price paid by the surrealists was dearer: their prestigious niche in art history continues to attract sycophants paying ritual tribute in the hope of preserving that most useful of all artistic dead ends, the romantic notion of the bourgeois rebel, uniquely transcending the rules and strictures of his or her time.

Notes

1. This text first appeared in *Afterimage* no. 10, 1982. All quotes from Epstein are taken from this issue unless marked otherwise.
2. David Bordwell, 'French Impressionist Cinema: Film Culture, Film Theory and Film Style', unpublished PhD Thesis, University of Iowa, 1974.
3. Ibid., pp. 106–8.
4. Ibid., pp. 112–13.

5. Serge Leclaire, *Démasquer le réel* Paris: Le Seuil, 1971), p. 77.
6. Quoted in J.-B. Pontalis, *Entre le rêve et la douleur* (Paris: Gallimard, 1977), p. 80.
7. Christian Metz, 'The Imaginary Signifier', in *Screen*, vol. 16 no. 2, Summer 1975.
8. Ibid., pp. 55–9.

Chapter 7

The Ophuls Text: A Thesis

The few reviewers and critics who attempted to deal with Ophuls' films all revert, regular as clockwork, to a handful of terms such as baroque style, camera virtuosity, rhythm, formalism, fascination, romanticism, nihilism, and so on. As Alan Williams has pointed out in his thesis on Ophuls,[1] the traditional film theories have been unable to cope with the latter's work. Starting with the idea that he must be an author, as opposed to a mere director, his work is then reduced to 'empty' formalisms or 'pure style', praised by the so-called *mise en scène* critics such as Jacques Rivette, or dismissed by moralists fixated on forms of content such as characters and themes.

Accepting this crude form/content opposition, other writers searched for profound statements about the human condition in selected combinations of style and story. The most intelligent and productive approaches (Brian Henderson, Victor Perkins and Andrew Sarris) have concentrated on the specific combinations in the director's work of sequence shots and montage, thus to some extent demonstrating why neither montage critics nor sequence shot critics such as André Bazin were able to find a way of reading the peculiar in-between strategies deployed in Ophuls' films.

A second set of terms that surfaces regularly in writing about Ophuls revolves around the argument that all his films focus on women, even if the original source material for the plot has to be pulled rather violently in that direction. The best examples of this are *Liebelei* (1932) and *Werther* (1938), where in each case a female character somehow gets to be privileged dramatically over the male protagonist. This notion relates, as will be argued later, to the fact that in his films, as well as in the rest of his work, women tend to be produced as pivots within intricate and elaborate narrative structures, turning them into privileged objects of the look: the look of the audience as well as that of intra-diegetic characters.

A third set of terms, produced mainly by content-oriented critics, relates to a contradiction between the filmed and the filming. For instance, Karel Reisz remarked in an essay in *Sequence*:[2] 'Ophuls is clearly fascinated by the world he depicts, but never allows its surface charm to obscure the price that has to be paid for its preservation. The social conventions, so pleasant to observe from a distance, conceal a rigid and merciless discipline.' This rigidity, this rigorous Order, transgression of which can bring death, is then depicted in the most fluid and flexible of ways, as if what was repressed by the rigorous social order re-emerges in the *mise en scène*. The most striking example of this is perhaps a structuring literalism in *Le Plaisir* (1952).[3] As a joke – and it is interesting that he should have chosen to put it in this way – Ophuls explained that the reason for the convoluted crane movement along the walls of the brothel in the Maison Tellier episode, peering through windows but never cutting to the inside of the house, was that the Maison Tellier was, precisely, a '*maison close*', literally 'a closed house' but a common French phrase designating a private brothel. Behind its windows and doors is locked away what a rigorous social morality excludes from its legal order.

So, the camera is on the side of the law (and of the people who cannot afford or pretend not to visit such places), but what has been excluded and repressed – in this case we see the repression and transformation of a verbal phrase combined with the inscription of socio-sexual repression – returns and energises the camera, moving it along as it obsessively circles its object of fascination, tracing the outlines of the gaps in the social fabric, catching glimpses of the forbidden areas where desire reigns. The tracks, dolly shots and crane movements constantly hold out the promise that in passing, or in the move from one position or look to another, the look finally may find and possess its object of desire, as for instance in the transition via the spyglass in *The Exile* (1947). But the object of desire evades the look, never offering itself to a close-up, to detailed scrutiny. The look searches but is never allowed the illusion of possessing its object.

It is also interesting to note that Ophuls appeared to be aware of the sexual implications of isolating a person for the look, the sexual implications of, for instance, cutting to a close-up of a woman, offering up her body for access by an investigatory and possessive gaze. In *Le Plaisir*, he shoots five prostitutes in a train in mid and long shots, always attempting to keep as many of them as possible in frame at the same time. The reason for this, Ophuls explained in an interview, by reference to yet another literalism, was that Maupassant's original story described the women as 'a bunch of flowers' and he was reluctant to 'pick' one of them.

The Ophuls film that turns entirely on this inscription of the look trying to take possession of its desired object is, of course, *Lola Montès* (1955). Here, the woman is explicitly put on show, offered to the fixed and fixing gaze of the viewer – the viewer in the film as well as the viewer of the film – with the camera playing endless veiling and unveiling games. But what the look finds is a mask, the woman as

masquerade, as screen. The film's narration and diegesis both fragment under the pressure of the desire to penetrate the body beyond
the mask and to possess that which, by definition, must always escape
if desire is to be sustained and death to be postponed. Every new
scene/seen promises to satisfy what the previous one promised, but
the look never quite finds its 'real' object, always landing on a stand-
in. Scene after scene is offered to the gaze, each constituting a trap for
it, something in which it can be trapped and lost, something to cap-
ture the eye by filling it yet nevertheless withholding what is actually
looked for, thus forever re-launching the wish to look again or to
look elsewhere, to move beyond. It is in this sense that Ophuls' films
engage with the cinema as spectacle or, in Stephen Heath's words,
'with the relations sustained in cinema, as cinema'.[4]

In Ophuls, cinema becomes a machine for captivating the look. It is
also in this sense that the function of the soundtrack in these films can
begin to be understood as the inscription of signifiers off-screen,
emphasising the unseen, that which has been withheld from the eye.
At important moments in *Letter from an Unknown Woman*,
Madame de ... and Lola Montes, the spectator is not shown the
performance which is heard on the soundtrack. Precisely that which is
socially and legitimately designated as 'to be looked at', is withheld.
The displaced presence on the soundtrack of the absent spectacle
emphasises the status of the image as a trap for the gaze, placing
cinema under the sign of the restless look at what is being socially or
legally withheld, reactivating cinema as a risky, eroticised institution
specifically designed to explore the nexus of look and desire, of scene
and seen. According to the rules of patriarchy, it is at this intersection
that the figure of the woman is produced as image. At the juncture of
order and the repressed, of the Law and the unconscious, woman is
produced as the signifier of desire. Moreover, this is a signifier representing the subject for that other signifier, the look, thus instituting
and producing the cinema spectator, that specific subject produced by
and for the cinematic institution and which, historically, has been the
object of such intense moral concern, not to say panic.

The ceaseless metonymy set in motion by the look, the endless
inscription of difference – the scene is never quite what is to be seen –
must be circumscribed and contained in some way for the film to
remain within a certain narrative formula, indeed for it to be able to
end at all. Interestingly, for a cinematic practice turning on the look, a
large number of Ophuls' films end with the inscription of a full stop
on the soundtrack (*Liebelei*, *Letter from an Unknown Woman*
(1948), *Madame de ...* (1953)). *Madame de ...* gives an especially
clear example of this: the duel is marked by the sound of a pistol shot
off-screen, present only as sound, in the same way as the social
spectacles referred to earlier are marked simply by sounds. In the duel
scenes, it is the sound that ends the film and not the image track,

which often spills over into an infinitely extendible epilogue signifying not so much a coming to rest as a freezing. In *Madame de ...*, this is the image of the couple on the beach, one of them in an invalid's chair, frozen into a static relationship for the rest of their lives as the film calmly lets the image track run out.

It isn't that there is no more to be seen, merely that from then on everything is endless repetition, sameness, immobility and loss. What the soundtrack puts an end to is the energising force of desire which drove the look, and the camera, from one scene to the next. The soundtrack halts this potentially infinite process by filling with a sound that gap between what was looked for and what was available to the look. It should not be a surprise that such a sound also signifies death.

The dialectic of order and excess turning on the pivot of the look at the female also makes its mark on three different levels in the films, one related to the narrative structure, the other two to the *mise en scène*. Firstly, as suggested earlier, the impact of the scopic drive on the narration fragments and distorts the latter. The linear, orderly telling of the story from beginning to end breaks open, turns back on itself, regresses and flashes back, as it tracks the memory of plenitude to be recovered in the future. The illusory expectation of a look at last satisfied produces a movement backwards into the future, expecting to recover, as the film unreels scene after scene, the lost cause of desire. A variant on this is the perpetual recommencing of the story as in *La Ronde* (1950), *Le Plaisir* and *La Tendre ennemie* (1936); or the renewal of the narrative trajectory and the repetition or the doubling of scenes as in *La Ronde*, *Madame de ...* and *Letter from an Unknown Woman*. Once more, the complex inscription of this aspect of the dialectic is to be found, not surprisingly, in the very same film that most directly engages with the cinematic representation of the look: *Lola Montes*.

Secondly, the dialectic of balance and symmetry on the one hand and of excess on the other is also to be found on the level of the arrangement of the pro-filmic event: characters will be placed in symmetric compositions with figures balancing each other or being balanced by the placement of objects within the frame, or in three-somes with the side figures looking at a central one. Even the sets reproduce this sense of symmetry in the form of double stairways, the shape of a circus tent, the entrance to a house, mirrors reflecting a figure, and so on.

At the same time, however, there is a proliferation of excessive detail filling up the image with impediments to the look, obstacles between scene and seen, as well as a proliferation of objects in the sets literally filling the image space to overflowing and offering a myriad of objects to the gaze. In this sense, the look is invited to wander through the scene, resting now on one object, now on another, while the overall composition offers the spectacle of fixed proportions harmoniously balanced in classically static relations, captivating the look and stopping it from wandering. The result is that the look is simultaneously subjected to two forces pulling it in different directions.

Thirdly, there is the conduct of the camera. It combines restlessness, a ceaseless movement the function of which I indicated earlier, with repeated movements often accompanying doubled scenes in the narrative: for instance, the station and church scenes in *Madame de ...* – a film in which nearly every element is doubled, echoed or inverted, either simultaneously via mirrors or through different narrative moments – or the repeated tracking shots in *Letter from an Unknown Woman*.

The camerawork also reproduces the stasis/process dialectic in relation to the pro-filmic event through the use of a moving camera to film a moving figure, both elements remaining equidistant and thus in a fixed, static relation to each other while the process, the excess, is displaced onto the background objects moving through the image (furniture, walls, trees, and so on). The clearest example of this occurs towards the beginning of *Madame de ...*, when the central character moves through her apartment at a frantic pace, but at a fixed distance from the camera that accompanies her movements. The furniture and the décor that provide the movement in the frame curiously echo the revolving landscapes which imbue a static railway carriage with an illusion of movement in the amusement park of *Letter from an Unknown Woman*. Each of these registers of textual construction inscribes simultaneously a breakthrough of excess, the transgression of a rigid and merciless discipline, as Karel Reisz puts it, and also the strategies to contain and recover, to neutralise through re-inscription or repetition what Order had to expel, to repress. In this sense, Ophuls' cinema can be seen as the dramatisation of repression, with the repressed returning and imprinting its mark on the representation, undermining and at times overwhelming that manifestation of secondary elaboration called a coherent scenario.

Notes

1. Alan Williams, 'Max Ophuls and the Cinema of Desire – Style and Spectacle in Four Films, 1948–1955', University of New York at Buffalo, 1977; a modified version was published by the Arno Press, New York, 1980. For problems posed by Ophuls to traditional genres of film criticism, see especially pp. 1–15.
2. *Sequence* no. 14, 1952.
3. For a discussion of 'literalisms', see Chapter 1. In this context, it refers simply to the literal production in the filmic text of a verbal metaphor.
4. Stephen Heath, 'The Question Oshima', in Paul Willemen (ed.), *Ophuls* (London: BFI, 1978); reprinted in Stephen Heath, *Questions of Cinema* (London: Macmillan, 1981).

Part Three

Chapter 8

An Avant-Garde for the 90s

In *Maeve* (John Davies and Pat Murphy, 1981), a series of political discussions interrupt but also irrigate what could be (mis)taken for a realist drama.[1] The first of these dialogues between Maeve, the lead character, and Liam, her republican boyfriend, is set on Cave Hill, the site where Wolf Tone and the Society of United Irishmen took their famous oath in 1795 to rid Ireland of the English. This historical event is not explicitly mentioned in the film in any way other than simply through the use of this particular location.

In Cinema Action's *So That You Can Live* (1981), there is a scene in which a couple are working in a little vegetable garden while the voice-over of their daughter informs us that the family tried gardening but, as with so many other things they undertook to supplement the family income, it didn't work out. In the background of the gardening scene is a hillside partially covered in thick forest, the results of a reforestation policy. In South Wales, reforestation uses up a large proportion of the available arable land and constitutes one of the most lucrative investments for London-based stock-market gamblers. In addition, people who only a few generations ago were transformed into an industrial working class are now caught up in a process of deindustrialisation which leaves them stranded in the countryside, forced to move elsewhere or to relearn farming skills. Neither of these options offers a solution for the immediate problems people in that situation have to face, especially when the prime farming land has been reserved for gamblers betting on the future price of wood.

In both films, the use of landscape requires what Raymond Williams, following Brecht, called 'complex seeing': the reading of landscape within the diegesis as itself a layered set of discourses, as a text in its own right. In these examples, landscape is not subordinated to character or to plot development. Instead, it is offered as a discursive terrain with the same weight, and requiring the same attention, as the other discourses that structure and move the text. This use of landscape is not to be read according to the habitual 'gestalt' type of image consumption, which is the customary tourist point of view privileged in all dramatic narratives, whether fiction or documentary.

Each of the two scenes mentioned, in their own way, activate the scenery, the landscape, and not merely as backdrop, as an atmospheric or symbolic setting referring to the psychological state of the characters or providing local colour. Nor is this scenery devised as a function of some spectacular action-space, rather it is deployed as a site where the dynamics of history can be read. In *Maeve*, the Cave Hill sequence not only demarcates the political dialogue from the main body of the narrative set in urban Belfast, it also connects with other types of activation of the landscape (and of cityscapes) within the film to form part of a landscape discourse that informs the film throughout. Even more importantly, Cave Hill evokes Wolf Tone and a particular anti-sectarian tradition in Irish nationalist politics: Tone was a Protestant working closely with Catholic organisations. This anti-sectarianism is, of course, directly relevant to contemporary Irish politics. The location thus not only frames the political dialogue in the film, it also situates that dialogue in a political history.

In addition, Tone's late-eighteenth-century democratic anti-sectarianism, strongly influenced by the ideals of the French Revolution, provides a further context for the very issues discussed by Maeve, a socialist feminist with an internationalist perspective, and Liam, a socialist and a critical supporter of the anti-imperialist dimensions of the Provisional IRA's nationalist politics. Tone's democratic nationalism may have been anti-sectarian, but it also represents a progressive tradition which nevertheless ignored the importance of class politics, and of the gender oppression which cuts across both the religious and class divide. As such, the Cave Hill location provides an essential historical dimension to the intricacies of current Irish politics, refuting – implicitly – the simplistically anti-imperialist support for the Provisional IRA's activities advocated by most of the radical left in England. Instead, the film acquires a dimension that stresses the linkage between religious, class and sexual politics at work synchronically and diachronically: synchronically in the scene of the film and in Ireland today; diachronically as the text unfolds and in the course of Irish history.

Walter Benjamin described such a condensed representation as a dialectical image, consisting of 'the numbered groups of threads that represent the weft of the past as it feeds into the present'.[2] Both *Maeve* and *So That You Can Live*, with their de-structuration of landscape into the traces of political and industrial archaeology, of history both in the past and in the making, can be understood as films exemplifying a new register of discourse in British film-making (although it might perhaps be safer to talk of a 'renewed discourse', since avant-gardes inevitably construct their own antecedents). This discourse is new in the sense of forming part of a growing trend, emerging in widely different areas of signifying practices, which appears capable of fundamentally displacing and renovating questions of the social circulation of meaning. It displaces them by shifting the focus away from the determining effects of textual procedures on subjectivity and towards the question of the social anchorage of meaning production.

This, in turn, allows for a renovation, a new avant-gardism of cultural practices, which is no longer caught in the realism-modernism dichotomy. Instead of starting from the question, 'How to speak?', this avant-garde starts from the question, 'How to understand social existence?' The latter question, in subsuming the former and subordinating it to the issue of social-historical over-determination, enables the relation between producer, text and reader to be conceptualised according to different priorities which differ from those inherent in the realism–modernism debate. In effect, such films demonstrate the debilitating aspects of that opposition, and stress the need for a fundamental rethink of those issues which the realism–modernism debate sought to address.

Modernism versus the Avant-Garde(s)
The current practice of equating modernism with the avant-garde, and even of using the two terms synonymously, is in fact a very recent phenomenon.[3] It was initiated in the USA after the Second World War and exported back to Europe in the 50s and 60s. This operation was so successful that today, even in Europe, many artists, historians and theoreticians make no distinction between the two terms. Such an equation is highly questionable. The very concept of an avant-garde, of a vanguard, implies a set of historical relations. Introduced as a phrase borrowed from military terminology by the French utopian socialists, the term implies questions such as: the vanguard of what, going where and to what purpose? In contrast, the notion of modernism reduces artistic practice to a set of formal characteristics, a set of procedures frozen into a specific generic practice and suggesting that modernism is a period style, as was impressionism or expressionism, or any other historically circumscribed style. The avant-garde, as a concept, is not prescriptive about the precise characteristics of any given art practice, while modernism is most definitely used as a normative category, distinguishing between objects on the grounds of attributes such as self-reflexiveness (allegedly within the text and not as a construction of the reader or viewer), immanence and indeterminacy. Modernism insists that these features be present in the form of experiments with visual perspective, narrative structure, temporal logic, and so on. The theoretical shadows of modernist procedures are concepts such as undecidability, deconstruction, decentring and specificity.

In the light of Benjamin's warning that 'In every era the attempt must be made to wrest tradition away from a conformism that is about to overpower it',[4] it is possible to distinguish between avant-gardism and modernism. Modernism represents, in the 20th century at least, the conformism that is constantly seeking to freeze and defuse into a mere repertory of techniques the critical adversariness deployed by the avant-garde tradition. A prime example of the conservative, conformist pressure exerted by modernism can be seen in the fate that has befallen Brechtian practice since the 50s, which, incidentally, is also the period when the term 'modernism' finally usurped the place of the avant-garde, emptying the latter term of any specific meaning. In 1952, when Brechtian practice was being reduced to a mechanical deployment of techniques of distanciation, Brecht protested: 'The question of choice of artistic means can only be that of how we playwrights give a social stimulus to our audience. To this end we should try out every conceivable artistic method which assists that end, whether it is old or new.'[5] The reduction of Brecht to a repertory of techniques constitutes such an example of modernism threatening to overpower an avant-garde attitude.[6]

It is possible, and indeed necessary, to elaborate Benjamin's rule in more historical terms and not to let his phrase stand simply as a universal conflict inherent in every artistic or intellectual practice at any time, and everywhere. Clement Greenberg's reformulation of Benjamin's rule from the conformist, modernist side of the fence, allows us to understand modernism not so much as a period style, as is so often implied, but as a dialectical tendency accompanying and counteracting manifestations of avant-garde practices, especially in the advanced industrial countries of the 20th century. Whereas the appropriate slogan for an avant-garde practice would be 'Tomorrow's art today', implying a close link between art practices and movements for social change – a relation that casts the avant-garde in the role of anticipating the art practices that would be part of the overcoming of capitalism in a socialist direction rather than the anticipation of further developments in a capitalist direction or the reactualisation of pre-capitalist tendencies – modernism's slogan would be 'Yesterday's art today and tomorrow'. While the avant-garde assumes – rightly or wrongly, and mostly in the form of wish-fulfilment – a symbiotic relation between artistic and political radicalness, modernism, in Greenberg's words, is designed 'to maintain or restore continuity [w]ith the highest aesthetic standards of the past', to restore 'levels of quality' which in turn are to be preserved by 'constant renewal and innovation'.[7] Modernism opposes change. It runs merely to stand still. As such, it is the incarnation of the conformist tendency at work in, or better, against any avant-garde practice.

Although there may be a superficial resemblance between modernism and the avant-garde due to former's appropriation of aspects and procedures of the latter, they are, in fact, two simultaneous but antagonistic tendencies. This does not prevent these two tendencies from coexisting within one movement, such as surrealism, or even within the work of one artist, such as Ezra Pound or Maurice Blanchot. In fact, an awareness of the inevitable coexistence of modernist and avant-garde tendencies within aesthetic ideologies should make it impossible to claim that any given single text, say Joyce's *Finnegans Wake*, performs one particular task, whether it be the dissolution of the unitary subject in writing, or its confirmation through the naturalistic representation of the single, embodied stream of consciousness which unifies the disparate voices and slippages of meaning deployed between the covers of the book. Any reading which pins a text to a single productivity or meaning necessarily disregards the fundamental split(s) inherent in the social-historical positions of both the producers and the consumers of such artefacts.

Modernism emerged in the latter half of the 19th century, when a radical industrial bourgeoisie sought to establish its ideological ascendancy over a weakening aristocratic absolutism. In the process, all kinds of bargains and ideological compromises were elaborated, as well as straightforwardly antagonistic ideological practices. The question must remain open, at least until the phenomenon has been studied in greater detail, as to the position of the bourgeois avant-garde within that heterogeneous formation all too readily and prematurely unified under the label 'modernism'.[8] A credible argument can be made for considering modernism as a peculiarly bourgeois compromise with the ideological world of the aristocracy, feeding upon the accommodationist tendency within the bourgeois revolution. Realism, and later naturalism, would then constitute the ideological practice of the radical bourgeoisie. In that case, modernism, even at the moment of its emergence, would already be on the conservative side of the bourgeois revolution, with realism and naturalism constituting the avant-garde tendencies associated with bourgeois struggles for social change – as demonstrated, for instance, in the way artists such as Zola lined up with Dreyfus against the feudal power structures of the French military establishment. However, at this stage, such a distinction, however likely, must remain tentative.

In the light of the historical emergence of modernism, the split between modernism and the avant-garde cannot be mapped simply onto the bourgeois versus working-class opposition. Both artistic practices are firmly middle-class, as all professional art practices are. As far as class positions are concerned, artists must be seen as middle-class intellectuals[9] and the divergence between the avant-garde and modernism as opposing tendencies within the middle-class intelligentsia, each of the conflicting currents engaging in a politics for social change oriented in diametrically opposite directions. One, as its name indicates, is a politics of modernisation, that is to say, a bringing up to date of values and procedures in order to establish, maintain or preserve a particular power-regime. Modernisation is a procedure to increase efficiency within a given framework of production and of values. The other is a politics of negation and transformation aligned with a process of change in a socialist direction, that is to say, a transformation instead of a modernisation.

The relevant distinction to be drawn, indeed to be insisted upon, is therefore not that between modernism and realism (as was the case throughout the 70s in journals such as *Screen*), but rather that between modernism and the avant-garde. The advent of the avant-garde could thus be dated at the emergence of a significant political split within the bourgeois intelligentsia. Whereas previously relations of force between sectors of the bourgeoisie and of the feudal aristocracy had been fought in terms of the opposition between realism and modernism, around the turn of the century a new force established itself as a major contender for political hegemony: working-class-based organisations pursuing a policy of socialist revolution. This new polarisation also inscribed a new split within the middle-class intelligentsia, superseding and displacing the old one: now there was a split between an intelligentsia oriented towards a socialist class politics (the avant-garde) and an intelligentsia dedicated to modernisation in order to 'maintain or restore continuity with the highest aesthetic standards of the past', as Greenberg put it.[10]

In this sense, the avant-garde emerges as part of the process that instituted a working-class politics as a major and explicit point of reference in the political-ideological spectrum at the end of the nineteenth century, achieving symbolic recognition in the period from 1905 to 1917. The entire period of the so-called historic avant-gardes, from 1905 to the Second World War, would then be marked by these conflicting tendencies within art practices, with notorious areas of ambiguity such as futurism, a heterogeneous phenomenon simultaneously opening out onto fascism and Bolshevism.

The common root of middle-class intellectual dissidence in the ambiguities of nineteenth-century romanticism provided ample opportunity for confusions, mixtures of, and overlaps between, the two opposing tendencies within the intelligentsia. But, in general, as Andreas Huyssen has argued in 'The Search for Tradition: Avant-Garde and Postmodernism in the 1970s':

> In modernism, art and literature retained their traditional 19th Century autonomy from everyday life. [T]he traditional way in which art and literature were produced, disseminated and received, is never challenged by modernism but maintained intact. Modernists emphasised time and again that it was their mission to salvage the purity of high art from the encroachments of modern mass culture. The avant-garde of the first three decades of this century,

146

however, attempted to subvert art's autonomy, its artificial separation from life and its institutionalisation as high art. [T]he avant-garde posited the reintegration of art and life as its major project.[11]

However, in their own ways, each of these tendencies devalued history. The avant-garde, in keeping with its roots in romanticism and utopian socialism, rushed headlong into the future, paying scant if any attention to the past. Modernism, in its Greenbergian adoration of eternal values, froze different art disciplines into timeless essences and promoted a fetishistic notion of specificity. From a political point of view, modernism and the avant-garde also had other points in common: they not only shared a rejection of history, but also agreed to define themselves almost exclusively in terms of strategies of signification. In this way, they both contributed to the production of 'subjectivity' as the central term of reference in artistic practice, relegating the non-artistic determinants of the formation of subjectivity to the margins, as factors to be taken into consideration, to be kept in the back of one's mind, but not of central importance to any understanding of artistic practices. It is, perhaps, in these shared presuppositions that the common class basis of modernist and avant-garde intellectuals can best be traced.

It is this close linkage which allowed Peter Wollen, in his now famous essay 'The Two Avant-Gardes',[12] to oppose the homogenisation of the avant-garde and modernism into a single stream, by insisting on the existence of, paradoxically, two avant-gardes, two trends. One of these trends is concerned with reflexiveness and semiotic reduction, foregrounding one category of signifiers or, more radically, the material substrata of given signifiers, thus defining art disciplines in terms of a movement towards the suppression or suspension of the signified. This 'avant-garde' corresponds to modernism. The other trend is described as reacting against purism, rejecting ontological presuppositions or investigations and in a concern with semiotic expansion, such as the use of mixed media, montages of different codes, signs and semiotic registers, the heterogeneity of signifiers also activating heterogeneous signifieds, and so on. This corresponds to an avant-garde approach.

The tendency towards semiotic reductionism clearly corresponds to the conservative impulse, explicitly articulated by Greenberg, to maintain the autonomy and the institutionalisation of high art. Its thrust is towards containing and limiting the challenges of the avant-garde by appropriating some of its terms and procedures (the 'modernising' of art practices) and then re-projecting those back into the traditional, reductively and a-historically defined categories of the 'specific' art disciplines and institutions. This should be seen in the light of the political shift away from the nineteenth-century absolutism—capitalism class opposition towards the twentiet-century capitalism—socialism antagonism. Modernism, associated with the former struggle, is reduced to operating a series of recovery manœuvres described as renovations or innovations. By re-inscribing avant-garde procedures back into the restrictive boundaries erected by theories seeking to establish the specificity of different art disciplines, modernism requires art practices to concentrate on repeating the terms of that specificity.

By characterising Peter Wollen's second avant-garde, that is, the avant-garde itself, exclusively in terms of semiotic expansion, the directionality of the semiotic strategies involved is removed from further analysis, since such an analysis depends on the historical-social anchorage and direction of the practices in operation, and not solely on the identification of certain formal procedures, however expansive. The question of directionality is important if we are to distinguish between practices and tendencies within the avant-garde: which tend towards an accommodation with modernism; and which constitute a movement towards extending the thrust of the avant-garde? Such a distinction would locate, for example, early and middle-period Godard on the modernist interface of the avant-garde, while some Straub/Huillet (for instance, *Lezioni di storia*, 1972; *Klassenverhältnisse*, 1983) subordinates a politics of signification to questions of historical analysis and would therefore point towards ways of developing the avant-garde in more productive directions.

What prompts me to rearrange Peter Wollen's two avant-gardes into an opposition between avant-garde and modernism is precisely the introduction of historical-conjunctural criteria, derived from an always necessarily provisional analysis constructed through an assessment of the forces at play in a given social formation. In this way, the avant-garde's rejection of purism and of ontological preoccupations in favour of an insistence on problems of reference (inherent in the refusal to bracket the signified and to be bound by notions of media specificity) can be understood as necessary preconditions for the elaboration of an artistic practice capable of representing the complexity of historical processes.

In his critique of Tim Clarke's essay on 'Manet's Olympia',[13] Peter Wollen summarised Brecht's opposition to traditional realism in this way:

[Realism] favoured the actual rather than the possible, and the observable rather than the unobservable. It was descriptive rather than explanatory. It effaces contradiction. It could not cope with the depiction of uneven development or over-determination. [Brecht] tried to develop an art on the basis of a montage of discourses, dealing separately and in different manners with different areas and levels of reality.

What is particularly important in this summary is not the critique of realism, but the implied argument for the things artistic practice should be able to do. As the earlier quotation from Brecht also makes clear, if the complexity of social-historical processes is to be represented as accurately and as effectively as possible, it would be wrong and debilitating to accept the limitations of a specificity imposed by any single art discipline. Consequently, by defining such a specificity as the essence of an art practice, and by requiring artists to deal primarily with that specificity, modernism actively militates against any effort to represent historical processes, either analytically or in some other way, and militates for the eternalisation and universalisation of nineteenth-century 'artistic' values, that is, ideologies – which is why it is conservative.

Specificity as Fetish

The ambiguities in the notion of specificity are confusing. There is a thin line between a descriptive definition of specificity and its unwarranted use as an evaluative category. If the descriptive definition of, for example, cinema is to be any good, it must be able to cover all films without distinction. The evaluative use of the term, however, introduces a pragmatic dimension and singles out certain films which direct attention to the features of that specificity. A complicated set of slippages is at work here. From the pedagogic demonstration of processes of cinematic enunciation present in any film whatsoever, from features to industrial training loops, the reader/viewer's learned ability to distinguish these processes, that is to say his or her theoretical competence, came to be attributed to the film itself as one of its effects. The real or claimed value of the reader's competence was transmuted into the film's value, instead of the latter being produced or at least recognised by the viewer. In other words, it is the reader/viewer's real or claimed value which such deconstructions read off from the film and then, modestly, present as the value of the text.

The slippage from a descriptive to a prescriptive use of specificity has now become extremely widespread in film journals. A host of deconstructive readings have been published purporting to show that films as diverse as *An Unmarried Woman* (Paul Mazursky, 1977), *Wide Angle Saxon* (George Landow, 1975), *La Femme du Gange* (Marguerite Duras, 1973) and *Tokyo Monogatari* (Yasujiro Ozu, 1953)[14] all draw attention to the specificity of cinematic enunciation and are to be valued for that reason. In fact, whenever a positive value judgment is required from a theoretical apparatus which is not designed to produce them, texts are now said to be ever so cinematically specific, riddled with fissures and chock-a-block with contradictions directing attention to processes of enunciation and requiring active readers. What is tactfully forgotten is that such a demonstration can be performed on all films without exception. It may perhaps be easier to accomplish with those films which engage our subjective fantasies and desires but that says absolutely nothing about their value. Except in the modernist ideology, of course, which prizes objects according to their ability to incarnate real or pretended cultural wealth, that is, according to their high art value, which is no more than the value of the consumer's social and educational status delegated to the object.

This abusive mobilisation of a prescriptive notion of specificity has been aided, or at least has not been counteracted, with the replacement of Metz's techno-sensoral definition of cinematic specificity[15] by Stephen Heath's more powerful elaboration of cinema as a specific signifying practice. The latter poses the text as the drama or the theatre (why not the sitcom?) of the subject-in-process and cinema as merely 'an institution of representing, a machine for the fabrication-maintenance of representation',[16] echoing the statement that literature, as a specific signifying practice, is to be regarded as 'theatre of language, theatre of the subject in language, in process'.[17] Such a definition need not lead straight to the institutionalised petrification of modernism, but it works on such a level of generality (un-specificity) that it can only facilitate such a tendency.

When Stephen Heath writes that:

> cinema is an institution of representation [and] it is as such that it is a crucial ideological statement, as such that it is developed and exploited, for a narration of the individual as subject in a narrative that is its mapping [w]ithin the limits of existing representations and their determining social relations[18]

what is missing from this overly abstract (but otherwise unobjectionable) definition is precisely the emphasis on the historicity of the processes of enunciation and representation that constitute the cinema as a representation-machine. History is present in that definition simply as a limit, as a still to be theorised articulation with an elsewhere of cinema: an articulation between cinema and the 'determining social relations' reduced to a mere set of constraints, an enclosure. The inscription of the historical-social into the enclosure as 'always already there' offers no solution to this problem. Such a formulation posits a constant co-presence of two terms, only one of which, cinema, is presented as a dynamic process. The other term, history, is reduced to a constant intimate but constantly untheorised companion, the theorisation of which is perpetually postponed because the very definition of cinema cannot conceive that 'specific signifying practice' in any terms other than those of the scene of the production of 'the' subject. The historical determinations within given conjunctures which bear on such a production are always invoked as topics for research in an ever receding future.

In this way, the political options for contemporary textual practices, as well as for theoretical endeavours, are posed exclusively in terms of an abstract, ahistorical notion of subjectivity, reducing the options to a binary opposition. Either the text is said to produce a sense of a unified subject, or it is said to disarticulate subjectivity, 'displacing the fixity of ideological formations, shifting subject positions [in a] kind of de-interpellation, a disfictioning in-of language'.[19] Displacing fixity for what purpose? Shifting subject positions in which direction? Faced with only two options, films will then be assessed strictly in terms of their operations of subject-unification (which is 'bad') or separation (which is 'good'), an option that gets us little further than Greenberg's notion of specificity and, moreover, gives added legitimacy to the slippage from a descriptive to a prescriptive use of specificity. The direction in which those operations of unification or separation work in a given social-historical dynamic becomes irrelevant because predetermined. This is why the theory of the articulation of the text and history, posed as a topic for future research, never gets off the ground: whatever form such a theory may take, its premises in the theory of signifying practices as 'theatres of the the subject in process' predetermine any possible results and make the research a waste of time.

As Stephen Heath has noted in the same context: 'This radical experience of the subject in language is fundamental to what we talk about as "modernism".'[20] Exactly: the way this radical experience of the subject in language and cinema is transformed into the analysis of the experience of the subject in history is fundamental to what we should talk about as the avant-garde. Modernism is indeed fixated on the experience of 'the' subject, radical or otherwise, always postponing or ignoring questions of the way in which that experience is implicated in, and determined by, particular dynamics of social change, and not just any old process of social change, because the social can change in a number of different directions, many of which are not especially desirable.

Putting it somewhat too crudely – but not much – the modernist posing of the radical experience of the subject in language as a sufficient political-cultural programme only leads to the conclusion that socialism will have been achieved when everybody has become an expert in the theory of 'specific signifying practices'. Education is very important, but to designate as the only possible road to socialism one particular academic discourse, however welcome and necessary in some respects that discourse is within the academia we have today, seems a bit excessive.

A Different Kind of Avant-Garde

By and large, the Second World War marked the end of the historical avant-gardes. It also marked the end of the heroic phase of revolutionary socialism in Europe. Whether 1968 represented a failed revolution or a successful modernisation movement still needs further analysis: both tendencies or possibilities were undoubtedly present, and the assessment will depend largely on which tendency is stressed in the efforts to explain events.[21]

In the USA, aspects of the European avant-gardes survived well into the early 70s, partly as a revolt against a modernism that had been thoroughly incorporated into the institutions of high art, to the point of taking on the role of cultural ambassador for a rapacious and bellicose capitalism during the Eisenhower and Kennedy regimes. But in the USA too, the avant-garde aspects of 'post-modernism' (a confusing term compounding the mystifying effects of the previous equation between modernism and the avant-garde) shone as a colourful death-mask, in Andreas Huyssen's phrase, of the avant-garde impulse buried in Europe after 1968.

The subsequent shift of avant-gardism from the area of art practice to the terrain of cultural theory, besides marking and confirming[22] the academicisation, that is, the modernisation of the avant-garde, also constituted a very positive development. Cultural theory operated a critical return of the avant-garde practices and searched for a way out of the dead end. It did so by combining the theoretical investigation of signification with a reassessment of Marxist theory itself. The cultural theory associated with socialist-feminist cultural politics in particular constituted a new avant-garde that re-posed the questions of signification in terms of a theory of the ideological, addressing the operation of the ideological in the social.

Feminism and especially associated work in film theory restated the questions of the avant-garde. But this time, the terrain of the avant-garde was no longer constituted in reference to art practices or in relation to established art disciplines: the relevant work went on in the interface between academia and the area of what used to be called popular culture – a development that had its ramifications within the fine art institutions as well as in other organisational contexts, of course. Claire Johnston's work in the 70s demonstrates this very clearly. An additional and crucially important benefit from this shift towards cultural theory was the emphasis on the historical dimension of signifying practices, including the analysis of the historical avant-gardes 'in context'.[23]

The ruthlessly modernist dictum of Henry Ford that 'History is bunk', an attitude largely shared by the historical avant-gardes and betraying the fact that both progressive and reactionary currents are warring with each other within art practices and discourses, became untenable as both the conventional left intelligentsia in Europe and the women's movement turned their attention to an examination of how they had wound up where they found themselves to be in the 70s. To find a way out of the 1968 impasse, the cultural left turned to a critical analysis of the historical avant-gardes, and to an equally critical consideration of Marxism's uneven engagement with ideological and cultural matters in the shape of Althusser's work. Feminists, who had even more cause to view Marxism critically, also turned to history in an attempt to identify or formulate principles and traditions of feminist struggles and politics. The convergence between the left and feminism can be seen as marked by the common focus on concepts such as subjectivity and memory throughout the 70s in Europe and in the USA.

The re-emergence of an avant-garde, and its attendant turn to history, was manifested in a variety of ways: massive exhibitions devoted to the historical avant-gardes, a flood of books and magazine articles devoted to those movements, the rethinking of the methodologies of historical enquiry itself, the proliferation of anthologies, of confessional literature and oral histories as well as other archival activities, the renewal of interest, especially by feminists, in utopian socialism, and so on.

Of course, this return to history was itself a highly contested area, as those who wished to learn from 1968 clashed with those who simply wanted to write out of history the progressive aspects and potential of 1968 and to return to the more familiar ways of thinking which had contributed in no small measure to the defeats incurred by the left both prior to and since the Second World War. Partly in conjunction with this emphasis on theories of ideology and questions of history, and partly at a tangent to it, some art practices emerged, or at least achieved visibility, addressing the same issues, although often from a different perspective.[24]

In cinema, the most positive aspect of this development can be found in a variety of films re-posing some of Brecht's questions regarding the relations between pleasure, knowledge and signification. But these films no longer asked those questions in terms of the modernism–realism debate, although this tended to be the way cultural theory addressed the issue. The mismatch led quickly to 'a prescriptive anti-realism which ignores the central question for a politics of cinema – that of the audience defined in social and historical terms', as Claire Johnston rightly pointed out.[25] Instead, it is the avant-garde side of Brecht, exemplified by the 1952 passage quoted earlier, which is reactivated: his requirements of what representations should try to achieve, which is a representation of the complexity of historical forces in such a way that they become comprehensible to, and connect with, the experience of audiences involved in trying to find a socialist exit from capitalism. In this sense, the new, nascent avant-garde, at least in the cinema, consists of precisely those films – and theories – which seek to challenge both the ossification of artistic procedures, however 'distancing', into modernist dogma, and the anti-historical tendencies within art and theoretical discourses. These films disavow neither the need to engage with cinema as a 'drama of subjectivity in process' nor the need for a politics of enunciation and representation. They do, however, insist on formulating that engagement in terms of, and in so far as it is pertinent to, the representation of 'history in process'.

Tracing the Political: Narrative

Peter Wollen, among others, has pointed out that feminist film and theory provide the major contemporary example of a sustained avant-gardist cultural politics.[26] But many aspects of the feminist avant-garde are shared by films made in dialogue with it, such as Godard's *Numéro Deux* (1975), as well as by the growing numbers of films made in the context of anti- and post-colonial movements which insist on the need to respect the cultural and the historical specificity of a particular social formation. Those films require that 'complex way of seeing', of reading, for which the old realist-modernist paradigm is totally inadequate. Films such as *So That You Can Live* deploy intricate patterns of montage within images, allowing, for example, landscapes to be read as palimpsests. Others deploy different strategies, but in each case what is at stake is the explication of a socio-cultural dynamic, the tracing of the political within a situation. This is attempted and sometimes achieved through a discourse which is 'in between' the conventions of modernism and those of psychological realism.

Both traditions turn on the issue of subjectivity: its assumed homogeneity (in the notion of character), or its inscription of fragmentation into the text (for example in Nick Roeg's films), its production in the place of the author who thus makes a bid for the status of Author (in, for instance, the case of Marguerite Duras), or its all-encompassing dictatorial rule (in Stan Brakhage) or its alleged elimination (in some of Peter Gidal's or Andy Warhol's work). At times, subjectivity is delegated to technology (in some films of Michael Snow), or allegedly subjected to nature (in the case of Chris Welsby), and so on.

The contemporary avant-garde – and that is why it is an avant-garde rather than another avatar of modernism – seeks to represent subjectivity as one, and only one, not necessarily important process within a situation over-determined by the forces that shape social existence. As such, it seeks to mobilise and transform the cultural knowledges and experience of the audiences it addresses. And it is in that context that narrative becomes an issue again, rather than simply a bad object to be disarticulated or eliminated.

Narrative, as the process through which the articulation of subject and history is elaborated in the text as well as in relation to the text, is thus unavoidable if one point of the discourse is precisely to trace the existence of the political within particular histories. However, a

154

different conceptual framework now presides over the construction of the avant-garde narrative. It is no longer the narrative that tells 'the sequence of events like the beads of a rosary'[27] nor the deconstruction of such a procedure, but a narrative that 'brushes history against the grain'.[28] It is a narrative that neither instructs nor absorbs, but one which leaves a space between production and consumption. The difference from the deconstructive approach lies in the nature of the knowledges summoned to that space. The avant-garde narrative no longer solely appeals to an interest in the way stories are constructed and told. Instead, it seeks to address an audience's knowledge and experience of history. As such, it is no longer a theory of discourse or of representation that is at stake, but instead an understanding of history, of social change.

The current avant-garde thus addresses an area of experience and knowledge which is no longer exclusively available to students of discourse or art theory. On the contrary, its primary audience is assumed to be interested in the dynamics of history, and the films then try to relate issues of signification to the problem of the representation of historical dynamics. In other words, the avant-garde narrative proceeds by means of dialectical images. As Susan Buck-Morss paraphrased Benjamin in a very useful essay:

> Neither content nor form of the bourgeois order of things was to remain untouched in Benjamin's war of demolition. But it was the conceptual platform that was exploded, not the material elements. When these were 'blasted out of the continuum of history', blown free of the codifying structures which entrapped them, it was necessary to catch them up again in a new, cognitive net before they disappeared in history completely. Here was the constructive moment of the dialectic. The elements of past cultures were drawn together in new 'constellations' which connected with the present as 'dialectical images.[29]

The contemporary avant-garde seeks to construct such cognitive nets.[30]

Some Conclusions

Although it may be premature to try to identify the main procedures characteristic of the current avant-garde,[31] it would appear that most of the films implicated deploy a double strategy: the splitting of both narrative and setting.

In conventional narrative, the diegetic setting (location, decor) is rigorously subordinated to plot and character development. Setting is deployed according to the dictates of psychological realism and motivation. It functions either as metaphor for a character's state of mind (critical terms used may range from 'bleak' to 'stormy' or 'wild'), as a picturesque backdrop ('colourful', 'luscious'), as a symbol for a character's environment in the sociological sense ('dehumanising', 'inhospitable') or simply as the necessary collection of props required to give a character a realistic space to inhabit.

None of the conventional uses of landscape, for instance, whether rural or urban, insist on offering the landscape as itself an active, multi-layered discursive space demanding to be read in its own right. Invariably, a tourist's point of view is adopted, as opposed to the point of view, for example, of those whose history is actually traced in the setting, or for whom the land is a crucial element in the relations of production governing their lives. The tourist sees in the landscape only mirrors or projections of his or her fantasms, and thus 'sees' landscapes exclusively in terms of a correspondence with subjective experience, either that of the tourist-author or that of his or her delegates in the narrative, that is to say, the characters.

The avant-garde narrative mobilises setting as another text, a space where a different historical dynamic can be traced, a dynamic proceeding with different historical rhythms and patterns of determination. Such a use of setting interacts with the other elements in the text in the same way that, for example, a written text inscribed in an image would interact with it: each of these texts has to be read, and a relation between them is to be constructed in that process of complex seeing; whereas in the tourist point of view, the setting merely doubles or supports, illustrates the desired construction of character and mood.

As a rule, the avant-garde narrative will oscillate between the use of a narratively motivated setting and the activation of the setting itself as an autonomous discourse. At times, this oscillation may even reverse the conventional hierarchy between narrative and setting, as in some of Chantal Akerman's films (*News From Home*, 1977; *Toute une nuit*, 1982). The activation of a landscape may require the mobilisation of cultural knowledges not readily accommodated into the discourse of film criticism. For instance, the farmer's knowledge of a type of land, or a knowledge widely shared among people inhabiting particular geographical spaces of the historical meanings that have accrued to those particular sites (as is often mobilised in Irish films such as *Maeve* or with the Roman streets in Straub/Huillet's *Lezioni di storia* and with the Vendée and the Egyptian sequences in *Trop tôt, trop tard*, 1981), allows for the reading of a discourse on history within the very use of the landscape – or the cityscape – itself, allowing narrative events to reverberate and to interact with or against an accompanying reading of history.

This may make such texts difficult to read, especially since we have learned to read landscape through profoundly ethnocentric and touristic eyes steeped in the iconographic traditions of landscape painting, home and holiday movies and snapshots, postcards, tourist brochures, travelogues and nature documentaries, and so on. But the relative inaccessibility of such avant-garde films is of a different order compared with that of traditional high-art modernist films and videos, which presuppose a familiarity of sorts with art history and erudite philosophical writings, or at least with some of the journalistic vulgarisations of these writings.

While there is nothing intrinsically wrong with such a requirement (why shouldn't films also be made for the educationally privileged?), the new avant-garde is able to engage with knowledges largely available outside of the universities. It is also able to engage with different class experiences, rearranging and transforming those experiences into new explanatory patterns, encouraging and even requiring a learning process oriented towards historically informed knowledges, rather than simply towards current aesthetic or philosophical fashion. As such, the avant-garde of today is in a better position than its historical precursors to achieve an art form that can teach us something about our own situation as well as providing a motivational connection to political action, or an outlet in praxis, as Benjamin put it.

The second level, that of narrative, is also split in its turn into a particular story on the one hand and its generic setting on the other. By generic setting I mean the inscription into the narrative of a history of discursive practices through references to the way specific aspects of the text figure in relation to other forms and traditions of representation. Prime examples of this would be the references to painting in Godard's *Passion* (1981), to oral literature in *Ceddo* (1976) or in *Maeve*, and to the conventions of direct cinema in *The Nightcleaners Part 1* (1975).[32] These references do not work simply as pointers towards other forms of representation: they also inscribe the hierarchical relations between, say, cinematic and painterly aesthetics, or between oral and imaged narratives. This process of splitting, of simultaneous and systematic bifurcations, can work as easily on the level of the enunciation as on that of the enounced, and inscribes a particular discursive regime into and against the prevailing genres of narrative representation.

This phenomenon is relatively familiar in that it has formed the major focus and prop for deconstructive readings. One significant difference, however, is that the avant-garde text is not condemned to constant and rigorous deconstruction, nor is it satisfied with playing deconstructive games in the margins of otherwise conventional mainstream narrative formats as, for example, in *Desperately Seeking Susan* (1985), where Susan Seidelman invokes the cultural prestige of Jacques Rivette's *Celine et Julie vont en bateau* (1974) but then proceeds to ignore and eliminate everything that made Rivette's film an extraordinarily productive critique of conventional narrative patterns. The new avant-garde deploys and foregrounds such splittings

only intermittently, since it is no more than a necessary but nevertheless secondary aspect of the discourse it deploys. A second difference
is that deconstruction, especially when practiced by epigones, usually
avoids the problem of the power relations between traditions of representation, contenting itself with the mere evocation of the historical
bric-a-brac stored in image traditions. A simple homogenisation/sep-
aration model cannot deal with such power relations, whereas the
avant-garde text assumes we are interested in precisely these hierarchical, determining and transforming relations.

This double splitting process, unequally present at any given
moment but equally present as structuring axes of the text as a whole,
allows for both overlaps with, and demarcations from, dominant and
modernist textual regimes alike. It engages with audience expectations but also brushes them against the grain. Such an in-between
discursive regime offers the possibility, at least, of posing at one and
the same time the problems of the historicisation of social as well as
of geographic space, together with the problems of representing such
spaces. This is a difficult strategy relying on complex seeing, which
affects the relations between film-makers and what or who they represent, as well as the relations between audiences and what or who is
represented. In this sense, the avant-garde is moving towards new
ways of constructing and telling (his)stories, 'des histoires'.

The argument put forward here would locate the contemporary
avant-garde in films such as *Fluchtweg nach Marseille* (Ingemo Engström and Gerhard Theuring, 1977), with its exploration of the interconnections between story and history, representation and subjectivity, its emphasis on critical analysis of a historical process still
active in the present and thus historicising contemporary questions of
subjectivity and representation. Other examples would be *Toute une
nuit* (Chantal Akerman, 1982) or *Crystal Gazing* (Peter Wollen and
Laura Mulvey, 1982), with their insistence on locating the dynamic
between stasis and repetition, and between process and difference, in
historically concrete and precise settings; *Die Reise nach Lyon* (Clau-
dia von Alemann, 1980) or the Vietnamese *Canh Dong Hoang* (aka
Land Laid Waste, Hong Sen, 1979), with their inscription of historical layers within settings, and their engagement with the very problem
of enouncing or constructing historical discourses which give their
full due to subjective factors, memory and desire – an engagement
articulated through the shifting relations between sound and image
tracks in stories that refuse the position of the professional, 'objective'
historian. Similar strategies are at work in Pat Murphy and John
Smith's *Maeve* and in Cinema Action's *So That You Can Live* and
Rocinante.

This is not to say that all these films are exemplary in all their
aspects, that they are all equally constructive in their exploration of
the interconnections between history, narration and cognition, nor

that they are all equally productive with regard to the elaboration of a socialist cultural politics. Nor is it to say that all aspects of modernism are simply and unequivocally to be dismissed at all times both in cinema and in the university. What is opposed or supported must depend on the situation and on the political options available and, to paraphrase Brecht, no device or strategy should be ruled out in this task. Besides, to essentialise devices deployed in modernism would be as objectionable as modernism's own mechanisation of, for instance, distanciation devices derived from Brecht. In other words, an avant-garde attitude must be taken towards modernism.

In addition, the demarcation lines are never absolutely clear-cut, precisely because they are always drawn within social practice, where the tension exists between the presentation and the appropriation of signifying practices. Not given textual characteristics, but rather the conjunctural effectiveness and the power (that is, the relative accuracy) of the historical analysis underpinning particular strategies of representation are the criteria for assessing cultural practices and for assigning them to modernism or to the avant-garde. We must be aware that even within any avant-garde, some would like nothing better than to go back to the mainstream, while others drag their feet and yet others may be trying to lead the group into a trap. The same tendencies, and more, are to be expected within the work of any avant-garde artist, even within any single avant-garde text.

What this tells us, to speak in historical shorthand, is that, for instance, Godard's still crucial ability to remind us of the facts of signification must now be seen as a necessary but secondary aspect within a cinema that doesn't just ask the question of cinema historically, but asks the questions of history cinematically.

Notes

1. This chapter draws heavily on the work of Claire Johnston published in *Screen*, vol. 22 no. 4, 1982.
2. Quoted in *New Left Review*, no. 128, 1981, p. 57.
3. This section draws heavily on the work of Andreas Huyssen published in *New German Critique*, no. 22. For a useful account of the avant-garde as a concept, see Nicos Hadjinicolau in *Praxis*, no. 6, 1982. However, that account does not break with the avant-garde/modernism equation and thus fails to address artistic practice as an intellectual practice. The result is a premature writing out of history of the ideological function and power of the different strata of middle-class intellectuals, eliminating at the same time their dialectical relation to socialist ideologies and struggle.

   Shortly after the publication of this essay, I became aware of Peter Bürger's *Theory of the Avant-Garde* (Minneapolis: University of Minnesota Press, 1984), which similarly attempts to distinguish between the avant-garde and modernism, and which overlaps with mine to a significant extent. Where I speak of 'conservatism', Bürger speaks of 'institutionalisation' regarding the modernist current.

4. Walter Benjamin, *Illuminations* (London: Fontana, 1973), p. 257.

5. John Willett (ed.), *Brecht on Theatre* (London: Eyre Methuen, 1964), p. 229.

6. See, for instance, the mechanical use of the notion of a politics of separation in 'The Politics of Separation', *Screen*, vol. 16 no. 4, 1975–6.

7. Quoted in John A. Walker, *Glossary of Art, Architecture and Design Since 1945* (London: Clive Bingley, 1977), p. 197.

8. See Michael McKeon, *The Origins of the English Novel* (Baltimore: Johns Hopkins University Press, 1987); T. J. Jackson Lears, *No Place of Grace – Antimodernism and the Transformation of American Culture 1880–1920* (New York: Pantheon Books, 1981).

9. Régis Debray, *Teachers Writers Celebrities – The Intellectuals of Modern France* (London: Verso, 1981).

10. What is at stake here is less the validity or the coherence of Greenberg's formulations than the fact that they achieved widespread adherence, indicating that his statements were accepted as a valid formulation of the cultural politics consciously espoused by a relatively large sector of especially American and US-oriented artists and intellectuals.

11. In *New German Critique*, no. 22, 1981.

12. Peter Wollen, 'The Two Avant-Gardes', in *Readings and Writings – Semiotic Counter-Strategies* (London: Verso, 1982).

13. *Screen*, vol. 21 no. 1, 1980.

14. For *An Unmarried Woman*, see Charlotte Brunsdon, 'A Subject for the Seventies', *Screen*, vol. 23 no. 3–4, 1982; for *Wide Angle Saxon*, see Vera Dika, 'Wide Angle Saxon – An Examination of the Film Viewer as Reader', *Film Reader*, no. 3, 1978; for *La Femme du Gange*, see Elizabeth Lyon, 'La Femme du Gange', *Camera Obscura*, no. 2, 1977; For Ozu, see Kristin Thompson and David Bordwell, 'Space and Narrative in the Films of Ozu', *Screen*, vol. 17 no. 2, 1976.

15. Christian Metz, *Language and Cinema* (The Hague: Mouton, 1974), pp. 224–35.

16. Stephen Heath, *Questions of Cinema* (London: MacMillan, 1981), p. 239.

17. *Sub-Stance*, no. 17, 1977, p. 74.

18. Stephen Heath, *Questions of Cinema*, p. 239.

19. *Sub-Stance*, no. 17, 1977, pp. 73–4.

20. Ibid., p. 69.

21. The coincidence between this fact and the collapse of the last absolutist empires – and of Britain's quasi-absolutist one – together with the surge of global dominance of, first, industrial and then, in the 60s, finance capital is worth noting. See also Chapters 10 and 11 on third cinema and on the concept of 'the national'.

22. A development aided by the powerful tendencies within Western Marxism transforming Marxism into a discourse on method. See Perry Anderson, *Considerations of Western Marxism* (London: NLB, 1976), especially pp. 25–48.

23. See, for instance, *Screen*'s issue on LEF, vol. 12 no. 4, 1971–2.

24. After all, theory circulates in different institutions from those presiding primarily over the circulation of art objects and practices.

25. *Screen*, vol. 22 no. 4, 1981, p. 55.

26. Peter Wollen, 'The Avant-Gardes: Europe and America', *Framework*, no. 14, 1981.

27. Walter Benjamin, *Illuminations*, p. 262.

28. Ibid., p. 256.

29. 'Walter Benjamin – Revolutionary Writer (I)', *New Left Review*, no. 128, 1981, pp. 56–7.

30. One of the film-makers working in the new avant-garde, Amos Gitai, describes his way of shooting as a process of 'trawling'. See also Chapter 9.
31. For preliminary explorations of this direction, see Chapters 9, 10 and 11.
32. For *Passion*, see Paul Willemen, '*Passion*', *Framework*, no. 21, 1983; for *Ceddo*, see Françoise Pfaff, *The Cinema of Ousmane Sembene – A Pioneer of African Film* (Westport, Connecticut: Greenwood Press, 1984); for *The Nightcleaners*, see Claire Johnston and Paul Willemen, 'Brecht in Britain – The Independent Political Film', *Screen*, vol. 16 no. 4, 1975–6; for *Maeve*, see Claire Johnston's contribution in *Screen*, vol. 22 no. 4, 1981.

Chapter 9

Bangkok—Bahrain—Berlin—Jerusalem: Amos Gitai's Editing

Rephrasing Ricoeur and Foucault in one of the most illuminating essays of the 80s about the dynamics at work in Euro-American cultures, Andreas Huyssen wrote:

> There is a growing awareness that other cultures, especially non-European and non-Western cultures, must be met by means other than conquest or domination. [T]his awareness will have to translate into a type of intellectual work different from that of the modernist intellectual who typically spoke with the confidence of standing at the cutting edge of time and of being able to speak for others. Foucault's notion of the local and the specific intellectual as opposed to the 'universal' intellectual of modernity may provide a way out of the dilemma of being locked into our own culture and traditions while simultaneously recognising their limitations.[1]

This quotation is perhaps too grandiose a way of opening a modest discussion of a few points triggered by viewings of Amos Gitai's extraordinary films, and particularly of his documentary *Bangkok–Bahrain* (1984) about the physical exploitation of Thai people's bodies, male and female, by different kinds of imperialisms (US, Europe, Arab). However, it allows me to begin by drawing attention to an increasingly pressing problem which faces cultural critics today: the fact that theory and criticism are intellectual practices very much tied to specific historical moments and geographical locations. In other words, what I feel energised enough to try to theorise, the issues I feel compelled to address and the terms in which I address them, are significantly determined by the situation in which I live and work. In my case, that is contemporary Britain. While this is a readily acknowledged truism for most intellectuals, it is also something rarely taken into account in the actual formulation of our work.

As a local and specific intellectual working in Britain, there is no escaping the fact of cultural heterogeneity, since the most vital aspects of cultural life here are to be found in the British Afro-Caribbean and British-Asian sectors (the plural is necessary because, as the compound terms suggest, the sectors do not constitute a homogeneous terrain). The cultural practices of Asian countries are also emerging as powerful challenges, although their impact, except for that of the Islamic reactionaries aligned (for whatever reasons) with the Iranian government, still seems less forceful.

In such a context, it is perhaps not surprising that intellectuals, faced with the need to meet other cultures in ways other than through conquest or domination, are tempted to succumb to a kind of traumatic aphasia. In England especially, intellectuals have played very murky roles in history, and the infamy of their politics has been used as a stick to beat all intellectual work without exception. This has made the life of the left intelligentsia in Ukania very difficult at the best of times. Over the last decade or so, throughout the 80s, the main response of those left intellectuals active in the 70s has been to try to efface themselves altogether, to abdicate the function and responsibilities of intellectual work. They are traumatised by the overwhelming atmosphere of anti-intellectualism, combined with the belated realisation of the contradictions inherent in the very position of being simultaneously an intellectual and on the left – that is, people who may have access to cinematic production, to video and to television, publishing, lecture platforms, and so on, but who are not aligned with the powers which control and occupy, in the military sense of the term, those media sites.

Whereas in the 1960s and 1970s there still existed a kind of confidence of speaking from the cutting edge of changing times and of cultural development in the formulation of theories of cultural struggles, that confidence, fortunately, has evaporated. Unfortunately, however, it left a vacuum in its wake as many of the intellectuals concerned tried to prosper, or were forced to find a way of surviving in the suffocating 80s. Now, the vast majority of British film- and video-makers, as well as the cultural critics, are either desperately trying to become invisible or to turn their coats and present themselves as celebrants of the consumer cultures associated with the triumph of finance capitalism in the Western heartlands. Examples of these trends can be found in Sean Cubitt's breathless ode to the adman's mental universe, *Timeshift* (Routledge, 1991), and in television programmes like *The Media Show* (Channel Four Television, 1987–91). For examples of intellectuals craving invisibility, see the numerous 'community' videos, often described as films, produced throughout Ukania.

Those opting for invisibility tend to delude themselves into believing that they function merely as channels for others to speak through, those others' being 'the oppressed', or some such category. Any suggestion that intellectuals have a responsibility, by virtue of their education and social position, to exercise their intellectual skills and knowledges in order to analyse the dynamics at work in their social formation, is dismissed as 'elitist'. Instead, they stand aside to clear the way for the voices of the particular group with which they have chosen to identify. At least, that is the fantasy. In fact, they do not stand aside at all, but occupy the media space with repeated calls for intellectuals to submit to the injunction that their skills are to be discarded in favour of expressions emanating from an allegedly popular consciousness, as if that consciousness was not already deeply marked by the discourses and products of the media industries in the first place.

The vast majority of those who might be left intellectuals no longer speak in that capacity. No doubt, there are some benefits to this stance: the voices coming through as a result are indeed often more interesting and intellectually astute than whatever the traumatised film- and video-makers might have come up with themselves. The negative effect, however, is more crippling: an almost terroristic imposition of the crudest types of populism takes the place of intellectual analysis. In England today, a malevolently paranoid anti-intellectualism seeks to stifle any critical intellectual work, especially work critical of consumer cultures[2], while journals, papers and television are teeming with celebrants of shopping and devotees of the short-term, rapid turnover (cultural) investment strategy characteristic of contemporary finance capital.

The brutalising effects of this development are particularly noticeable in the area of documentary film-making, where many community and other 'left' media practitioners consider it almost a crime for a film-maker to assume responsibility for his or her discourse and to be seen to be shaping an analytical discourse in the form of a film or a television programme. A case in point is the negative reaction from the liberal and left intelligentsia to the four-part film, *Nicaragua* (1985), shown on Channel Four and made by the best documentary film-maker working in Britain today, Marc Karlin. What seemed to be most objectionable was the film-maker's inclusion in the films of an exploration of the issues involved in the representation of Nicaragua, filmically or photographically, by non-Nicaraguans. Karlin had committed the cardinal sin of questioning the terms in which we produce and consume images.

It is because of the profoundly damaging effects of these developments that I want to turn to the work of the Israeli film-maker Amos Gitai, who is elaborating, alongside his work in fiction, a kind of essayistic film-making particularly relevant to us in Europe (but elsewhere also) in the late 20th century.

In a situation in which television has become virtually the only source of money, as well as providing the main channels of exhibition for film, different registers of audiovisual discourse are emerging with different implications as to the mode of attention they invite and require. Gitai's films are made with television money and mostly transmitted via television, but they nevertheless require a cinematic mode of attention. That is to say, they require a considerable amount of concentration over extended periods of time, close attention being paid to editing patterns, camera movements, composition in depth and lighting patterns.

Traditionally, editing has been used and discussed as a way of limiting ambiguity, as a way of making sure that viewers follow and receive as exclusively as possible the sense which film-makers want the viewers to receive. In other words, editing is used primarily to impose, as far as this is possible, a reading. More recently, in music-television and other types of television advertising, editing has been subordinated to the music track and is used to enjoin people to 'stop making sense' and to absorb and live by 'moods'. Both the imposition and the prevention of sense-making illustrate the manipulatively authoritarian aspect of editing which was given one of its most sophisticated formulations in Eisenstein's early writings and in his theory of montage. The issue of editing's implicit authoritarianism was the bone of contention between, for instance, Eisenstein and Bazin, who argued for Christian Democratic sequence shots and deep-focus compositions.

Although it is true that editing is a manipulative technique staking out the path the reader/viewer is supposed to follow, the matter is slightly more complex, as Eisenstein himself acknowledged in his discussions of colour and frame composition. The point is that in cinema a multiplicity of codes operates to generate meaning, of which the cuts propelling viewers from one bundle of meanings to another is perhaps the main but not the only one. Moreover, these cuts acquire meaning only in relation to the disposition, the montage, of signifying elements within the shots, so that it might be more accurate, as far as cinema is concerned anyway, to talk of the orchestration of meaning.

Again, the current and increasingly dominant forms of television seek to reduce the complexity of this orchestration by reducing the pertinent field of vision, and therefore of potential meanings, almost exclusively to the human face and torso. The result is the near total loss of any notion of cinema, as television-derived aesthetics swamp all forms of audiovisual discourse: actorial 'character' drama narrated in close shots or advertising-inspired kitschy showiness are the norm. Engagement with a sense of place or time has to make way for an exclusive focus on quirky individuals. Time and again, we are forced to detour through an identification with some allegedly interesting character or person if we are to be granted access to the socio-cultural forces that structure the situations these characters inhabit. Worse: most of the time we are denied any access at all to some engagement with the forces shaping the world we live in, as we are stuck with our noses up against samples of warm and wonderful humanity emoting in close-up.

Gitai's films, together with those of a number of other prominent but still fairly unfamiliar film-makers such as Chantal Akerman, Ousmane Sembene, Ritwik Ghatak and David and Judith McDougall, deploy a type of orchestration of meaning not often discussed but crucially important for the artistic as well as the intellectual value of the medium. In Gitai's films, as in Mark Karlin's, the authorial voice is neither authoritarian nor effaced. Instead, the films are marked by a strategy of address that tries to mobilise meanings rather than impose them. It works with the cultural and the political knowledges assumed to be present in the viewer, calling on non-automatic, non-normative ways of deciphering one's environment. The process of meaning production is activated by working with, as well as upon, the viewer's skills and knowledges, trying to re-articulate them into better, more complex and more comprehensive ways of making sense of and with the materials presented. The viewer is not manipulated, and neither is he or she left to her 'own' devices, which invariably are the devices made available and strenuously advocated by the daily press and televison's cultural functionaries. Instead, a kind of dialogue is set up between film-maker and viewer in which the film-maker proposes a way of making sense, but simultaneously invites critical attention to the way this is done, regularly pausing to allow the reader/viewer to check the proceedings.

This in-between way of proceeding – in between intellectual and mood manipulation – is rather difficult to define or even to describe. An example may help to clarify the point. Think of a medium long shot held for a considerable length of time, with or without camera movement, such as a sequence shot. During the viewing of such a shot, complex changes occur in our mode of attention to what is depicted as we begin to take in aspects of the scene normally overlooked (that is aspects of the scene we have been dis-habituated from attending to), such as background details, changes of light, ambient sounds, landscape details, and so on. The scene comes alive as our relation to the seen is activated as a significant component of our viewing experience. The cognitive value of the scene changes as we work with the whole range of the materials on offer.

Often, the effect of such a scene or of a sequence shot will be to allow the characters in it (if there are any) to begin functioning 'in context', as we begin to become aware of the environment within which the character operates and which, precisely because we are given the opportunity to attend to the environmental details, co-determines in important ways the nature and status of that character itself. In such a sequence, individuals are allowed to be seen as social beings existing within, and marked by, very specific geo-social circumstances. We are no longer forced to detour our attention through 'identification' with a character in order to gain access to the fiction or to the signified world. The emotional relation between character and viewer is no longer at the centre of the picture. Instead, the relation between a character and its context, presented perhaps not as all-determining but at least as very significant, becomes the focus of attention. The emotive realism banking on character identification has thus been bypassed and its equally restrictive obverse, the fore-grounding of the processes of enunciation, is thus avoided as well. In other words, this strategy of address is neither realist nor modernist in the traditional senses of those terms in cultural theory.

Instead of requiring us to submit to the inexorably sequenced bits of meaning strung together fast enough to disallow any attention to the textures and to the actual substance of the meanings and moods we are asked to undergo, this type of orchestration relies on complex interactions, spread over time, between a scene and its viewer. One could almost call it dialogic if that term had not been rendered mean-ingless by its fashionable over- and misuse. In the spaces where we notice the processes of construction, the film-maker says 'I' and addresses us as interlocutors as well as witnesses. The marks of enun-ciation are there, as they are in conventional modernism, but contrary to the modernist styles, they are subordinated to the essayistic dis-course and the referential argument that discourse is conducting. In this sense, Gitai's films present a discourse about a topic in the form of an argument, rather than an order, addressed to us. The film does not shrivel into empty rhetoric if we disagree with aspects of the argument: we can still work with the materials presented in order to formulate other arguments, other 'senses'.

Moreover, the argument presented is embedded in such richly and complexly detailed sets of relations deployed at a pace that allows for contemplation and reflection, that the authorial voice is itself some-what displaced. It is no longer a case of the author, with or without the use of voice-over narration, marshalling images and sounds to buttress his or her argument, but rather of the presentation of perti-nent along with ancillary facets of a set of interconnected issues about which the authorial voice offers a by no means continuously clear-cut position. The author can thus assume full responsibility for the dis-course constructed without having to hide behind either a bogus neutrality (as in, for example, Fred Wiseman's documentaries) or the pyrotechnics of flashy enunciation strategies (as in some films of Godard, for example), these being the two best-known alternatives to the routinely authoritarian practices of 'social concern' films. Gitai provides a nudging, essentially friendly kind of discourse, acknow-ledging the presence alongside him of the viewer and assuming a shared interest in the attempt to understand, to make sense of the particular social processes the film is about.

After making *Ananas* (*Pineapple*, 1983), a documentary using one particular commodity to trace relations of exploitation, imperialism and resistance in the era of transnational capitalism, Gitai made *Bangkok–Bahrain* (1984) about the exploitation of Thai men and women. He shows and discusses the dislocations brought about in Thailand by the US attack on Vietnam and then goes on to discuss the use of female and male Thai bodies, the former in the Bangkok sex-tourism industry, the latter in the Middle Eastern construction industry, which has its own brand of pimps in the form of traffickers in migrant labour. Up to this point, the film proceeds with fairly long, meandering shots, sometimes with a static camera as we listen to someone's story. The camera has remained primarily observational, in the position of a visitor who is not always welcome and who tactfully keeps his distance.

Then we encounter an extraordinary sequence shot. It starts with a televisual framing of a trafficker seated behind a desk as he is interviewed on camera. He is lit in the standard television manner in medium close-up as he replies to some questions about his unsavoury job. Then, as the film-maker asks a question referring to a previous conversation not shown in the film, the camera hesitantly but doggedly pans right and reveals the man's wife, sitting in the corner of the room, not properly lit at all and obviously expecting to remain out of the frame. Pinned to the wall by the camera movement, she responds to the question. But suddenly, the whole situation has been changed by this obvious infringement by the film-makers of an agreement that must have been made prior to filming: the agreement not to film her, demonstrated by the absence of professional lighting.

To debate whether this agreement was made explicitly or not is beside the point, since the initial set-up and the lights make it clear that she was in a no-film area. The pan, resulting in the 'badly lit' image of the wife, the hesitation before her reply, the phrasing of the question referring to a previous conversation, the confusion shown by the husband as the camera shifts away from him: all this suddenly addresses the viewer, telling us something about repression, censorship and the difficulty of filming social relations in operation, as it were. It also reveals that the conventional television-style image was based on the suppression of an essential bit of information: the man was to be filmed as if his discourse was 'open', spontaneous and autonomous, with nothing to hide.

In addition, the length of the sequence gives the viewer plenty of time to absorb the implications, on various levels, of the changes brought about by the pan. The film-maker's choices are made available for scrutiny, but more importantly, the interviewed individuals have ceased being simply individuals: they have been transformed into agents in and of a social situation. They have become representatives of a social order which includes and produces them. One could

168

say that they have come to function as signifiers of a repressive order and an exploitative system hiding in plain sight. Conventional television techniques would have required the adherence to the obfuscations set in place by the interviewees, or would have lit the whole room and used fast stock to enable the handheld camera to roam throughout the room without hitting any unlit areas. Either option would have significantly impoverished the scene, aesthetically as well as intellectually, if those two aspects can be separated at all.

The camera movement marks a shift from the dialogue between film-maker and filmed people, which is the standard contract we see in operation in nearly all television, to a three-way relationship between the filmed, the filmers and the viewers, inserting that relationship in its turn into the whole problem of 'filming social relations'. In that sense, it is a critique of television documentaries and current affairs programmes, as well as of the propagandistic moralising characteristic of the populist videos which lack any sense of the dimensions of *mise en scène* essential to any notion of critical 'social' film-making. It may be worth mentioning that after this audacious shot, Gitai and his crew quickly went to the airport and left the country: during the interview, we learn that the man interviewed was an ex-cop and a former censor, while his wife described herself as involved in the security business. This sequence shot is an example of a courageous (left) intellectual at work with cinema. He does not tell us what to think, but leaves us in no doubt as to what he thinks while providing a complex representation of a situation for us to argue with. Neither are the filmed people reduced to pawns in the film-maker's discourse of self-righteous indignation: they are allowed to have their say and are shown as *metteurs en scène* themselves, that is, as people who not only engineer other people's lives, but who advocate an alternative kind of *mise en scène*.

The pan also stresses something few films and virtually no television programme ever acknowledge: the relation of otherness *vis-à-vis* the filmed which a film-maker experiences, but usually hides in the finished product. The images are not illustrations of a preformed discourse on the topic, whether delivered on the soundtrack or not. Instead, Gitai shows us a way of making sense of an unfamiliar situation while participating in it, and he takes the viewer into his confidence, provided we are prepared to pay attention to the modes of enunciation and their implications. To arrange the same sequence into a series of separate, edited shots would have destroyed its productivity and made it into a sequence of bits dished out for us to follow obediently, linearly, ingesting whatever the film-maker wants us to swallow before getting a chance to reflect on the situation itself.

A little later in the same film, Gitai resorts to a different strategy but achieves a very similar effect. He shows a series of fairly brief shots depicting workers, in which each time the filmed people give only one single piece of information: their nationality. No other interaction between filmers and filmed appears possible and the otherness of the film-makers is writ large. As if exasperated by this inability to establish contact with the workers (the owner of the building contracting firm in Bahrain does freely interact with the film-makers), the sequence culminates in a shot in which the camera appears to be encased in a dark space, leaving only a small square of light with the heads of a few workers peering into the dark space below them, that is, towards the camera. One worker can be seen stretching his neck to get a better look at the camera, which seems torn out of any social context. It is removed from the scene, which is somewhere beyond the small square of daylight up above. Together with the viewer, who shares the camera's position and point of view in his or her own kind of dark, asocial space, gazing at a lit square high in front of his or her eyes, the camera becomes an object of curiosity rather than an investigator.

This sudden reversal of the camera's position and authority sets up a dialogue with the viewer, also barred from interaction with the filmed workers, but simultaneously enables the film-makers to engage in a dialogue with the workers, as if the removal of the film-makers and their camera from the social relations at work in the area was the price that had to be paid in order to enter into such a dialogue. After that shot, it is no longer necessary to specify at length in the film that the film-makers were allowed to work in Bahrain as long as they did not actively interact with the workers: that point has been made in the very *mise en scène* of the shot, signalling the gulf between 'us' (film-makers and viewers) and 'them' (the dislocated workers subjected to an extremely repressive situation).

In each of these two examples, the viewer's anticipated thoughts about the situation have been worked into its very mode of presentation. He is taking for granted our interest in critical, analytical looking and he assumes we will accord the images and sounds a degree of critical attention not normally given to television images, even though that is where the film will be seen by most people. He banks on a cinematic mode of attention in the sense that he relies on the fact that the forms of the discourse, such as at times quite small changes in the position of the camera, the pacing of the shots or their place in a particular sequence, will be noticed and thought significant. If we do not give these aspects of the discourse their full weight, the complexity of the social mechanisms filmed will escape us as well. We are not told what to think and neither are we asked to discover everything by ourselves (which always was a particularly cowardly and hypocritical aesthetic ideology anyway). Gitai films in a conversational mode, including his interlocutors in the process. Should a viewer refuse, or be too damaged intellectually to engage in this conversation, the films are transformed into somewhat slow, rather disorienting documentaries.

At the same time, this strategy has the merit of refusing to adopt a touristic point of view: the film-maker inviting the viewer to attend to his ruminations illustrated by local colour shots linking bits of talking-head footage, as is customary in the vast majority of social concern videos, as well as in television journalism. Gitai thus shows up the insufficiencies, filmic as well as political and intellectual, that cripple both the dominant, touristic forms of documentary current affairs television and the currently most widely practised alternative form of journalism: the pretence of effacing the voice of the film-maker in favour of the 'authentic' voice of the people – an alternative that is at best hopelessly naive.

Finally, there is one more point I would like to make arising out of Gitai's film-making. Current debates in Euro-American film theory make a lot of play of point-of-view shots as ways of positioning the viewer in relation to the filmed. In many respects, discussions and analyses of point of view have taken the place of the former discussions about subjectivity and editing. Gitai's films, amongst others, show that it is most decidedly *not* through point-of-view shots that we are mobilized, but through the differences between, for instance, one point of view and another, even within the one shot. The dialogue with the viewer, which is the film's mode of address, is to be traced in the pattern of differences, in the shifts between markers such as point of view manifested in the body of the text. That is where we learn who the film-maker thinks he or she is talking to, and what he or she thinks we know or are interested in.

Gitai's films assume an audience that is cine-literate in the best sense of the term: an audience that is interested in concentrating on the audiovisual discourse, on the way it is formulated, as much as it is interested in finding out how social relations have shaped whatever is being filmed. The films most definitely do not presuppose that we are concerned only with looking at the strangeness of others, nor is the viewer assumed to want to judge the people represented as goodies or as baddies. On the contrary, the films begin to make sense only when we regard the people represented as social creatures rather than as individuals in the conventional sense. We are not invited to give moral value judgments on the people, but rather to understand why and how they have come to be the way they are (by extension, the films ask us the same question). In other words, people are represented as shaped by social existence in all its contradictoriness, with all the consequent possibilities for change that such a view implies, since the social itself is presented as a field in constant flux. Nothing is more alien to a Gitai film than the populist presentation of oppressed people as idealised victims. Even the historicity of film-making itself, the fact that different social formations circumscribe different practices and possibilities of filming, is part and parcel of Gitai's cinematic practice.

Although these techniques were developed in the context of a documentary practice, its lessons apply just as much to fiction cinema, where a subtle orchestration of time and space can be used to convey a sense of place, opening up the setting, the cityscapes and landscapes, to an awareness of historically accrued meanings. Gitai achieved this in his first feature film, *Esther* (1986), by setting a biblical story in a recognisable and memory-laden part of contemporary Haifa, giving the viewers ample opportunity to savour the political sense generated by the mobilisation of this particular place for this particular story. In his next feature, *Berlin–Jerusalem* (1989), Gitai charts what happens to utopian desires while simultaneously affirming the need to have them. With impressive images (courtesy of Henri Alekan and Nurith Aviv), Gitai tells of the expressionist poet Else Lasker-Schüler's yearning for an idealised Jerusalem, and of the Bolshevik Mania Shochat, who went to Palestine and helped set up a rural co-operative, eventually becoming the main left opposition figure in Ben Gurion's Israel.

Instead of trying to re-stage the familiar Weimar iconography, Gitai uses a kind of cinematic shorthand, evoking the period through references, activating our memory banks full of representations of the period and the place. As he conjures up the Weimar setting in beautifully stylised sequences, Gitai simultaneously rearranges our perception of the Weimar period by putting into place three different but connected spaces. Our collective imaginary, made up of half-remembered films, photographs and paintings, provides the broadly historical setting. This imaginary space is then displaced and somehow hollowed out by the menacingly empty and shadowy spaces surrounding the poet in the first half of the film, while her private sense of claustrophobia and oppression is evident from the cramped and cluttered spaces of her private life. In two strongly emotional moments, Else escapes from these imbricated spaces: when she goes to the seaside and when she buries her son in a wintry graveyard, a moment marked by the complex tracking shot looking up through leafless trees at a pale sky.

The Mania plot-strand is also spatially circumscribed, from the trek across the foggy mountains to the place where the small group of pioneers set up their farming collective. From then on, the real but understated drama is in the way that their farm-space intersects with the Palestinian spaces around it. The film charts the gradually increasing sense of separation, together with the way such an isolated group living in back-breakingly difficult circumstances tries to weld itself together. Mania is the one with the most politically acute sense of the contradictions and dangers involved in such an attempt to act out utopian wishes: however much the members of the collective try to divest themselves from previous ways of living, people cannot but bring with them cultural and personal ways of being and thinking which undermine the utopian aspirations.

In the end, the political battle is over the way a particular state organisation seeks to enshrine and contain these tensions. The film ends more or less where the tragic dimension of the Israeli state begins, having shown that there were different options for that state. The relevance of the film to current political issues cannot be underestimated. It is the most explicit cinematic statement to date of a position which receives all too little exposure in either cinema or television: by showing the ideological as well as the experiential elements that were – and are – active in the formation of the Israeli state, Gitai points to the possibility and indeed the necessity of a *different* state formation, adjusted more realistically to the actual needs and conditions prevailing in the area. The film is neither pro-Israeli nor pro-Palestinian. In that respect, Gitai's film is a contribution to the growing debate about what it means to be an Israeli citizen and what the options in fact are.

Other films made elsewhere (in Taiwan, India, Ireland) are also concerned with cinema's ability to render the complexities of time-space relations in such a way as to make us recognise spaces in which history can be seen at work, transforming spaces into places shaped by the encounter between social forces, personal experience and landscape. Gitai's films blur the distinction conventionally made between documentary and fiction: the sophisticated use of settings and location developed in his documentary practice is transferred into his features. At the same time as raising the question of the relation between the telling of particular stories and contemporary historical issues, this strategy brings that thorny problem into sharp focus by directly addressing the generation, and the historical-geographical reach, of a particular set of cultural forms such as, for instance, biblical texts. In this way, the films also ask the question, rarely raised in cinema, of the social construction of audiences, while exploring the social construction of cultures.

Hollywood and mainstream television solve those questions by reducing the cultural milieu to a picturesque backdrop for its dramas of individual character (and even those individuals are presented in exceedingly vague terms in order to make them internationally consumable). This reduces cultural meanings to those available to the average tourist. On the other hand, Euro-American experimental cinema contents itself with addressing specific subcultures while trading on generalities about art and aesthetic ideologies familiar throughout the West. Gitai, in common with a Kumar Shahani or a Ritwik Ghatak (at least in this respect), asks fundamental questions about the social aspects of cinema: at what point does a cinema betray its audiences by expecting them to become tourists in their own cultures? What is the effective geographical reach of the cultural materials a film is fashioned from and which it addresses? How can one mobilise culturally specific meanings without at the same time restricting audiences to uneconomic levels?

It is obvious from these questions that the answers imply political and ideological analyses rather than (or as well as) economic-industrial judgments. In effect, Gitai's films open up a whole new perspective on cinema itself: a new way of assessing how films are shaped by the tensions between their industrial and their cultural aspects.

I would like to close by stressing that in my view Gitai is a rare film-maker, one of an as yet small number whose work comes across both on television and in cinema by practising and requiring a fundamentally cinematic mode of attention to the audiovisual representation of social situations. In other words, he shows that television does not have to be as brutalisingly reductive as it is at the moment. In addition, his approach to essayistic film-making respects the otherness of specific socio-cultural formations, but he does not allow himself to be traumatised by that otherness. His kind of conversational film-making offers one way out of the dilemma of being a local-specific intellectual locked into his or her own culture while being sufficiently outside of that culture to recognise its limiting boundaries. It may not be the only way out, but it is the only one that I can point to as an example which today's British film-makers could considerably benefit from. I suspect that his approach could also hold valuable lessons for film-makers elsewhere.

Notes

1. 'Mapping the Postmodern', *New German Critique*, no. 33, 1984.
2. See, for instance, Valerie Walkerdine's contribution to *Formations of Fantasy* (London: Methuen, 1986).

Chapter 10

The Third Cinema Question

With the major political and economic changes experienced in both the Euro-American sphere and in the so-called Third World since the 70s, the issue of cultural specificity, that is to say, the need to know which specific social-historical processes are at work in the generation of cultural products, and the question of how precisely social existence over-determines cultural practices, have taken on a new and crucial importance. The complexity of the shifting dynamics between intra- and inter-national differences and power relations has shown simple models of class domination at home, and imperialism abroad, to be totally inadequate.

In addition, the ethnocentrism of 70s cultural theory developed into a crippling handicap[1] which under the pressure of current political and economic policies has caused Euro-American cultural theory to stagnate. Or worse, to degenerate into a naively sentimental leftism including its Third Worldist variant, or into 'post-modernism', with its contradictory thrust towards a pre-industrial nostalgia and towards bringing cultural-educational practice in line with the corporate cultures required for the new phase of the market economy and with its entrepreneurial ideologies.

Cultural activists outside the white Euro-American sphere, while taking note of 70s theory and its genuine achievements, have continued their own work throughout this period, formulating both in practice and in theory – in so far as these can be separated – a sophisticated approach to questions of domination/subordination, centre/periphery and, above all, resistance/hegemony. This work is of fundamental importance today, not only because of its ability to unblock the dead ends of 70s cultural theories, but also and primarily because it opens out onto new practices of cinema: a cinema no longer captivated by the mirrors of dominance/independence or commerce/art, but grounded in an understanding of the dialectical relationship between social existence and cultural practice.

In the light of the Edinburgh Film Festival's engagement with critical issues throughout the 70s, it also seemed the appropriate place to initiate a critique of current European approaches to popular culture by proposing that the notion of Third Cinema is more relevant to contemporary cultural debates than some kind of 'post' rhetoric. The conference's implied polemical position had a double thrust. By turning to Third Cinema, it implied that left cultural theory in the UK and in the USA had become a serious handicap, in that it had become hypocritically opportunist (see for example, the proliferation of attempts to validate the most debilitating forms of television and cinema, with academics cynically extolling the virtues of the stunted products of cultural as well as of political defeat), or had degenerated into a comatose repetition of 70s deconstructionist rituals.[2]

The turn to Third Cinema with all its Latin American connotations also repeated a gesture which had proved extremely productive in the early 70s: then, a determined and systematic injection of 'foreign' cultural theories ranging from Althusser to Brecht, from Eco to the Soviet Formalists and from Lacan to Saussure had proved capable of reanimating the petrified body of English cultural criticism. Faced with a relapse into a state of suspended animation or, worse, a reverting to 'left labourism' of the most parochially populist type,[3] the conference was designed to draw attention to different, non-English approaches to cultural politics.

Mainly because the productivity, and the not to be underestimated genuine achievements, of British cultural criticism in the 70s must be seen as stemming from a salutary anti-Englishness, and because the current degeneration of cultural theory correlates exactly with a renewed accommodation with English cultural populism, the turn to Third Cinema can be seen as a rejection of parochialism as well as a critical engagement with the positive aspects of 70s theory. The political-cultural trends of the 80s have demonstrated the need for a drastic reappraisal of the terms in which radical practice had been conceived in the 70s: questions of gender and of cultural identity received new inflections, and traditional notions of class-determined identity were seen to be as inadequate as the forms of syndicalist struggle that corresponded to them.[4]

Some of the issues raised at the Edinburgh conference, such as the questions of Brechtian cinema and of cultural identity, received a new urgency, but were now posed in a different context where not the radical white intelligentsia but the militant black cultural practitioners constituted the cutting edge of cultural politics and innovation. Their terms of reference were derived from a wide variety of sources and included 70s theories of subjectivity and Marxism, in addition to the work of Fanon, C. L. R. James, black American writers and activists, Latin American and African film-makers, West Indian, Pakistani and Indian cultural traditions and intellectuals, and so on. The cultural practices grounded in those – from an English point of view – 'other' currents, together with the impact of a whole

176

series of physical acts of collective self-defence and resistance, offer the best chance yet to challenge and break down the ruling English ideology described so vividly in all its suffocating decrepitude in Tom Nairn's classic essay on 'The English Literary Intelligentsia'.[5]

The notion of Third Cinema (and most emphatically not Third World Cinema) was selected as a central concept in 1986, partly to re-pose the question of the relations between the cultural and the political, and partly to discuss whether there is indeed a kind of international cinematic tradition which exceeds the limits of both the national-industrial cinemas and those of Euro-American as well as English cultural theories.

The latter consideration is still very much a hypothesis relating to the emergence on an international scale of a kind of cinema to which the familiar realism versus modernism or post-modernism debates are simply irrelevant, at least in the forms to which Western critics have become accustomed. This trend is not unprecedented, but it appears to he gaining strength. One of its more readily noticeable characteristics seems to be the adoption of a historically analytic, yet culturally specific, mode of cinematic discourse. It is best exemplified by, for instance, Amos Gitai's work, Cinema Action's *Rocinante* (1986), Angelopoulos's *O Thiasos* (1975), the films of Souleyman Cissé, Haile Gerima and Ousmane Sembene, Kumar Shahani's *Maya Darpan* (1972) and *Tarang* (1984), Theuring and Engström's *Fluchtweg Nach Marseille* (1977), the work of Safi Faye, the recent films of Yussif Chahine, Yang De-Chang's (Edward Yang) *Taipei Story* (1985), Chen Kaige's *Yellow Earth* (1984), the work of Fong Yuk-Ping (Allen Fong), the two black British films *Handsworth Songs* (1986) and *The Passion of Remembrance* (1986) and the Brazilian films of Joaquim Pedro de Andrade and Carlos Reichenbach.

The masters of this growing but still threatened current can be identified as Nelson Pereira dos Santos, Ousmane Sembene and Ritwik Ghatak, each summing up and reformulating the encounter of diverse cultural traditions into new, politically as well as cinematically illuminating types of filmic discourse, critical of, yet firmly anchored in, their respective social-historical situations. Each of them has refused to oppose a simplistic notion of national identity or of cultural authenticity to the values of colonial or imperial predators. Instead, they have started from a recognition of the many-layeredness of their own cultural-historical formations, with each layer being shaped by complex connections between intra- and inter-national forces and traditions. In this way, these three film-makers exemplify a way of inhabiting one's culture which is neither myopically nationalist nor evasively cosmopolitan. Their film work is not particularly exemplary in the sense of displaying stylistically innovative devices to be imitated by others who wish to avoid appearing outdated. On the contrary, it is their way of inhabiting their cultures, their grasp of the relations between the cultural and the social, which founded the search for a cinematic discourse able to convey their sense of a diagnostic understanding (to borrow a happy phrase from Raymond Williams) of the situation in which they worked and to which their work is primarily addressed.

Third Cinema
The notion of a Third Cinema was first advanced as a rallying cry in the late 60s in Latin America and has recently been taken up again in the wake of Teshome Gabriel's book *Third Cinema in the Third World – The Aesthetics of Liberation* (1982).[6] As an idea, its immediate inspiration was rooted in the Cuban Revolution (1959) and in Brazil's Cinema Novo, for which Glauber Rocha provided an impetus with the publication of a passionate polemic entitled 'The Aesthetics of Hunger' (or 'The Aesthetics of Violence').[7] But as Michael Chanan reminded us in his introduction to *Twenty-five Years of the New Latin-American Cinema*,[8] even at that stage the elaboration of an aesthetic felt to be appropriate to conditions in Latin America drew on the ideals of such far from revolutionary currents as Italian neo-realism and Grierson's notion of the social documentary, as well as on various kinds of Marxist aesthetics. What is becoming clearer now is that the various manifestos and polemics arguing for a Third Cinema fused a number of European, Soviet and Latin American ideas about cultural practice into a new, more powerful (in the sense that it was able to conceptualise the connections between more areas of socio-cultural life than contemporary European aesthetic ideologies) programme for the political practice of cinema.

Two particular aspects of neo-realism and of the Griersonian approach may have recommended themselves to the many Latin American intellectuals who studied in Europe, who included such influential figures as Fernando Birri, Tomas Gutierrez Alea and Julio Garcia Espinosa, all of whom studied at the Centro Sperimentale in Rome. Firstly, both neo-realism and the British documentary were examples of an artisanal, relatively low-cost cinema working with a mixture of public and private funds, and enabling directors to work in a different way, and on a different economic scale, from that required by Hollywood and its various national-industrial rivals. Secondly, contrary to the unifying and homogenising work of mainstream industrial cinemas, this artisanal cinema allowed, at least in principle and sometimes in practice, a more focused address of the 'national', revealing divisions and stratifications within a national formation ranging from regional dialects to class and political antagonisms.

What the Latin Americans appear to have picked up on was the potential for different cinematic practices offered by the European examples, rather than their actual trajectories and philosophies.

178

Consequently, they did not follow the evolution of neo-realism into European art-house cinema, nor the relentless trek of the British documentary via Woodfall into the gooey humanism of television plays and serials, with debased forms of the Griersonian documentary, lacking that genre's acute sense of aesthetic stylisation, surviving in stunted forms in the backwaters of the British state-funded video sector.

The term Third Cinema was launched by the Argentinian film-makers Fernando Solanas and the Spanish-born Octavio Getino, who had made *La Hora de los Hornos* (1968) and published 'Hacia un Tercer Cine' ('Towards a Third Cinema').[9] This was followed by the Cuban Julio Garcia Espinosa's classic avant-gardist manifesto, 'For an Imperfect Cinema' (written in 1969),[10] which argued for an end to the division between art and life and therefore between professional, full-time intellectuals such as film-makers or critics and 'the people'. This utopian text, foreshadowing policies advocated during the Chinese Cultural Revolution, was followed by numerous writings both in Latin America and in post-68 Europe, in which notions of Third Cinema, Third World Cinema and Revolutionary Cinema tended to get lumped together to the point where they became synonymous.

Simultaneously, in North Africa a number of texts appeared advocating approaches similar to the ones outlined in the Latin American texts: in 1967–8, in Cairo, a few critics and cineastes published the manifesto 'Jamaat as Cinima al jadida' ('Movement of the New Cinema') and in Morocco the journal *Cinema 3*, founded by Nourdine Saïl, also published Third Cinema arguments. As Ferid Boughedir has pointed out, other manifestos followed in the early 70s: 'Cinima a Badil' ('Alternative Cinema'), published in 1972 on behalf of a number of Arab cineastes in the Egyptian journal *At-Tariq*; the 'First Manifesto for a Palestinian Cinema' in 1972, issued at the Damascus Festival, and the 'Second Manifesto' issued later that year at the Carthage Festival, among others.

However, in the public reception of these manifestos a number of crucial distinctions, often only marginally present in the founding texts written under the pressures of urgent necessity, seem to have been overlooked.

Firstly, the authors of the classic manifestos forcefully state their opposition to a sloganised cinema of emotional manipulation. Any cinema that seeks to smother thought, including a cinema that relies on advertising techniques, is roundly condemned. Sanjines even accuses such strategies of going against revolutionary morality. In other words, a cinema that invites belief and adherence, rather than promoting a critical understanding of social dynamics, is regarded as worse than useless. All authors, from Birri to Espinosa and even the mystically inclined Glauber Rocha, stress the need for a cinema of lucidity. The widely expressed antagonism towards professional intellectuals is in fact an opposition to colonial and imperialist intellectuals, and this antagonism is never used to devalue the need for the most lucid possible critical intelligence to be deployed as a crucial part of making films. What is at stake here is the yoking together of the cognitive and the emotive aspects of the cinema. As Espinosa put it, this cinema is addressed 'in a separate or co-ordinated fashion at the intelligence, the emotions, the powers of intuition'.

A major lesson to be learned from these manifestos is thus that they consistently warn against drifting into anti-intellectualism or, worse, into shoddy intellectualism, emphasising the need to learn. What they do condemn is a particular kind of middle-class intellectual, not intellectual activity *per se*. The intellectuals condemned are only those whose 'expertise has usually been a service rendered, and sold, to the central authority of society', as Edward Said has put it.[11]

Secondly, the manifestos refuse to prescribe an aesthetics. The authors broadly agree about which aesthetic forms are inappropriate or are even damaging, but they also refuse to identify a particular formal strategy as the only way to achieve the activation of a revolutionary consciousness. Following Brecht, who vigorously protested against the attempt to elevate the use of 'distanciation devices' into an obligatory procedure, the Latin Americans insisted on the legitimacy of any procedure which was likely to achieve the desired results, that is, an analytically informed understanding of the social formation and how to change it in a socialist direction. In Espinosa's words: 'Imperfect cinema can make use of the documentary or the fictional mode, or both. It can use whatever genre, or all genres. [It] can use cinema as a pluralistic art form or as a specialised form of expression.' Solanas and Getino talk about 'the infinite categories' of Third Cinema, and the Bolivian film-maker Jorge Sanjines notes that the forms of revolutionary cinema must change as the relations between author and people change in particular circumstances. There are no general prescriptions other than negative ones in the sense that certain roads have been explored and found to be dead ends or traps. Glauber Rocha once recalled Nelson Pereira dos Santos quoting a line from a Portuguese poet: 'I don't know where I'm going, but I know you can't get there that way.'

One of the main differences between Third Cinema and the European notion of counter-cinema is this awareness of the historical variability of the necessary aesthetic strategies to be adopted. Whatever the explanation – and the weight of the modernist tradition in the arts may be a crucial factor here – and regardless of the political intentions involved, the notion of counter-cinema tends to conjure up a prescriptive aesthetics: to do the opposite of what dominant cinema does. Hence the descriptive definition of dominant cinema will dictate the prescriptive definition of counter-cinema. The proponents of

Third Cinema were just as hostile to the industrially and ideologically dominant cinemas but refused to let them dictate the terms in which they were to be opposed.

To be fair, the two main UK counter-cinema theorists, Peter Wollen and Claire Johnston, never argued that the strategies and characteristics of counter-cinema should be canonised and frozen into a prescriptive aesthetics. They pointed to the importance of cinematic strategies designed to explore what dominant regimes of signification were unable to deal with. Theirs was a politics of deconstruction, not an aesthetics of deconstruction. The difference is worth noting: a politics of deconstruction insists on the need to oppose particular institutionally dominant regimes of making particular kinds of sense, by excluding or marginalising others; an aesthetics of deconstruction proceeds from the traumatic discovery that language is not a homogeneous, self-sufficient system. Allon White put it most succinctly:

> Only for those who identify language as such with Saussurean *langue* does it appear paradoxical and impossible that dispersal, *différance*, lacks, absence, traces and all the modes of radical heterogeneity should be there at the heart of discourses which pretend to be complete. Much of the time, deconstruction is rediscovering in texts, with a kind of bemused fascination, all the indices of heteroglossia which Saussure excluded from consideration in his own model, by consigning them to the trash can of *parole*. To discover that rationality (the logic of the signified) may be subverted by writing itself (the logic of the signifier) seems to put the 'whole Western episteme' into jeopardy, but is in fact a fairly trivial business.[12]

The politics of deconstruction, then, insists on the need to say something different; an aesthetics of deconstruction dissolves into endlessly repeated difference-games, into the Varietal Thesis, as Meaghan Morris once put it. Nevertheless, even a politics of deconstruction is circumscribed by its attention to the limits of dominant regimes of signification, whereas the Third Cinema polemicists avoided that trap, though admittedly at the price of rather unhelpfully homogenising 'dominant cinema' itself. This mistake was later corrected by Nelson Pereira dos Santos's *O Amuleto de Ogum* (1974) and *Na Estrada da Vida* (1979), which show what can be done with a selective redeployment of the dominant cinema's generic elements while refusing to reduce the films to, or to imprison them in, that 'varietal' relationship. Dos Santos's films do not quote elements of the dominant cinema in order to provide a nostalgic updating of a kind of cinema now associated with the past; he proposes instead a transformation of cinema which refuses to jettison all the components and aspects of dominant cinema merely because they form part of an unacceptable cinematic regime.

Thirdly, and most importantly, the Latin Americans based their notion of third cinema on an approach to the relations between signification and the social. They advocated a practice of cinema which, although conditioned by, and tailored to, the situations prevailing in Latin America, cannot be limited to that continent alone, nor for that matter to the Third World, however it is defined. The classic manifestos are fairly ambiguous on this point, making rather cursory references to Asian and African cinemas, as well as to the work of Chris Marker or Joris Ivens. The clear, though not often explicitly stated implication is that although Third Cinema is discussed in relation to Latin America, the authors of the manifestos see it as an attitude applicable anywhere. Solanas took the opportunity to clarify the issue.[13] It is worth quoting him at some length since he corrects many misconceptions that have accrued to the notion of Third Cinema:

> First cinema expresses imperialist, capitalist, bourgeois ideas. Big monopoly capital finances big spectacle cinema as well as authorial and informational cinema. Any cinematographic expression [l]ikely to respond to the aspirations of big capital, I call first cinema. Our definition of second cinema is all that expresses the aspirations of the middle stratum, the petite bourgeoisie. Second cinema is often nihilistic, mystificatory. It runs in circles. It is cut off from reality. In the second cinema, just as in the first cinema, you can find documentaries, political and militant cinema. So-called author cinema often belongs in the second cinema, but both good and bad authors may be found in the first and in the third cinemas as well.
>
> For us, Third Cinema is the expression of a new culture and of social changes. Generally speaking, Third Cinema gives an account of reality and history. It is also linked with national culture. [It] is the way the world is conceptualised and not the genre nor the explicitly political character of a film which makes it belong to Third Cinema. Third Cinema is an open category, unfinished, incomplete. It is a research category. It is a democratic, national, popular cinema. Third Cinema is also an experimental cinema, but it is not practised in the solitude of one's home or in a laboratory because it conducts research into communication. What is required is to make that Third Cinema gain space, everywhere, in all its forms. But it must be stressed that there are 36 different kinds of Third Cinema.

Of course, these definitions beg a great many questions, the most immediate one being that of the viewers: is it possible to see a First

Cinema film in a Third Cinema way? In Europe, most Third Cinema products appear definitely to have been consumed in a Second Cinema way, bracketing the politics in favour of an appreciation of the authorial artistry. A pessimist might argue that the deeper a film is anchored in its social situation, the more likely it is that it will be 'secondarised' when viewed at a geographical or at a temporal distance, unless the viewers are prepared to interest themselves precisely in the particularities of the socio-cultural nexus addressed, which is still a rare occurrence.

In most, perhaps even in all countries, Third Cinema is exhibited, promoted and reviewed as part of the art cinema. This would not be such a big problem if the bulk of the art cinema did not consist of Euro-American and indeed of, for instance, Indian Second Cinema. So, not only the place and the time of exhibition have a decisive impact, but the industrial context also militates against Third Cinema. In addition, reviewing and other promotional practices try to limit even more the ways in which films can be received by reducing the specific aspects of Third Cinema to familiar patterns of Second Cinema consumption. An extra kick in the teeth is then provided by critics deploying a left-populist rhetoric to contrast Third Cinema negatively to both the first and the Second Cinemas on the grounds that only the corporate cultures of the movie business and of its industrially accredited authors can really be described as anything other than elitist.[14]

Another point of interest is that the categories elaborated above by Solanas are not aligned with Marxist notions of class, presumably since all film-makers would then have to be seen as middle-class entrepreneurs, which is indeed what they are, even when making films clandestinely. Espinosa tackled that problem by arguing that no film-maker should be a full-time professional. Instead, Solanas aligns First, Second and Third Cinemas with three social strata: the bourgeoisie, the petty bourgeoisie and the people, the latter including industrial workers, small and landless peasants, the unemployed, the lumpenproletariat, students, and so on. As a category, 'the people' seems to be used as a catch-all term designating all who are left after the bourgeoisie and most of the petite bourgeoisie have been deducted. This gives Third Cinema a basically negative definition.

Moreover, if First Cinema is a capitalist-industrial-imperialist cinema and Second Cinema an individualist-petty bourgeois or unhappily capitalist one, Third Cinema is definitely presented as an anti-capitalist and therefore a socialist cinema. But the possibility of an anti-capitalist cinema drawing inspiration from a pre-capitalist, feudal nostalgia is not taken into account: some anti-capitalist currents are worse than capitalism, as was demonstrated by 'left' Nazism, and by the totalitarian aspects of religiously inspired social movements and counter-cultures. Neither did the authors of the manifestos always avoid attributing an essentially revolutionary consciousness to 'the people', the oppressed: as if the experience of oppression itself did not also have ideologically damaging effects, which is why a cinema of lucidity is such an essential prerequisite for a socialist cultural practice.

The manifestos also omit any mention of an aristocracy or of caste divisions, as if those groupings simply didn't count in the cultural configuration. While this may be true to a large extent in Latin America, this approach is most certainly a handicap when considering Asian countries, not to mention European or African ones and their systems of social stratification. Moreover, neither ethnic nor gender divisions are acknowledged in any of the manifestos, which confuses matters still further. These aspects of the Third Cinema texts do reinforce the impression that it was a notion developed by Latin Americans for Latin Americans and that the general applicability of the idea was added as an afterthought.

However, even though in this respect Third Cinema is not defined with precision, two characteristics must be singled out as especially useful and of lasting value. One is the insistence on its flexibility, its status as research and experimentation, a cinema forever in need of adaptation to the shifting dynamics at work in social struggles. Because it is part of constantly changing social processes, that cinema cannot but change with them, making an all-encompassing definition impossible and even undesirable. The second useful aspect follows from this fundamental flexibility: the only stable thing about Third Cinema is its attempt to speak a socially pertinent discourse which both the mainstream and the authorial cinemas exclude from, or marginalise within, their regimes of signification. Third Cinema seeks to articulate a different set of aspirations out of the raw materials provided by the culture, its traditions and art forms, the complex interactions and condensations of which shape the national cultural spaces inhabited by the film-makers as well as their audiences.

Lineages

The Latin American manifestos must also be seen in the context of Marxist or Marxist-inspired cultural theories in general, for which they mark a significant additional current with linkages passing both through Cuba and through Italy, as well as developing home-grown traditions of socialist and avant-gardist thought. The most direct connections in this respect, for a European reader, are with German cultural theory of the 1930s, with Brecht and also with Benjamin.

The relation with Brecht has been referred to earlier and may seem obvious, but the Benjamin connection is less well known. Susan Buck-Morss, one of the most perceptive and best informed commentators on Benjamin's work, drew attention to his statement about history writing which, *mutatis mutandis*, also applies to cinematic discourses

184

and evokes the relationship which Solanas and Getino posited between film-making and the context within which film-makers work. In her essay 'The Flaneur, the Sandwichman and the Whore: The Politics of Loitering',[15] she quotes Benjamin: 'The events surrounding the historian and in which he takes part will underlie his presentation like a text written in invisible ink.' Similarly, underlining phrases from the *Passagenwerk*, she describes a mode of inhabiting one's culture which comes close to the ideas put forward in the manifestos, except that Benjamin uses a characteristic metaphor to sum up the approach:

> In the face of 'the wind of history [t]hinking means setting sails. How they are set is the important thing. What for others are digressions are for me the data that determine my course.' But this course is precarious. To cut the lines that have traditionally anchored Marxist discourse in production and sail off into the dreamy waters of consumption is to risk, politically, running aground.[16]

Even though they criticise the mobilisation of emotive responses without provision of an analytic perspective aimed at evoking possible strategies for change, the Third Cinema manifestos do not mention Benjamin's theory on dialectical images. Nevertheless, it is clearly present in their margins when they stress the relations with the viewer as being the productive site of cinematic signification. Paraphrasing Benjamin, one could say that once the sails are set, it is not within the cinematic discourse, but rather in the spaces and the tensions between the referential world it conjures up and the real, that the cognitive process is propelled.

Finally, in a direct parallelism with the aspirations of the Latin American cineastes, Benjamin wrote that he saw his work as one of educating 'the image-creating medium within us to see dimensionally, stereoscopically, into the depths of the historical shade'.[17] Perhaps these echoes of Benjamin can be explained by the fact that 'It is in Benjamin's work of the 1930s that the hidden dialectic between avant-garde art and the utopian hope for an emancipatory mass culture can be grasped alive for the last time', according to Andreas Huyssen in the best book to date on contemporary cultural dynamics, *After the Great Divide*.[18] He should have added 'in the West', because the work resurfaced and continued in Latin America and in India in the 60s, although in modified forms.

In fact, the lineage goes back to the Soviet avant-gardes. Espinosa echoes Bogdanov's insistence that art practices must address the 'organisation of emotion and thought'. Rocha's violently emotional work echoes Tretyakov's reliance on shock to alter the psyche of the recipient of art. The Latin Americans' emphasis on lucidity echoes

Brecht's confidence in the emancipatory power of reason, something he shared with many Soviet artists allied to Lunacharsky's Commissariat of the Enlightenment and their 'goal to forge a new unity of art and life by creating a new art and a new life' in one and the same movement. There are, then, clear continuities running from the Soviet artists via Tretyakov to Rocha, via Brecht to Solanas and via Benjamin to . . . Edward Said?

However, it would be misleading to overlook the differences between the Brecht-Benjamin nexus and the Latin American manifestos. In the displacement of the political-cultural avant-garde from Europe to Latin America, some themes fell by the wayside, while others were modified. Technological utopianism was the first casualty, as evidenced by Espinosa's notion of a technologically, as well as financially poor cinema as being the most effective way forward for artists opposed to the Hollywood-dominated consciousness industries. The recourse to poor technology (for example, black and white 16mm handheld camera techniques as opposed to studio technology, and so on) had become a necessity not only in Latin America, but also for all those who wished (and still wish) to contest the industrial cinema's domination.

Secondly, compared to the Soviet and to the German socialist avant-gardes, the Latin Americans put an extraordinary, almost desperate stress on the need for lucidity in the struggle for a renewed attempt to integrate art and life. It is easy to see how changes that had come about since the 30s could give rise to a feeling of desperation in this respect. As Andreas Huyssen has put it:

> The legitimate place of a cultural avant-garde which once carried with it the utopian hope for an emancipatory mass culture under socialism has been pre-empted by the rise of mass mediated culture and its supporting industries and institutions. It was the culture industry, not the avant-garde, which succeeded in transforming everyday life in the 20th century. And yet – the utopian hopes of the historical avant-garde are preserved, even though in distorted form, in this system of secondary exploitation euphemistically called mass culture.[20]

The Latin American, Asian and African film-makers were, and largely still are, caught between the contradictions of technologised mass culture (its need to activate emancipatory wishes in order to redirect or defuse them by invoking an array of pleasures organised so that the dominant pleasures become associated with conservative or individualist gratifications), and the need to develop a different kind of mass culture while being denied the financial, technological and institutional support to do so. Since the culture industry has become extremely adept at orchestrating emotionality while deliberately

186

atrophying the desire for understanding and intellectuality, it makes sense for the Latin American avant-gardes to emphasise lucidity and the cognitive aspects of cinema, thus reversing the hierarchy between the cognitive and the emotive, while of course maintaining the need to involve both.

The third main difference is due to two absences in Latin America. One is the absence of a powerful fascist culture with its aesthetisisation of politics, as exemplified in Nazi Germany. In Latin America, political power has been wielded in more nakedly repressive ways, perhaps because the populist ideologies required by national-fascist regimes would never be successfully passed off as a domestic aspiration: imperialist forces were too obviously in play for that strategy to work.

The second absence is the experience of Stalinism's rigorous subordination of cultural workers to the requirements of the elite of the Party bureaucracy. Whatever could be said of Cuba's cultural policies, the effervescence of Cuba's cinema in the 60s was such a welcome contrast to the cinemas of other 'existing socialisms' that the shortcomings of prevailing Marxist theories of culture were not a major issue for Latin American cultural practitioners. The Allende period in Chile only reinforced this optimism for a while. Consequently, the Latin Americans were better able to reconnect with the emancipatory drive of 20s and 30s cultural theory than their European counterparts, who had been traumatised by the experience of World War II, and by the degeneration of the once revered Soviet regime. For them, the dangers inherent in the avant-garde rhetoric about the fusion of art and life were all too apparent. It took the Latin Americans' reformulations under different circumstances, and in the context of a wave of successful independence struggles, to put the question back on the political-cultural agenda. Their emphasis on lucidity also functioned positively in that respect as a warning against subordinating the critical-cognitive dimensions of cultural work to the emotive-utopian harnessing of popular aspirations to a (necessarily) centrally dictated strategy of a political party (if that party is at all serious about gaining power).

Finally, the Latin Americans also pioneered, alongside their filmmaking work, a Third Cinema critical practice which proceeded from the same impulses towards historical lucidity, something which the Europeans never achieved as far as cinema was and is concerned. Not only did the cineastes write manifestos, they also engaged in a critical reconstruction of their cinematic histories. In conjunction with them, historian-critics such as Paulo Emilio Salles Gomes and Jean-Claude Bernardet in Brazil consistently worked towards a type of criticism that sought to understand individual texts and contemporary trends in film-making in relation to the historical processes, institutions and struggles from which these texts and currents received their formative impulses. It took longer for those critical practices to travel to Europe than it took the films. Only recently, and indirectly, has the critical equivalent of Third Cinema gained ground in the West and, not surprisingly, it is mainly, but not exclusively,[21] practised by critics and theorists who themselves try to reconnect with, as well as extend, aspects of 30s German cultural theories: examples include some of Fredric Jameson's work,[22] the work of Eric Rentschler, Miriam Hansen, writers associated with the US-based journal *New German Critique*, the writings of Luke Gibbons and of Alexander Kluge. In Britain, the work on British and Irish cinema published by the Ireland-based John Hill and the writings of Peter Wollen come to mind, along with Claire Johnston's essay on *Maeve*,[23] as all too rare examples. Perhaps fittingly, this return to critical theory went together with a rediscovery of the massive importance of a Soviet theoretician's long neglected work: that of Mikhail Bakhtin.

Third Cinema Today

Recently, Teshome Gabriel reformulated some of the Third Cinema theses, pointing out that:

> Third Cinema includes an infinity of subjects and styles as varied as the lives of the people it portrays. [Its] principal characteristic is really not so much where it is made, or even who makes it, but, rather, the ideology it espouses and the consciousness it displays.[24]

Although still confining it de facto to so-called Third World countries, nearly always overlooking Asia (which may be due to the difficulty of obtaining prints for study rather than to oversight), Gabriel's unambiguous affirmation that Third Cinema can be practised anywhere opens the way towards a different conceptualisation of Third Cinema and its contemporary relevance. Instead of either Epstein's notion of *photogénie* or difference theory (the 'varietal thesis'), which are theories of consumption, Third Cinema refers to production, and its corresponding theory of consumption would then be Bakhtin's theory of reading, including its emphases on inner speech and the profoundly social aspects of discourse.

However, perhaps because of his committed internationalism, Gabriel risks contradicting himself by not facing head-on the question of the national. If Third Cinema is as varied as the lives of the people it portrays (I would prefer to say: as varied as the social processes it inhabits), it must follow that it espouses nationally specific forms, since the lives of people are governed and circumscribed by histories and situations made 'nationally specific' by the very existence of the boundaries framing the terrain where a particular government's writ runs, by the legal and educational systems in place there, and so on. Nevertheless, in Gabriel's 'Towards a Critical Theory of Third

World Films', Third Cinema and a Third World cinema expressive of Third World needs are still equated. Whether or not China, India or South Korea can meaningfully be regarded as Third World areas, Gabriel's essay raises a serious problem: is it theoretically possible to find a unifying aesthetic for non-Euro-American cinemas? If the answer is 'yes', as his analyses tend to suggest, then Third Cinema is undoubtedly not nearly as varied as the lives of the people it portrays. But, going one step further, the way Gabriel seeks to substantiate the argument for a unifying aesthetic leads to two conflicting results. Firstly, and in spite of a stated contrary intention, Third Cinema is once more defined in terms of its difference from Euro-American cinema, thus implicitly using Hollywood and its national-industrial rivals as the yardstick against which to measure the other's otherness.

Secondly, Gabriel demonstrates also that the various non-Euro-American cinematic regimes organise time and space in their own specific ways. That is to say, using a Bakhtinian term, non-Euro-American cinema is characterised by a different chronotope. In his study of Bakhtin's work, Tzvetan Todorov defined the chronotope as 'the set of distinctive features of time and space within each literary genre'.[25] Bakhtin himself was a little less restrictive. He talked about an image of 'historical time condensed in space,'[26] and of:

> the ability to see time, to read time, in the spatial whole of the world and, on the other hand, to perceive the filling of space not as an immobile background, a given that is completed once and for all, but as an emerging whole, an event – this is the ability to read in everything signs that show time in its course, beginning with nature and ending with human customs and ideas (all the way to abstract concepts). [T]he work of the seeing eye joins here with the most complex thought processes.[27]

Consequently, chronotopes are time-space articulations characteristic of particular, historically determined conceptions of the relations between the human, the social and the natural world, that is, of ways of conceptualising social existence. Gabriel's argument that a different chronotope determines the narrative images and rhythms of non-Euro-American cinemas is convincing. However, his analysis stops short of specifying how, for instance, the chronotope of Ghatak's films, with their intricate interweaving of historical, biographical, natural and emotional temporal rhythms, not to mention musical and speech rhythms, in spaces disrupted by edges and boundaries themselves condensing historical and symbolic meanings, differs from Joaquim Pedro de Andrade's telescoping of historical, allegorical and fantasy times in *O Homem do Pau-Brasil* (1982), or from the representation of historical time in terms of the relation between linear-evential time and cyclical-ritual time in a space divided according to varieties of sacred-profane oppositions, as in Sembene's *Ceddo* (1976).

Secondly, the chronotopes of neither the First nor the Second cinemas are as homogeneous as Gabriel's argument (and the use of the term Euro-American in these notes) would suggest. Chantal Akerman and Bette Gordon's films each in their own way deploy space-time worlds at variance with dominant Euro-American cinemas. Similarly, some of Mario Bava's horror films operate within the confines of fantasy time and logic (in which the narrative is propelled by the working through of a single, highly condensed but basically fantasy structure[28] whereas Roger Corman's work is marked by the imbrication of sacred-ritual and profane-linear time structures[29] although both tend to use space in very similar ways).

Then there is the question of the differences between the chronotopes of commercial Indian cinemas and those of the Japanese, Hollywood or Latin American ones. In addition, there appear to be marked differences between black British and black American films, in spite of their shared opposition to Hollywood. These differences relate more directly to the varying relations between these films and their respective 'host' cinemas, a relationship which also informs the differences between British and American independent political cinemas in general. For example, the black British cinema can be seen as organising time-space relations differently from both dominant and experimental-independent British cinemas, and this complex differentiation from its immediate industrial-social-cultural context is a more pertinent (over-)determining process than, for example, any reference to black African cinemas. Moreover, within the black British cinema there are further important distinctions to be made between films drawing on Asian and on Caribbean cultural discourses and histories.

Gabriel's homogenisation of the Third Cinema chronotope into a single aesthetic family is thus premature, although the analysis of the differentiation between Euro-American cinema and its 'other' constitutes the necessary first step in the politically indispensable and urgent task of expelling the Euro-American conceptions of cinema from the centre of both film history and critical theory. The difficulties of such a project are not to be underestimated, as is demonstrated by the consistent shorthand usage of the term Euro-American in this discussion: readers of these notes are bound to have some idea of what is meant by that term, while a distinction between Islamic and Buddhist cinemas is likely to be received with puzzlement, although it is in all probability an apposite distinction to make.

The National
One important factor which programmes Gabriel's premature re-homogenisation of Third Cinema, after his insistence on its infinite variability, is his principled but costly avoidance of the national

question. The effectiveness with which the national socio-cultural formations determine particular signifying practices is not addressed. Admittedly, the national question itself has a different weight in various parts of the globe, but the forced as well as the elective internationalism of cinema – especially of a cinema with inadequately developed industrial infrastructures – tends to bracket national-cultural issues too quickly. And yet if any cinema is determinedly national, even regional, in its address and aspirations, it is Third Cinema.

Since Hollywood established its dominance in the world market, from about 1919 onwards,[30] the call for a cinema rooted in national cultures has been repeated in a variety of ways, perhaps most vocally by national bourgeoisies cynically invoking the 'national culture' in order to get the state to help them to monopolise the domestic market.[31] Initially, these calls took the form of arguments for an authorial cinema, within a national industry if possible, outside of its institutions if necessary. The split between a national-dominant cinema competing with Hollywood and a national authorial cinema – which also existed within Hollywood, as Solanas acknowledged – has been mirrored in the split between a politically oriented militant cinema opposing mainstream entertainment cinema, and a personal-experimental cinema opposing the literariness of author-cinema, even if these categories have tended to overlap at times. These mirror-divisions have developed since the mid-20s each giving rise to its own institutions, but none being able to challenge the industrial-political domination of Hollywood.

At best, some countries (especially in Asia) have managed to prevent Hollywood from destroying their local film industry, but even these countries have failed to make a significant international impact. The post-Second World War era up to 1975 (the Vietnamese victory over the US) has been characterised by intense struggles over national film cultures, and has seen the rise of authorial cinemas, while the dominant industrial cinemas' ideological and economic functions within national, as well as in international, capitalist structures have shifted towards television.

In countries without advanced film production sectors, the question of the national was also and immediately a political question, that is to say, the question of national liberation and the right to speak in one's own cultural idioms. But although these questions are fairly recent as far as cinema is concerned, they had been rehearsed for over a century in relation to literature, the fine arts, theatre, music, and so on.

The West invented nationalism, initially in the form of imperialism, as states extended their domination over others, creating at one and the same time the hegemonic sense of a national culture and the problem of national identity for the colonised territories. The issue of national-cultural identity arises only in response to a challenge posed by the other, so that any discourse of national-cultural identity is always and from the outset oppositional, although not necessarily conducive to progressive positions. This holds true for the colonising nation, as well as for the colonised one(s) it calls into being. The responses to this reciprocal but antagonistic formation of identities fall into three types.

The first option is to identify with the dominant and dominating culture, which is easy for members of the metropolitan intelligentsia such as the infamous Thomas Macaulay, who disguised armed and economic force under the cloak of cultural superiority. This option is less comfortable for the colonised intelligentsia, who may aspire to the hegemonic culture, but can never really belong to it. However, the rewards for such an aspiration are sufficiently attractive for many of them to pursue it with vigour: there is the promise of advancement under colonial rule and of becoming the 'national' leadership to which a retreating coloniser will wish to bequeath power.

The second option is to develop the antagonistic sense of national identity by seeking to reconnect with traditions that have been lost, or have been displaced or distorted by colonial rule or by the impact of Western industrial-military power. In spite of the undoubted mobilising power of such national-populist ideologies, this option presents considerable difficulties and dangers. The main ones derive from the need to (re)invent traditions, to conjure up an image of pre-colonial innocence and authenticity, since the national-cultural identity must by definition be founded on what has been suppressed or distorted. The result is mostly a nostalgia for a pre-colonial society which never existed, full of idyllic villages and communities peopled by authentic (for which, read 'folkloric') innocents in touch with the 'real' values perverted by imperialism or, in the most naive versions, perverted by technology.

Alternatively, particular aspects of some culture are selected and elevated into essentialised symbols of the national identity: the local answer to imperialism's stereotypes. Mirroring imperialism's practices, such efforts mostly wind up presenting previously existing relations of domination and subordination as the 'natural' state of things. And then, of course, there are the political monstrosities that occur when such idealised and essentialised notions of national identity achieve some kind of power: for example, the wholesale massacres of 'others', those 'others' being required to define the national identity and to function as scapegoats for the fact that the original idyllic existence still seems as far away as ever.

African and Asian as well as Latin American intelligentsia have negotiated these problems for a very long time and have come up with a variety of solutions, among which are Third Worldist types of internationalism (the displacement from national identity to continental identity), the controlled mixture of feudalism and advanced capitalism as practised in Japan, the displacement of the national to the racial (negritude, for example), and so on. In the second half of the twentieth century, however, together with the widespread struggles for national liberation and independence, a different approach has gained strength. Although often still riddled with residues of backward-looking idealisations of what the 'original' culture must have been like before the impact of Western rapaciousness, this third option has refused both national chauvinism and identification with the aggressor in favour of a more complex view of social formations and their dynamics, including the fraught relationship with the West. As the Moroccan Zaghloul Morsy has put it: 'Whether we try to refute it, liberate ourselves from it or assent to it [t]he West is here with us as a prime fact, and ignorance or imperfect knowledge of it has a nullifying effect on all serious reflection and genuinely artistic expression.'[32]

It is one of the contentions of these notes that the opposite holds true as well: Asian, African and Latin American cultures are with us as a fact, and ignorance of them has an equally nullifying effect on all serious reflection ... in the West. While the bourgeois nationalist intellectuals of the liberated countries talked about effecting a synthesis of East and West or of North and South in order to forge a new hegemony, militant intellectuals rejected that illusion and opted for a rhetoric of becoming: the national culture would emerge from a struggle waged by the existing people, and not by the idealised figment of a ruralist fantasy. It is in this process of struggle that the intellectuals would find a role. In that context, liberation did not refer to the freeing of some previously existing but temporarily suppressed state of culture. On the contrary, political and economic liberation would be a necessary precondition for the emergence of a popular culture, a point most cogently made by Solanas when he stressed the experimental nature of Third Cinema. In each case, the specific circumstances of the country involved – its pre-colonial as well as colonial history, and so on – would determine the particular shape and dynamics of the culture once it has been freed to evolve according to its own needs and aspirations.

Consequently, the question of the national became not irrelevant but secondary: the primary task was to address the existing situation in all its often contradictory and confusing intricacy with the maximum lucidity. The expression of cultural and national identity, as well as personal identity, would be an inevitable by-product in the sense that a discourse about and addressing particular social processes would necessarily bear the imprint of those processes in the same way that any discourse bears the imprint of those it addresses, along with the traces of the (over-)determining forces that shape it. Cultural identity no longer precedes the discourse as something to be recovered. It is by trying to put an understanding of the multifarious social-historical processes at work in a given situation into discourse that the national-cultural-popular identity begins to find a voice. Tradition(s) can no longer be seen as sacred cows: some are to be criticised, others to be mobilised or inflected - an attitude exemplified by Sembene's and Cisse's work.

Nationalist solidarity thus gives way to the need for critical lucidity, which becomes the intellectual's special task. His or her contribution becomes the provision of a critical understanding likely to assist the struggles at hand. As Louis Althusser put it in a letter to Régis Debray: '[Intellectuals] are entrusted by the people in arms with the guardianship and extension of scientific knowledge. They must fulfil this mission with the utmost care, following in the footsteps of Marx, who was convinced that nothing was more important for the struggles of the workers' movements and those waging those struggles than the most profound and accurate knowledge.'[33]

Edward Said formulated it in this way: 'The history of thought, to say nothing of political movements, is extravagantly illustrative of how the dictum "solidarity before criticism" means the end of criticism.' And he went on to say: 'Even in the very midst of a battle in which one is unmistakably on one side against another, there should be criticism, because there must be critical consciousness if there are to be issues, problems, values, even lives to be fought for.'[34] So, although the national may indeed not be the most important issue, to skip the question altogether and slide directly towards an international aesthetic also eliminates the defining characteristics of Third Cinema itself: the aim of rendering a particular social situation intelligible to those engaged in a struggle to change it in a socialist direction.

That the question of the national cannot be divorced from the question of Third Cinema is also evident from an example which most Third Cinema theorists tend to overlook in spite of the striking similarities presented by it: the cultural practice advocated at Santiniketan in India in the 20s and the 30s. The institution founded in Bengal by Tagore developed an aesthetic on the interface between nature and culture, unifying the Janus-faced relationship of the artist to both under the terms of the 'environment' and the 'living tradition'. It saw culture as layered into regional specificities, while insisting on a critical inter-nationalism. In Geeta Kapur's words:

As an artist, Rabindranath's commitment to the living tradition came first and foremost through his creative choices, through his working the great range of artistic forms [as] for example his use as a poet of Upanishadic verse, Baul songs and folk lullabies. At the same time he enjoined his colleagues to resist spiritual and aesthetic (as for that matter political) codification of forms on any rigid national or ethnic grounds, to open themselves out to the world art movements, thus enlivening their own practice and making it internationally viable and contemporary. This after all would be the best test of a living tradition. At Santiniketan, a concerted attempt was made to organise the liberating effects of such an orientation towards the complexities of a contemporary environment and of vernacular vocabulary and skills into a coherent aesthetic approach which was deeply embedded in the Indian national independence movement. The political and the cultural were fused into a radical curriculum in which students at Santiniketan were introduced to craftsmen at work. They were encouraged to re-work traditional materials and techniques and the objects produced were exhibited and sold in local fairs [an equivalent of the exhibition practices associated with Third Cinema and its screenings at informal popular gatherings as well as in student milieux and in radical institutions] with the hope of recycling the taste and skills of craftsmen-artists into the urban middle class milieu with the young artist forming a double link. A new Indian sensibility was to be hypothesised, created, designed. [Popular art] inclined them to visual narratives (derived from the great myths as well as from tribal fables), to hybrid figural iconography and swift stylistic abbreviations.[35]

Summing up the pedagogic approach of Nandalal Bose, 'the most courageous artist of the nationalist period', Geeta Kapur emphasises that this constituted a practice of 'images derived from popular sources serving political-populist purposes with a radical effect on both'.[36]

The dialogic relation with the popular, the stress on the vernacular, the double reference to both the regional and the international, the hybridisation practices, the recourse to the most inexpensive means of artistic production, the project of creating a new national culture – all these features recur in the writings of the Third Cinema polemicists. In addition, the Cuban as well as the Indian varieties of this current were deeply embedded in anti-imperialist struggles for national-cultural as well as political and economic autonomy.

This should not, of course, obscure the differences between Santiniketan and the Latin Americans, the most obvious of which are the latter's overtly Marxist approach and the fact that the political practice of a capital-intensive, inherently 'modern' mass-media technology such as cinema required a drastic reconceptualisation of the nature of the dialogue with the popular. Moreover, Santiniketan is not the only antecedent of Third Cinema in this respect: the Brazilian theatrical and literary avant-gardes of the 20s, especially those associated with Oswald de Andrade, the Pau Brasil and the Anthropofagia manifestos, come to mind, as do the Mexican muralists in the 30s, and so on, all of which address similar sets of tensions and contradictions. In that regard, the references to Italian neo-realism and to Grierson in the manifestos cannot be taken at face value. They function as a symptom of the productive cultural hybridisation inherent in the position from which the Latin American cineastes speak, rather than as a designation of origins.

Finally, the absence in that context of references to Jean Rouch also speaks volumes. Rouch is a reference for African film-makers as opposed to Latin American ones, except for the rather jokey allusions in the Brazilian comedy *Ladroes de Cinema* (Fernando Cony Campos, 1977). His absence from the classic Third Cinema manifestos thus operates as a marker of the marginalisation of African cinemas by the Latin Americans at the time. The argument that it might have been overlooked because of Rouch's ethnographic rather than explicitly political discourse would not be very convincing, since Griersonian social democracy and its admiration for strongly centralised (but benevolent) state authority does figure in the texts in spite of its dubious politics. Moreover, Rouch can be seen as a most intriguing father-figure for Third Cinema, more so than Ivens or Marker, since it is with *Moi un noir* (1957) that he invented an African Third Cinema style of film-making, and that precisely because of the dialogic relation set up between Rouch and his main protagonist, 'Robinson' (Oumarou Ganda), which structures the filmic process, its stylistic aspects along with its fiction.[38] It is significant that Rouch's film, and the emergence of a Third Cinema in Africa, date back to the very year in which Ghana became the first African state to gain independence from its colonising power.

The connection between Rouch and Paulin Soumanou Vieyra could also be seen as significant in this respect. Vieyra started making Third Cinema type films in France and in Senegal in the late 50s. But neither his films nor his writings became a reference point for Third Cinema polemics, confirming the marginalisation of African cinema in favour of the Europe–Latin America axis.

Bakhtin

For the theoretical elaboration of the interplay between utterances and their socio-historical setting(s), the most useful inspiration available to date is the work of Mikhail Bakhtin. In particular, his concepts of dialogue, otherness and the chronotope provide productive ways in which Teshome Gabriel's pioneering work might be built upon, allowing us to rethink the whole issue of cultural politics in the process. Although Bakhtin does not directly address the question of the national, he is very much concerned with the issue of socio-historical specificity. His discussion of discursive genres outlines the way he poses the problem:

The work is oriented, first, towards its [r]ecipients, and towards certain conditions of performance and perception. Second, the work is oriented towards life, from the inside, so to speak, by its thematic content. [E]very genre has its methods, its ways of seeing and understanding reality, and these methods are its exclusive characteristic. The artist must learn to see reality through the eyes of the genre. [T]he field of representation changes from genre to genre [i]t delineates itself differently as space and time. This field is always specific.[38]

Bakhtin then goes on to make another link by defining genre as a fragment of collective memory:

Cultural and literary traditions are preserved and continue to live, not in the subjective memory of the individual nor in some collective psyche, but in the objective forms of culture itself. [I]n this sense, they are intersubjective and interindividual, and therefore social. [T]he individual memory of creative individuals almost does not come into play.[39]

Bakhtin's translators, biographers and commentators, K. Clark and M. Holquist, emphasise the proximity of such an approach to cultural tradition to Bakhtin's concept of the chronotope: 'In each place and period a different set of time/space categories obtained, and what it meant to be human was in a large measure determined by these categories. The Greeks saw time as cyclical, for example, while the Hebrews assigned greatest value to the future.'[40] The component parts of discourses-utterances are themselves 'socialised':

Within the arena of [e]very utterance an intense conflict between one's own and another's word is being fought out. Each word is a little arena for the clash of and crisscrossing of differently oriented social accents. A word in the mouth of a particular individual is a product of the living interaction of social forces. The reason for this is that no utterance can be attributed to the speaker exclusively; it is the product of the interaction of the interlocutors, and, broadly speaking, the product of the whole complex social situation in which it has occurred.[41]

Bakhtin goes so far as to characterise individual utterances as corridors in which echo a multiplicity of voices, a corridor shaped by the interaction, whether direct or indirect, delayed or anticipated, between interlocutors, so that what is actively unspoken or what is simply, silently assumed exerts as effective a determining force upon the discourse as the speaker's project. In addition to the interlocutors and to the social situation – itself alive with remembered, half-remembered, anticipated and temporarily dormant discourses – there is the echo of the generic whole, which resounds in every word that functions within it. However, Bakhtin's plurivocal cultural spaces do not present some egalitarian jostle of intersecting voices of the type that deconstructive notions of intertextuality evoke. On the contrary:

> Just as [social diversity] is constrained by the rules imposed by the single state, the diversity of discourses is fought against by the aspiration, correlative to all power, to institute a common language. [T]he common language is never given but in fact always ordained, and at every moment of the life of the language it is opposed to genuine heterology.[42]

Cultural specificity is thus never a closed, static terrain; it is never a systemic whole like a code:

> Culture cannot be enclosed within itself as something ready made. The unity of a particular culture is an open unity [in which] lie immense semantic possibilities that have remained undisclosed, unrecognised, and unutilised.[43]

The clear implication here is that, just as there is a hierarchy imposed upon the diversity of discourses, the institutionalised exercise of power bears upon exactly which semantic possibilities shall remain unrecognised or unutilised. In the case of cinema, this means that social power has its word to say in what kind of discourses are made, as well as in how people read them, a point made earlier in relation to the promotion and the reviewing of Third Cinema films as Second Cinema ones. The silence of the oppressed may be an active form of resistance, a refusal. It may also be the result of a socially induced incapacity to activate certain registers of meaning, the exercise of social power having succeeded in blocking access to a number of semantic possibilities. It is important to stress this particular effect of power, since it is often overlooked by people who study the way consumers use products of the cultural industries: questions of pleasure are often emphasised at the expense of an examination of the stunting and restrictive effects of dominant discursive regimes which constantly repeat the prohibition of certain types of making sense.

Having sketched the parameters of a possible typology of the dynamics shaping cultural formations, Bakhtin makes some particularly challenging points with far-reaching implications, especially for the community-oriented populist tendencies currently dominant among left cultural practitioners in the UK as well as in the US. In a short journalistic piece he warned:

> In our enthusiasm for specification we have ignored questions of the interconnection and interdependence of various areas of cul-

ture; we have frequently forgotten that the boundaries of these areas are not absolute, that in various epochs they have been drawn in various ways; and we have not taken into account that the most intense and productive life of culture takes place on the boundaries of its individual areas and not in places where these areas have become enclosed in their own specificity.[44]

This warning helps to explain the sterility of classic modernist positions but also, and more importantly, of attempts to enclose cultural practices within class or ethnic or gender specificities. This point is developed into a fully-fledged critique of practices that advocate identification between the intellectual artist and 'the people' or any other social grouping. In the following quotation, Bakhtin refers to attempts to understand 'foreign' cultures, but his remarks apply with equal force and pertinence to social strata other than one's own, regardless of whether these strata are defined in terms of class, ethnicity or gender:

There exists a very strong, but one-sided and thus untrustworthy idea that in order better to understand a foreign culture, one must enter into it, forgetting one's own, and view the world through the eyes of this foreign culture. [O]f course, the possibility of seeing the world through its eyes is a necessary part of the process of understanding it; but if this were the only aspect [i]t would merely be duplication and would not entail anything enriching. Creative understanding does not renounce itself, its own place and time, its own culture; and it forgets nothing. In order to understand, it is immensely important for the person who understands to be located outside the object of his or her creative understanding – in time, in space, in culture. In the realm of culture, outsideness is a most powerful factor in understanding. [W]e raise new questions for a foreign culture, ones that it did not raise for itself; we seek answers to our own questions in it; and the foreign culture responds to us by revealing to us its new aspects and new semantic depths. Without one's own questions one cannot creatively understand anything other or foreign. Such a dialogic encounter of two cultures does not result in merging or mixing. Each retains its own unity and open totality, but they are mutually enriched.[45]

One must be 'other' oneself if anything is to be learned about the meanings of limits, or borderlines, of the areas where the most intense and productive life of culture takes place.

Trinh T. Minh-ha, in an equally provocative introduction to a special issue of *Discourse*, echoes Bakhtin's concern with the productivity of otherness:

Otherness has its own laws and interdictions. [A]nd difference in this context undermines opposition as well as separatism. Neither a claim for special treatment, nor a return to an authentic core (the 'unspoiled' Real Other), it acknowledges in each of its moves the coming together and drifting apart both within and between identities. What is at stake is not only the hegemony of Western cultures, but also their identities as unified cultures: in other words, the realisation that there is a Third World in every First World, and vice-versa.[46]

Remembering Bakhtin's point about the unequal power relations between discourses, these considerations lead us far from the postmodern or the multiculturalist free play of differences, the republican carnival of voices, towards a politics of otherness as the precondition for any cultural politics. If outsideness is the prerequisite for creative understanding, it also follows that outsideness is a position as threatening as it is productive. Threatening for the 'insider', whose limits become visible in ways inaccessible to him or her; productive precisely in so far as structuring limits, horizons, boundaries become visible and available for understanding.

If we return to the Latin American manifestos through the prism of Bakhtin's theories, their insistence on a lucid presentation of social forces and of reality, coupled with the pursuit of socialist aspirations, can be seen in a somewhat different light. Viewed from this perspective, Third Cinema is a cinema neither of nor for 'the people', nor is it simply a matter of expressing opposition to imperialism or to bourgeois rule. It is a cinema made by intellectuals who, for political and artistic reasons at one and the same time, assume their responsibilities as socialist intellectuals and seek to achieve through their work the production of social intelligibility.

Moreover, remembering Edward Said's point about the need for criticism, their pursuit of the creative understanding of particular social realities takes the form of a critical dialogue – hence the need for both lucidity and close contact with popular discourses and aspirations – with a people itself engaged in bringing about social change. Theirs is not an audience in the Hollywood or in the televisual sense, where popularity is equated with consumer satisfaction and where pleasure is measured in terms of units of the local currency entered on the balance sheet. Theirs, like Brecht's, is a fighting notion of popularity, as is clear from Solanas's insistence on Third Cinema being an experimental cinema engaged in a constant process of research. And like Brecht, the Latin Americans reserve the right to resort to any formal device they deem necessary to achieve their goals, as shown by their refusal to strait-jacket themselves into a codified Third Cinema aesthetic.

Speaking in the forms of cinema, that is, of making films, or in other genres of audiovisual discourse, this necessarily means entering into a dialogue, not only with the historical uses of these genres – since these discourses inevitably reverberate in, for example, Third Cinema's sound-image articulations – but also with the power re-lations enshrined in those historical uses of dominant narrative regimes, along with the entire cultural networks within which the experiences of making and viewing are located. Third Cinema is most emphatically not simply concerned with 'letting the oppressed speak with their own voices': that would be a one-sided and therefore an untrustworthy position. Those voices would only speak the experi-ence of oppression, including the debilitating aspects of that con-dition. Third Cinema does not seek to induce guilt in, or to solicit sympathy from, its interlocutors. Instead, it addresses the issue of social power from a critical-but-committed position, articulating the joining of 'the intelligence, the emotions, the powers of intuition', as Espinosa put it, so as to help achieve socialist ideals.

Because of the realisation of the social nature of discourse, the Third Cinema project summons to the place of the viewer social-historical knowledges, rather than art-historical, narrowly aesthetic ones. These latter knowledges would be relevant only in so far as they form part of the particular nexus of socio-historical processes addressed. As for Third Cinema and otherness or outsideness, it is no accident but rather a logical consequence that a sense of non-belong-ing, non-identity with the culture one inhabits, whether it be nationally defined, ethnically or in any other way, is a precondition for 'the most intense and productive aspects of cultural life'. Although that may be too strong a formulation, since it obviously is possible to be 'other' in some respects and to be 'in and of' the culture at the same time, the fact remains that it is in this disjuncture, in this in-between position, that the production of social intelligibility thrives, at least as far as socialist cultural practices are concerned. The price paid for such a position is invariably the hostility of representatives of the hegemonic culture, whether these are active apologists for the ruling ideologies, opportunists seeking to profit from celebrations of cor-porate culture (such as most post-modern critics) or merely guilty intellectuals who hope to wash away the taint of their middle-class position by abdicating all intellectual responsibilities. But that hos-tility is actively to be welcomed as an indication that we are on the right track.

What is at stake, from my point of view, in the re-actualisation of the Third Cinema debates in the UK in the 80s, is the conviction that outsideness-otherness is the only vantage point from which a viable cultural politics may be conducted in the UK. The negotiation of the problems involved in otherness as a positional necessity is the precon-dition for a critical-cultural practice in Britain, as witnessed by the work of black film-makers, who now constitute the most intellectually and cinematically innovative edge of British cultural politics, along with a few 'others' such as Cinema Action (the makers of the most intelligent film about Englishness in the 80s, *Rocinante*), Marc Karlin (whose television programmes on *Nicaragua* (1984) constitute an example of Third Cinema's adaptability to televisual modes of discourse) and some film-makers such as Pat Murphy and Thaddeus O'Sullivan who move between Ireland and the UK.

While the work of these film-makers seems to have little in common from a formal, aesthetic point of view, they nevertheless share a systematic demarcation from the genres to which they ostensibly belong: *Burning an Illusion* (Menelik Shabazz, 1981) is as different from the prevailing social-realist dramas as *Territories* (Isaac Julian, 1984) is from modernist-experimental video and film-making; *Rocinante* is as different from road movie romances as *Anne Devlin* (Pat Murphy, 1984) or *December Bride* (Thaddeus O'Sullivan, 1991) are from films with strong heroines, and so on. In each case, the difference is not generated by a surfeit of formal innovation, or by the pursuit of a marketable variation on a theme, but because the prevailing generic codifications are too restrictive for the articulation of their social-analytical purposes.

Together with these film-making activities, theoretical-critical work also needs to address its Englishness, its parochial limits, its ethnocentricity and insularity. This requires a particular emphasis to be given to otherness, to the dialogue with unfamiliar cultural practices and traditions, while refusing to homogenise every non-Euro-American culture into a globalised 'other'. The challenge to English aspirations towards universality is not to pose a counter-universality, but actively to seek to learn about, as well as promote, other ways of making sense. When we learn how the work of Ritwik Ghatak, Kumar Shahani or Carlos Reichenbach is 'specific' to the cultural formations that produced them, perhaps we will learn to see better how our home-grown theories and films bear the imprint of an incapacitatingly restrictive Englishness (Americans may substitute their own -ness where appropriate). Therefore, the notion of Third Cinema is relevant to the UK in its exemplification of an approach to the relations between the social and the cultural, and for its very 'otherness' in the sense of something it is necessary both to learn from and about: to learn from Third Cinema film-makers and intellectuals while endeavouring to make more breathing space within the UK for the emergence of otherness as a challenge to the English Ideology.

Consequently, my primary aim in drawing attention to the issues which the notion of Third Cinema allows me to raise is an attempt to help change the (film) culture which I inhabit by evoking a historical narrative, of sorts. This narrative is intended, firstly, to conjure up an anticipated, desirable but necessarily utopian image of what socialist critical-cultural practice might or should be, and, secondly, to help create a space for what is truly 'the best of world cinema' within my own socio-cultural formation.

Notes

1. For an elaboration of this point, see Chapter 8. A particularly damaging aspect of that theoretical work is only now becoming manifest. Although presented in assertive, even combative language, the work elaborated in the 70s was profoundly experimental, a fact underlined by the proliferation of essay titles proclaiming their status as 'notes towards' something or other. Nevertheless, with the premature academic institutionalisation of that work, the essays were often presented as 'theoretical knowledge', and taught as such to students in the 80s. One of the unfortunate results of this practice was brought home to me by a doctoral thesis on Indian social melodrama which came from a reputable English university. The author had taken Anglo-American notions of melodrama as relatively accurate accounts of filmic melodrama and then found that the Indian films he wanted to consider did not really fit those patterns. Consequently, instead of using this lack of fit as a symptom of the inadequacy of the taught notions of melodrama, he proceeded to define as 'specifically Indian' those aspects of the films which did not fit the Anglo-American model of melodrama. The result was a most interesting piece of work which simultaneously criticised (implicitly) and confirmed (explicitly) the notions of melodrama currently dominant in film and media studies. That orthodoxy clearly functioned as a serious brake on the student's insight, signalling that the extant work on melodrama needed to be rethought drastically.
2. For particularly virulent examples, see Val Walkerdine, 'Video Replay – Families, Films and Fantasy', in Victor Burgin, James Donald and Cora Kaplan (eds), *Formations of Fantasy* (London: Methuen, 1986); also Sean Cubitt's *Timeshift – On Video Culture* (London: Routledge, 1991). For deconstructivist rituals, see virtually any 'reading' of films or of television programmes in *Screen, Wide Angle, Cinemaction* or *Iris* in the 80s.
3. See for instance, the ideology of 'community' in current independent film and video circles, the populist assumptions vitiating most 'audience studies' and the celebrations of *Rocky* and US as well as British soaps.
4. In fact, the whole notion of 'late capitalism' had come unstuck in the early 80s, as cultural theory finally began to register the reverberations of the abandonment of the Bretton Woods agreement in 1971, consolidating the victory of finance capital over industrial capital and initiating the era of Capitalism Triumphans. The complex shifts this engendered, the exact forms of which would have to be studied in detail in each specific socio-cultural formation, provide a far more useful explanatory framework than any amount of post-modern phraseology.

   For a discussion of the post-Bretton Woods framework, see M. T. Daly and M. I. Logan, *The Brittle Rim – Finance, Business and the Pacific Region* (Victoria: Penguin Books Australia, 1989).
5. *Bananas*, no. 3, 1976.
6. *Third Cinema in the Third World* (Ann Arbor, Michigan: UMI Research Press, 1982).
7. *Revista Civilizacâo Brasileira*, no. 3, 1965.
8. Published by the BFI and Channel Four Television, London 1989. This pamphlet contains the translation of all the major Latin American manifestos

mentioned in this paper and is the source of subsequent quotes unless specified otherwise.

9. *Tricontinental*, no. 13, 1969.
10. *Cine Cubano*, no. 66–7, 1970.
11. Edward Said, *The Writer, the Text and the Critic* (London: Faber & Faber, 1984), p. 2.
12. 'Bakhtin, Sociolinguistics and Deconstruction', in Frank Gloversmith (ed.), *The Theory of Reading*, Sussex, 1984, pp. 138–9.
13. 'L'Influence du troisième cinéma dans le monde', *CinémAction*, Paris, 1979.
14. Pam Cook's review of Yvonne Rainer's film *The Man Who Envied Women* (1985) in *The Monthly Film Bulletin*, no. 643, 1987, provides a particularly sad example of this trend.
15. *New German Critique*, no. 39, 1986.
16. Ibid., p. 107.
17. Ibid., p. 108.
18. *After The Great Divide* (Bloomington: Indiana University Press, 1986), p. 16.
19. Ibid., p. 12.
20. Ibid., p. 15.
21. See for example Meaghan Morris on *Crocodile Dundee* in *Art & Text*, no. 25.
22. Jameson's reliance on Ernest Mandel's notion that we are living in the era of late capitalism is a corrosive flaw in his work. A far more credible argument is that capitalism has only recently – in the 50s, after a three-hundred-year conflict culminating in two world wars and the collapse of the last empires – achieved a position of supremacy consecrated by the victory of finance capital over an ascendant industrial capital. Consequently, the mix of emer-gent and residual cultural forms, especially in the West, consists primarily of retrogressive anti-capitalist forms of resistance, rather than of attempts to short-circuit or by-pass capital's triumphal trek. The consignment of absolu-tist cultural forms into the distant past, rather than confronting them as still very much present in a variety of mixed and residual forms, does not allow Jameson to distinguish between socialist and reactionary forms of anti-capi-talism in his allegoric approach to literary and to cinematic practices. There-fore, he cannot distinguish between Third Cinema and Second Cinema, the former seeking to prepare a socialist exit from capitalism, the latter seeking to find a lucrative niche within it for its absolutist-romantic hangover. For the economic context of this argument, see note 4.
23. See the first part of Chapter 8.
24. Teshome Gabriel, 'Towards a Critical Theory of Third World Films', reprinted in Paul Willemen and Jim Pines (eds), *Questions of Third Cinema* (London: British Film Institute, 1989).
25. *Mikhail Bakhtin: The Dialogical Principle* (Manchester: Manchester Univer-sity Press, 1984), p. 83.
26. *Speech Genres & Other late Essays* (Austin: University of Texas Press, 1986).
27. Ibid., p. 24.
28. For instance, *Sei Donne Per l'Assassino*, Mario Bava, 1964.
29. Paul Willemen, David Will and Mike Wallington (eds), *Roger Corman: The Millennic Vision* (Edinburgh Film Festival, 1970).
30. Kristin Thompson, *Exporting Entertainment – America in the World Film Market, 1907–34* (London: BFI, 1985).
31. Prior to 1919, the universalist ambitions of cinema entrepreneurs were emphasised. See, for instance, Thomas Elsaesser (ed.), *Early Cinema. Space-Frame-Narrative* (London: BFI, 1990). Also, Miriam Hansen's contribution

to *New German Critique*, no. 29, 1983. Subsequently, the universalist argument was deployed in the context of attempts by a national-industrial cinema to establish or maintain itself as a multinational industrial cinema.

32. Mikel Dufrenne (ed.), *Main Trends in Aesthetics and the Sciences of Art* (New York: UNESCO, 1979), p. 40.
33. Régis Debray, *A Critique of Arms* (Harmondsworth: Penguin Books, 1977), p. 267.
34. Edward Said, *The Writer, the Text and the Critic*, p. 28.
35. Geeta Kapur, *K. G. Subramanyam* (New Delhi: Lalit Kala Akademi, 1987), pp. 17–18.
36. Ibid., p. 19.
37. See Jim Hillier (ed.), *Cahiers du Cinéma*, vol. 2 (London: BFI/ Routledge & Kegan Paul, 1986), pp. 223–5.
38. Quoted in Tzvetan Todorov, *Mikhail Bakhtin: The Dialogical Principle*, pp. 82–3.
39. Ibid., p. 85.
40. *Mikhail Bakhtin* (Cambridge, Mass.: Harvard University Press, 1984), p. 278.
41. Ibid., p. 220.
42. Quoted in Todorov, *Mikhail Bakhtin: The Dialogical Principle*, p. 30.
43. Ibid., p. 57.
44. Mikhail Bakhtin, *Speech Genres & Other Essays*, pp. 5–6.
45. Ibid., p. 2.
46. *Discourse* no. 8, 1986–7, p. 3.

In the introduction to *The Archibald Paradox – A Strange Case of Authorship*,[1] Sylvia Lawson formulated the paradox besetting the central figure of her book, J. F. Archibald, the editor of *The Bulletin* at the turn of the century in Australia, in the following terms:

> The Archibald paradox is simply the paradox of being colonial. [T]o know enough of the metropolitan world, colonials must, in limited ways at least, move and think internationally; to resist it strongly enough for the colony to cease to be colonial and to become its own place, they must become nationalists.

I would like to approach this paradoxical tension between the national and the international from a slightly different perspective: that of multiculturalism and the concern with national specificity as it relates to film studies.

In each socio-cultural formation, these tensions must, by definition, be played out in different ways. But the terms in which these tensions are presented will have a family resemblance. Consequently, some of my remarks may seem to rehearse well-worn lines of argument. Nevertheless, the issues of the national and the international, and indeed of the colonial and the imperial, are present in film studies in specific ways, ways different from those adopted, for instance, in anthropology or in comparative literature. Although the structural method of analysis migrated from linguistics into film theory via the anthropology of Claude Lévi-Strauss, it is only fairly recently that some anthropologists have begun to take on board questions of textual functioning and subjectivity which have become commonplace in film theory, issues such as the constructed-and-constructing nature of all discursive practices. And while the traumatic aspects of the relativist binge that followed from that recognition are mercifully beginning to recede in film theory (while still holding sway in television studies), the vanguardist anthropology of someone such as George Markus is still incapacitated by the discovery that anthropological discourse is also 'discourse'. As for comparative literature, regardless of its many historical deficiencies, it must be acknowledged that comparative studies in cinema do not as yet exist. What is worse, given the current insufferably ethnocentric bias of film theory, it may well be a while before this urgently needed discipline of comparative cinema studies displaces the kind of film studies currently being inflicted on university and college students.

Both the terms 'cross-cultural' and 'multicultural' already point to the first problem, in the sense that they suggest the existence of discrete, bounded cultural zones separated by borders which can be crossed. The term 'multicultural' in addition suggests that cultural zones continue to exist within a given country as small, self-contained pockets or islands, miniature replications of an alleged community's allegedly original national culture, as repositories of some cultural authenticity to be found elsewhere in time, in space or both.

In Ukania – Tom Nairn's suggestive term for the ossified, incompletely modernised monarchical state known as the United Kingdom[2] – one hears references to, say, the Bangladeshi, or the Irish or indeed the Asian communities, as if a given 'ethnic' community had simply transposed a national culture from 'there' to 'here'. This multicultural ideology has some positive, but also some exceedingly negative consequences for a country's cultural life and policies.

One very negative result is that 'ethnic' groups will be imprisoned, by arts funding bodies and by local government practices, within a restrictive and fossilised notion of culture. In this way, such groups are condemned to repeat the rituals of ethnic authenticity, regardless of how uncomfortable many members of those so-called communities may feel with them. One of the political effects of such policies is that administrators and local politicians tend to recognise 'community' spokespeople who represent the more conservative and nostalgically 'traditionalist' sectors of 'the communities' in question. A further consequence is, perhaps ironically, to encourage the practice of a 'traditional' culture separated from the social conditions by and for which cultural forms are shaped and, in so doing, to fetishise the separateness of the cultures thus called into being. In this respect, multiculturalist policies are in fact designed to create a kind of cultural apartheid.

By insisting on the discreteness and the separateness of the 'other' cultures, the host culture conspires with the conservative upholders of an imagined 'ethnicity' to draw lines around those 'other' cultural practices, ghettoising them. And in that way, the host culture can reaffirm its own imaginary unity and the illusion of its own specialness and authenticity. In this context, I would like to draw attention to the brilliant work of the late Eric Michaels in relation to Australian Aboriginal cultures, and particularly to his short talk entitled 'Postmodernism, Appropriation and Western Desert Acrylics'.[3] There,

207

Eric Michaels argued against the notion that Aboriginal art should be locked into some ethnographic notion of authenticity and irremediable otherness. Instead, he pointed to the modernity, indeed the critical post-modernity in some respects, of the work of many Aboriginal artists as they engage with their critics, with the market, and reflexively comment on their own contemporary production practices as Aboriginals living in a late twentieth-century Australia, which in its turn is part of broader cultural processes and institutions, such as the international art market and its power centres.

Although we can all agree that cultural zones are far from unified, homogeneous spaces, this should not lead us to deny or unduly relativise the existence of borders. The existence of borders is very real, and although their meaning and function are changeable, their effectiveness has not diminished in the least.

At one level, it does indeed make sense to try to construct a notion of national culture by way of a spatial commutation test. The culture would then be defined in terms of the things that change in 'the whole way of life' (Raymond Williams) or 'the whole way of struggling' (E. P. Thompson) when a national frontier is crossed. For instance, abortion may be legal on one side of a border and not on the other. Similarly, legal and other institutional arrangements, such as those relating to film and television finance and censorship, may be vastly different as well. In federal structures such as India, the United States, the former USSR or Australia, there are different inflections to this problem because of the imbrication of national and state institutions, but the problem of the borders of the nation-state remains, as is demonstrated by the importance of passports for bestowing a national identity upon individuals, with the consequent legal regulation of immigration and the whole panoply of issues implied by the notion of citizenship.

On the other hand, the construction of a cultural matrix in such a geo-structural way does not account for the sense of temporal continuity that is attributed to national cultural formations. The comparative study of, say, independent British cinema in the 30s and in the 70s is not regarded as a form of cross-cultural studies. The intervention of the Second World War, and of a host of other socio-political and economic changes, apparently does not constitute a sufficient temporal boundary for us to be able to talk of different cultural formations. My question would then be: what model of social functioning is able to account for the differences, as well as the connections, between temporal periodisations and geographical demarcations?

Perhaps we should begin by becoming more aware of the unholy complicity between periodisation in history and the drawing or the crossing of geographical boundaries. The invasion of Australia, and the declaration of a bicentenary period, is only one example of this complicity. The tendency to date England back to the invasion of 1066 is another, as is the tendency to regard the Second World War and its large-scale redrawing of the world map as the most significant temporal watershed of the 20th century. It would be foolish to deny that the War is indeed a very significant marker in all kinds of respects. The point is that in other respects, such as for instance the periodisation of capitalism, the Second World War is not such a significant marker. The liquidation of nineteenth-century absolutist empires took over fifty years, and the triumphant consolidation of capitalism on a global scale happened some time between the mid-50s and the late 60s, while the triumph of finance capital over industrial capital took even longer and was not consolidated until the 80s.[4]

This point is worth making to show that there are temporal rhythms and periods which, although implicated in and affected by geographic changes, do not coincide with them. The synchronicity of geographical and temporal periods at work in most national histories has to be produced at some cost: the loss of perspective on the very forces that construct the vicissitudes of 'the national' in the era of international dependency.

The notion of cultural specificity that may be deployed against the universalising ethnocentricity at work in film studies, works at the level of this geo-temporal construction of the national. The question of cultural specificity can be posed on other, social community levels (and these community levels may themselves be transnational, as are some constructions of gender- and class-based politics). But in film studies, the issue of specificity is primarily a national one: the boundaries of cultural specificity in cinema are established by governmental actions implemented through institutions such as censorship and its legislative framework, industrial and financial measures on the economic level, the gearing of training institutions towards employment in national media structures, systems of licensing governed by aspects of corporate law, and so on.[5] For the purposes of film culture, specificity is a territorial-institutional matter, and coincides with the boundaries of the nation state: the terrain governed by the writ of a particular government.[6]

As a rule, the effectiveness with which national socio-cultural formations, that is to say, state-bound unities, determine particular signifying practices and regimes is not addressed. This is a problem for a number of reasons. One result is that it encourages confusion between, on the one hand, the discourses of nationalism as objects of study or as a political project, and, on the other hand, the issue of national specificity. Compared to the US black films, the black British films are strikingly British, and yet in no way can they be construed as nationalistic. They are part of a British specificity, but not of a British nationalism: especially not if you remember that British nationalism is in fact an imperial identification, rather than an identification with the British state. To complicate matters further, an identification with the British state is in fact English nationalism, as opposed to Welsh, Cornish or Scottish nationalisms, which relate not to a state but to nations, and are recognisable by their demand for autonomous governments, even if that autonomy may be qualified in various ways.

A second area of confusion is the relation between a concern with national identity and the specificity of a cultural formation. For instance, the concern with notions of Australianness and with national identity was a temporary component of the dominant registers of Australian cultural specificity. That concern started to decline after the so-called bicentennial celebrations and resurfaced, in a different form, in the early 90s, around notions of republicanism. This simply means that the specificity of the Australian cultural formation has changed over the last decade and now generates other motifs and discourses. In that sense, the concern with socio-cultural specificity is different from identity searches and debates. The specificity of a cultural formation may be marked by the presence but also by the absence of preoccupations with national identity. Indeed, national specificity will determine which, if any, notions of identity are on the agenda.

So, the discourses of nationalism and those addressing or comprising national specificity are not identical. Similarly, the construction or the analysis of a specific cultural formation is different from preoccupations with national identity. I would go further and suggest that the construction of national specificity in fact encompasses and governs the articulation of both national identity and nationalist discourses. Nationalist discourses forever try to colonise and extend themselves to cover, by repressively homogenising, a complex but nationally specific formation. Thankfully, they are also doomed to keep falling short of that target. In that sense, nationalism is the shadow side of imperialism: it is an ideology generated by imperialism as its own counter-body, and it is in some ways even more repressively homogenising than that of the empire it seeks to undo – perhaps necessarily so if nationalism is to undo its imperial yoke successfully.

At the same time, in art and media studies, insufficient attention is paid to the determining effects of the geographically bounded state-unity, and this encourages a kind of promiscuous or random form of alleged internationalism, which I would prefer to call an evasive cosmopolitanism masking imperial aspirations. Another, more polemical way of putting this is to say that the discourse of universalist humanism is in fact an imperial and a colonising strategy. If we accept that national boundaries have a significant structuring impact on national socio-cultural formations (please note that I have written 'a significant impact' and not that these boundaries are the only determinations, nor necessarily the most important ones in all circumstances: merely that they are real and significant), this has to be accounted for in the way we approach and deal with cultural practices from 'elsewhere'. Otherwise, reading a Japanese film from within a British film studies framework may in fact be more like a cultural cross-border raid, or worse, an attempt to annex another culture in a subordinate position by requiring it to conform to the raider's cultural practices.[7]

Such practices are an acute problem in film studies for three main reasons. The first is that academic institutions are beginning to address the film cultures of non-Western countries.[8] This expansion in academia's disciplinary field creates job and departmental growth opportunities. The result is that scholars formed within the paradigm of Euro-American film theory are rushing to plant their flags on the terrain of, for instance, Chinese, Japanese or Indian film studies. In that respect, those scholars and departments are actively delaying the advent of a genuinely comparative film studies by trying to impose the paradigms of Euro-American film and aesthetic theories upon non-European cultural practices. In the process, the very questions concerning the production of specific socio-cultural formations mentioned earlier, are marginalised or ignored.

The second reason for film theoretical malpractice can be found in the assumed universality of film language. This illusion is promoted to ignore the specific knowledges that may be at work in a text, such as shorthand references to particular, historically accrued modes of making sense (often referred to as cultural traditions). As an example, we might remember the controversy generated by Antonioni's use of the close shot in his film on China,[9] or the different ways in which notions of realism are deployed in relation to various types of melodrama in Asia. Further examples can be found in films which engage with the connotations generated by particular landscapes within particular cultures, or with the differing meanings attached to, for instance, images of industrialisation. It is regarding this set of issues that notions of Third Cinema can most productively be deployed. Similarly, since the Hollywood model of character narration is accepted as the norm in Euro-American film studies, the modes of studying Hollywood narrative and its counter-cinemas have been presented as equally universal and normative, duplicating and confirming the position of the economic power enjoyed by Hollywood.

The third reason is the forced, as well as the elective, internationalism of film industries themselves. The capital-intensive nature of film production, and of its necessary industrial, administrative and technological infrastructures, requires a fairly large market in which to amortise production costs, not to mention the generation of surplus for investment or profit. This means that a film industry – any film industry – must address either an international market or a very large domestic one. If the latter is available, then cinema requires large potential audience groups, with the inevitable homogenising effects that follow from this, creating an industrial logic which, if played out at a national level, will benefit from the equally homogenising project of nationalism. The economic facts of cinematic life dictate that an industrially viable cinema shall be multinational or, alternatively, that every citizen shall be made to contribute to the national film industry, regardless of whether they consume its films or not.

If the question of national specificity is posed in this context, it is at the level of national and governmental institutions, since they are the only ones in a position to inflect legislation and to redistribute tax revenues. And that fact has unavoidable consequences for the social power relations that govern the kind of cinema thus enabled. Consequently, a cinema which seeks to engage with the questions of national specificity from a critical, non- or counter-hegemonic position is by definition a minority and a poor cinema, dependent on the existence of a larger multinational or nationalised industrial sector (most national cinemas operate a mixed economic regime, but that does not alter the argument: it merely creates a little more breathing space for film-makers). By the same token, a cinema addressing national specificity will be anti- or at least non-nationalistic, since the more it is complicit with nationalism's homogenising project, the less it will be able to engage critically with the complex, multidimensional and multidirectional tensions that characterise and shape a social formation's cultural configurations.

This leads us to the ironic conclusion that a cinema positively yet critically seeking to engage with the multi-layeredness of specific socio-cultural formations is necessarily a marginal and a dependent cinema: a cinema dependent for its existence on the very dominant export and multinational-oriented cinema it seeks to criticise and displace. This too is a paradox worthy of Archibald, because this marginal and dependent cinema is simultaneously the only form of national cinema available: it is the only cinema which consciously and directly works with and addresses the materials at work within the national cultural constellation. The issue of national cinema is then primarily a question of address, rather than a matter of the film-makers' citizenship or even of the production finance's country of origin.

Cultural Specificity as an Analytical Construct

For the Soviet cultural theorist Mikhail Bakhtin, there are three kinds of interpretation which correlate with three different ways of framing relations with other socio-cultural networks.[10]

The first is a kind of projective appropriation (my term). This happens when the reader/viewer projects him or herself, his or her belief world, onto the texts. The most common example of this practice happens when a theoretical or interpretative framework elaborated for and within one cultural sphere is projected onto the signifying practices of another cultural sphere. To project early twentieth-century Western novelistic criteria of psychological verisimilitude onto 40s commercial Indian films would be one such example. Another would be the assumption that Leavisite or Baudrillardian aesthetic ideologies are universally applicable norms. Projective appropriation accompanies efforts to internationalise a restrictive regime of making sense. It is concerned with conquering markets, eliminating competition and securing monopolies.

The second type is what I would call ventriloquist identification. This is the obverse of projective identification and happens when someone presents him or herself as the mouthpiece for others, as if the speaker were immersed in some ecstatic fusion with the others' voices and were speaking from within that other social or cultural space. The fantasy at play here, in the realm of film studies as well as in filmmaking, is that of the middle-class intellectual or entrepreneur who is so traumatised by his or her privileged education and access to expensive communications technology that he or she feels compelled to abdicate from intellectual responsibilities and to pretend to be a mere hollow vessel through which the voice of the oppressed, the voice of other people, resonates. The attitude remains the same regardless of whether those other people are defined in terms of class, gender, ethnicity, religion, nationality, community or whatever. Ventriloquism is the monopolist-imperialist's guilty conscience: it allows him or her to remain an authoritarian monopolist while masquerading as 'the oppressed'.

The third type, predictably, avoids both these undesirable but very widespread attitudes. It does not appropriate the other's discourse, it does not subordinate itself to the other's discourse and neither does it pretend to be fused with it. With increasing frequency, this third practice is described with the Bakhtinian phrase: the dialogic mode. Unfortunately, this is a complete misunderstanding of Bakhtin's notion of dialogism, which is in fact an inherent characteristic of all language and of all communication. In other words, it is completely meaningless to try to distinguish one practice from another by calling one dialogic and the other, presumably, monologic. It is worth pointing out that Bakhtin revised his work on Dostoevsky in the light of this insight into the social nature of language itself, and tried to distinguish between the ways in which texts activated their inherently dialogic aspects.

More useful is Bakhtin's notion of creative understanding and the crucial concept of alterity, of otherness, which he introduces into his theories. Bakhtin argues for a necessary alterity, and this aspect of his work is far more important, though usually overlooked, than the now fashionably inflated reference to The Dialogic.

To clarify this point, I would like to repeat the quote from Bakhtin on creative understanding, or, as Raymond Williams called it, diagnostic understanding:

> There exists a very strong, but one-sided and thus untrustworthy idea that in order better to understand a foreign culture, one must enter into it, forgetting one's own, and view the world through the eyes of this foreign culture [this is what I called ventriloquist identification]. Of course, the possibility of seeing the world through its eyes is a necessary part of the process of understanding it; but if this were the only aspect [i]t would merely be a duplication and would not entail anything enriching. Creative understanding does not renounce itself, its own place and time, its own culture; it forgets nothing. In order to understand, it is immensely important [t]o be located outside the object of creative understanding, in time, in space, in culture. In the realm of culture, outsideness is a most powerful factor in understanding. [W]e raise new questions for a foreign culture, ones it did not raise for itself [this is worth stressing since it is almost always overlooked: film- or videomakers do not engage critically with, for instance, the community group they work with]; we seek answers to our questions in it; and the foreign culture responds to us by revealing to us its new aspects and semantic depths. Without one's own questions, one cannot creatively understand anything other or foreign. Such a dialogic encounter of two cultures does not result in merging or mixing. Each retains its own unity and open totality, but they are both enriched.[11]

My own conclusion from Bakhtin's discussion of creative understanding is that one must be other oneself if anything is to be learned about the meanings of other cultures, of another culture's limits, the effectiveness of its borders, of the areas where, in another memorable phrase of Bakhtin's, 'the most intense and productive life of culture takes place'.

It must be stressed that for Bakhtin, creative understanding requires a thorough knowledge of at least two cultural spheres. It is not simply a matter of engaging in a dialogue with some other culture's products, but of using one's understanding of another cultural practice to re-perceive and rethink one's own cultural constellation at the same time. If the critical study of, say, Chinese or Indian cinemas is not also aimed at modifying our Euro-American notions of cinema, then why study these cultural practices at all? Simple curiosity does not sound like a persuasive answer to such a question.

Bakhtin and Film Studies
Bakhtin's three ways of relating to other cultural practices can be neatly illustrated by the way in which Western film critics and other

214

film writers, including Indian ones, regrettably, approach commercial Indian cinema.

The first and most widespread approach is a demonstration of Bakhtin's first type of interpretation: projective identification. It deploys a scornful amusement at Indian commercial cinema, marvelling at the infantile eccentricities of an intellectually underdeveloped mass audience supplied with entertainment by a film industry that matches its quaintly simple-minded naiveté. The criteria used to justify such a discourse invariably erect a mid-twentieth-century European bourgeoisie's notions of art into a self-evident, universally applicable norm against which to test the rest of humanity's degree of civilisation. Increasingly, a variant of this approach can be found in the writings of advocates of the post-modernist persuasion, who project the modalities of finance capital's corporate cultural forms (corporate raiding and short-term investments in diversified portfolios for quick profits) onto 'the global culture'.

The second approach mirrors this process of projective identification, but simply operates an ethical inversion of the terms. Anglo-American notions of popular culture are projected onto the Indian cinema and, suddenly, the products of the Indian film industry become examples of 'the people's culture' in exactly the same way that, for instance, Hollywood is said to be a site of the people's culture in the West. Such an inversion of projective identification corresponds with Bakhtin's second type of relation, which I called ventriloquist identification. It validates the commercial Indian cinema by pointing to the vast box-office takings of its more lucrative products. Something that such large numbers of people want to pay for must be popular culture. To dismiss the cultural products involved is to dismiss those who derive pleasure from them. On the other hand, to validate the products is to identify with the downtrodden people who enjoy them.

An unfailing characteristic of this populist position is the constant reference to pleasure in its discourses. In fact, such a position equates units of pleasure with units of the local currency as they appear on the balance sheet of a business enterprise. It also fails to distinguish between the various types of pleasure that can be derived from cultural practices or objects: for instance, the pleasures of mastery, of submission, of repetition, of difference, of narcissism, and so on. Consequently, the populist position is also blind to the way in which particular cultural-economic practices seek to bind specific pleasures to specific types of product, while ruling other pleasures out of order. In discussions of popular culture in Ukania and in the US, the pleasures of understanding are nearly always outlawed or stigmatised by associating them with, for instance, 'white middle-class male values', a phrase deployed as a kind of ritual curse, but which has little if any explanatory value.

Before going on to talk about Bakhtin's third type, involving a necessary outsideness, a transitional subcategory has to be taken into account. This subcategory corresponds to the traditional scholarly approach to the history of the Indian cinema, chronicling trends and formulating historical narratives, while avoiding, to some extent at least, legitimising or instrumentalising positions. The value of this approach depends on the quality of the historiographic skills deployed. Admittedly, these narratives are often riddled with elements of the populist and of the projectivist tendencies, which does not make life any easier for the reader who has to unravel the useful leads from a hopelessly tangled discursive web. However, this scholarly approach is still to be welcomed for its efforts to provide much-needed information, even though its narratives must be treated with extreme caution.

This is a transitional moment in the process of engagement with otherness, because it still maps the familiar Western reductive paradigms onto, for instance, the development of the Indian film industry. But to the extent that the effort is genuinely scholarly, this type of historiography is also bound to register areas of difference where the object of study resists the interpretative framework projected upon it. For instance, Barnouw and Coomaraswamy's history of the Indian cinema[12] uses Lewis Jacobs's *The Rise of the American Film*[13] as its main model. But whereas Jacobs offers a standard romantic version of the way in which the industry destroys individual genius (Chaplin, Stroheim, Welles), Barnouw and Coomaraswamy find themselves stuck for individual geniuses in the Western mould (until Satyajit Ray). Consequently, they promote powerful actors and studio bosses as the individuals of genius: genius-entrepreneurs, rather than genius-artists. In this way, they have difficulty assessing the value of Guru Dutt or of Ritwik Ghatak, since both operated in relation to India's commercial and traditional (but already inflected by industrialisation) aesthetic practices.

Bakhtin's third type of encounter is only now beginning to be attempted.[14] It is an approach which concentrates on the need to understand the dynamics of a particular cultural practice within its own social formation. However, that social formation is simultaneously taken as an historical construct, and thus as an object of transformation rather than a given essence hiding deep within the national soul. In this way, the analyst's own socio-cultural formation is brought into focus as an historical construct, equally in need of transformation. The engagement with other cultural practices can (and in my view must) thus be geared towards the unblocking, or the transformation, of aspects of the analyst's own cultural situation.

In a way, we are talking here about a double outsideness: the analyst must relate to his or her own situation as an other, refusing simple identifications with pre-given, essentialised socio-cultural cat-

216

egories. At the same time, such identifications with group identities 'elsewhere' must be resisted as well, since the object of study is precisely the intricate, dynamic interconnections of processes which combine to form a social formation, or perhaps better and following Walter Benjamin's terminology, a socio-cultural constellation.[15]

Some of the forces at work in such a constellation will tend towards the containment of elements likely to challenge its fragile and always provisional cohesion, others will tend towards the consolidation of unequal balances of power, still others will promote collusion with, or resistance to, the reigning balance of power, and so on. Identities, whether subjective or group ones, are riven as well as constituted by such processes-in-tension. Indeed, identities are the names we give to the more or less stable figures of condensation located at the intersection of psycho-social processes.

With such an approach, it becomes possible to ask questions outlawed by populist instrumentalism as well as by projectivist appropriation. In the case of the Indian cinema, it allows us to address questions regarding the mobilisation of pre-capitalist ideologies, and capitalist but anti-imperialist tendencies, among urban workers and underclasses; about the operative differences between central and regional capitals, and so on. It allows us to envisage the possibility that in some circumstances (but which ones?), bourgeois cultural trends may have a greater emancipatory potential than anti-capitalist ones which hark back to an idealised fantasy of pre-colonial innocence.

More importantly, the outsideness approach requires us to conceptualise texts and other practices as potentially comprising many different, even contradictory strands: some aspects of a text may pull in one direction, while others will pull in a totally different direction, with yet others exerting pressure in diametrically opposite directions, and so on. For me, the fundamental question to ask of a film is: in which direction does this particular bundle of discourses, on balance and in the present situation, seek to move its viewers or readers? Obviously, answers to that question will always be provisional and context-dependent, that is to say, dependent on the context within which these questions and answers are meant to achieve a degree of productivity.

Finally, a caveat may be in order. Although it is necessary for Western intellectuals to address, for instance, Indian cinema with one eye on their own situation, their other eye must remain focused on the potential effects of their discourses within the Indian situation. This uncomfortably cross-eyed mode of operation is absolutely vital if Western intellectuals, however well intentioned, are to avoid obstructing the work of Indian comrades and their allies. The unfortunate facts of imperialism mean that the power relations between Indian and Western intellectuals are still uneven. This is clearly evident, for instance, from the fact that Indian film-makers can secure production finance at least partly on the strength of their reputation in the West.

Consequently, Western intellectuals, in their efforts to draw attention to particular aspects of cultural practices in India likely to assist desirable developments in Western cultural practices, must be careful not to lend inadvertent support to work which, in India, obstructs the very positions they are trying to support. Differences between Ireland and Ukania require a similar approach, as do differences between East and West Germany. If this cross-eyed dialectic is forgotten, the term 'specificity' loses any meaning and with it any notions of 'creative understanding' or of 'diagnostic understanding' go out of the window. That would be unfortunate, since a position of double outsideness, hybridity and in-between-ness is the precondition for any useful engagement with 'the national' in film culture.

Notes

1. Sylvia Lawson, *The Archibald Paradox – A Strange Case of Authorship* (Victoria: Penguin Books Australia, 1987).
2. Tom Nairn, *The Enchanted Glass – Britain and its Monarchy* (London: Radius, 1988).
3. In Sue Cramer (ed.), *Postmodernism: A Consideration of the Appropriation of Aboriginal Imagery* (Brisbane: Institute of Modern Art, 1989).
4. This paper was written in the summer of 1989, before Eastern Europe's surrender in the Cold War.
5. See, for instance, the discussions about legislative measures reported in *Filméchange*, the most informative French media publication to emerge in recent years. See also Pat Mellencamp's recent work on media case law in the US, presented in a brief discussion at the International Communications Association Annual Conference in Dublin, 1990 (publication forthcoming); see also Jane Gaines, 'Superman and the Protective Strength of the Trademark', in Patricia Mellencamp (ed.), *Logics of Television* (Bloomington: Indiana University Press, 1990).
6. For an exposition of the arguments I am opposing in this section, see 'Narrating the nation' in Homi K. Bhabha (ed.), *Nation and Narration* (London: Routledge, 1990).
7. See, for example, my remarks on David Bordwell's analysis of Ozu's work in Chapter 2.
8. See, for instance, the setting-up of the Asian Film Studies Association in the USA and the proliferation of conferences devoted to Asian film studies in 1989–1990.
9. For a detailed commentary on this episode, see Sam Rohdie, *Antonioni* (London: BFI, 1990).
10. Mikhail Bakhtin, *Speech Genres & Other Late Essays* (Austin: University of Texas Press, 1986).
11. Mikhail Bakhtin, 'Response to a Question from Novy Mir Editorial Staff', in *Speech Genres & Other Late Essays*.
12. E. Barnouw and S. Krishnaswamy, *Indian Film* (New York: Columbia University Press, 1963).

218

13. Lewis Jacobs, *The Rise of the American Film – A Critical History* (New York: Teachers College Press, University of Columbia, 1939).
14. See my remarks on the Third Cinema approach to criticism in Chapter 10.
15. Quoted in Susan Buck-Morss, 'Walter Benjamin – Revolutionary Writer; Pt. 1', *New Left Review*, no. 128, 1981, p. 57.

Part Four

Chapter 12

Through the Glass Darkly:
Cinephilia Reconsidered

In British cultures, the selection of cinema as an object of study has never been associated with cinephilia. In other words, the desire for cinema has never been accepted as a sufficient reason. Those who manifestly did show signs of such a desire have been forced to find alibis for it in order to be allowed to practise it in public. Whereas, for instance, in France there has been a consistently intelligent and vocal resistance against this imposition ever since the theorists of *photogénie* in the 1920s, in Britain compliance with the social demand to cover up the manifestations of desire for cinema has been the rule for nearly a century. The social demand to cover up can be explained in a number of ways, most of them originating in the class connotations attached to the encounter between the amateur techno-fetishism of the inventors and the fairground which gave rise to cinema. Especially since the resulting art form was immediately mobilised for the relentless industrialisation of culture which coincided with and has been a key weapon in the bourgoisie's victory over feudal absolutist social formations (at the cost of two 'world' and countless 'minor' wars) in the first half of the century. Initially, the alibis for loving cinema were provided by ethnographic and political discourses, accounting for the decidedly sociological odour attaching to many discussions of cinema right into the present. The most prominent of these discourses has taken two distinct forms. The first one, quantitatively as well as chronologically, is the moral panic discourse which in successive waves has gripped large sectors of the lower middle class, caught between the Scylla of romantic humanism (developed by a declining aristocracy as a compromise with a rising mercantile bourgeoisie) and the Charybdis of populist entertainment ideologies (negotiated between industrial capital and the mass consumers it needed and created). Since both cultural forms are equally threatening to this social sector, moral panics have been orchestrated on cultural terrains in order to secure an area where, with appropriate state backing, the

223

lower middle class can defend itself against the ravages of aristocratic ideologies while escaping, at least in fantasy, the need to face up to the radical dimensions of a culture in which the gratification of desire includes questioning established legality and morality. Hence the hypocrisy of defending both market notions of culture and censorship.

The second form most commonly given to the sociologically inclined alibi is simply an inversion of the moral panic idiom, accepting all its presuppositions about the relationship between films and people's minds but emphasising the medium's potential for exerting a beneficial influence. See, for instance, the endless 'bleeding heart' tele-movies and documentaries as well as most so-called radical film-making. Hence the various demands for a directly political use value for cinema. In either avatar, the desire for cinema is encompassed by a socio-political framework that excludes the very possibility of relating to cinema in any terms other than socio-political productivity manifested in the modification of behaviour.

In Britain, the first major attempt to subvert this framework merely replaced the old alibi with a new one: the literary ideology. Henceforth, films were to be valued, not for their beneficial or deleterious effects on impressionable minds but according to the degree in which a film approximated literary standards. As a political move to obtain legitimation for cinema within the British context, this substitution, carried out by critics and historians as diverse as Ernest Lindgren in the late 40s, *Sight and Sound* in the 50s and *Movie* in the 60s, proved to be a successful ploy. It grafted cinema onto the romantic humanism which was the dominant ideology in the apparatuses of state until the late 70s.

This orthodoxy, coexisting uneasily with the populist entertainment ideologies advocated by the more radical wings of the entrepreneurial bourgeoisie, was challenged in its turn from the early 70s onwards when more radical sectors of the English bourgeoisie sought to impose a more ditect equation between cultural value and market value. At present, vestiges of the old literary humanism can still be found in the film columns of the daily and weekly papers. Television's coverage of the cinema has long since capitulated to Rupert Murdoch's idea of what 'viewers' should accept as cultural value.

Unfortunately, critiques of the humanist-literary orthodoxy in film criticism were proposed mainly by intellectuals detouring through cinema in order to circumvent and to loosen the blockages preventing direct challenges to the dominant ideology in universities' literary departments. Another challenge to the literary ideology was mounted mainly by modernist film-makers who suggested cinema was to be valued according to its approximation of concerns prevailing in discussions of the plastic arts. Although these challenges did clear some space for new approaches to cinema, none directly recognised the central importance of fantasy as a way of accounting both for the films themselves and for our relationship to them. This development emerged from a desire to look at films through the prism of psychoanalytic theory and was activated primarily by feminist film theorists in the mid-70s (as far as Britain is concerned).

However, even though the recourse to psychoanalysis did allow the questions of cinephilia to be addressed, the importation of psychoanalytic terminology was a costly business both for film theory and for psychoanalytic theory. The cost was the erasure of concepts such as transference and resistance from both theoretical discourses. Since the practice of psychoanalysis is inconceivable without these two terms, the psychoanalytic theory mobilised by and for film theory was seriously flawed, to say the least. On the other hand, the absence of these two key concepts allowed critics freely to delegate their neuroses to the films where they would then be 'read'. In effect, this reduced the films to the reader's screen memories. Since then, the relation between psychoanalysis and film theory has been reversed: instead of using random bits of psychoanalytic theory to generate readings of films, now bits of films are used to introduce readers to psychoanalytic theory (cf. the work of Slavoj Zizek).

With the rapid ossification of a film theory prematurely ensconced in academia where it has been tailored to the requirements of curricula and with the turn to television in the later 1970s, even the productive potential of the challenges to the sociological and the literary ideologies has been neglected as old film theory was served up as new television theory. The 'alternative' derived from the plastic arts discourse degenerated into the scavenging of the half-understood detritus of fine arts debates and advertising hype for an amateurish but resolutely careerist bricolage passed off as 'postmodern' media theories.

Now that cinema and film theory are threatened with extinction, a variety of new options for approaching cinema can be conceived. The main one, practised with great skill by, for instance, Peter Wollen, is to begin seeing film in a historical context where it can be integrated into a broad-ranging analysis of cultural histories. Another one, able to coexist with the historical approach, is exemplified by the work of Serge Daney. His critical practice revolved around questions of cinephilia, that is to say, around explorations of the desire that sustained cinema and which is now being rerouted in alignment with the requirements of what Daney dismissively called 'the audio visual', or, in more familiar Anglo-Saxon terms, the needs of the communications industries dominated by advertisers and hardware manufacturers.

Discussing these issues with an Australian colleague, Noel King, we decided to use the format of the interview to try and clarify, at least in our own minds, what it might mean to think about the desire for cinema, that is to say, about cinephilia. These exploratory discussions were held in London in September 1992 and constitute no more than a preliminary reconnoitering of the terrain.

NK: We have been talking for a couple of days about cinephilia and why it is of interest to you at the moment. I realise you're still working out exactly what it is about cinephilia that interests you, and that you are still in the process of deciding how you want to talk about it. But it's already clear that it is a question of how cinephilia relates to the cinematic system in terms of broader issues concerning representation. And it's also clear that it involves the way cultural discourses circulate in particular historical conjunctures. Furthermore, it seems that cinephilia, for you, has some sort of connection with your 1981 essay on 'Epstein and Photogénie'.[1] So, could you begin by setting out in broad terms your interest in notions of cinephilia?

PW: First of all, it has to be understood that my current interest in notions of cinephilia is programmed by a number of other problems. I am still giving these thoughts room to play, and I do not yet feel I have arrived at any conclusions to which I would want to attach a longer-term value. It is work that needs to be done and which addresses a number of neurotic knots in current film cultures, but I'm still trying to locate the actual import of notions of cinephilia. It may well be that the very notion of cinephilia is a displacement, a smoke-screen for something else. After all, that has been the case for most widely-used terms in the film-critical vocabulary. Most of them have turned out, in some sense, to be displacements.

NK: For example?

PW: Montage. It's such a vague concept. It means that things are being put together and it thereby deflects attention from what is being put together. The whole debate is based on false premises, as is shown by the varieties of possible 'montages' in, for instance, music video, or when orchestrating fields in depth within a sequence shot, to give just two examples. Discussions of montage generally avoid thinking about exactly what is being montaged. I also think the so-called debate between realism and modernism that was conducted in the 60s and 70s, but much earlier in literature and in the fine arts, also operated on false premises because it assumed a truly fanciful periodisation of history. The other example I could give nowadays is postmodernism. Those are all displacement terms which link into a lot of totally different, sometimes mutually exclusive preoccupations. A particular term is widely circulated, widely taken up, and then someone comes along and tries to give it an essential definition, which is not the point because the whole reason for the term being in

226

circulation in the first place is that it can cover different fields without specifying what is meant. As soon as you look at it more closely, it vanishes, like sand between your fingers. So cinephilia might well prove to be one of those terms.

NK: With the case of postmodernism, you have a reasonably constrained set of debates as to whether it's an historical period, a set of textual forms, a cultural logic, a genre of theoretical discourse, a machine for generating a set of binary relations to other 'isms' (modernism, Marxism, feminism, postcolonialism). To that extent, it might resemble the currency given to terms such as 'new historicism' or 'neo-pragmatism' within North-American literary-cultural criticism. But cinephilia, for me, names a regularity of critical description. You find anyone, from a 50s or 60s French critic writing in *Cahiers du Cinéma* or *Positif* through to someone writing now in *Film Comment* or *Cinema Papers*, all of them targeting films in a particular way. And that's what interests me. Across the apparent diversity of cinephilic practice one finds a regularity of critical description. There is always the fetishising of a particular moment, the isolating of a crystallisingly expressive detail and so on.

PW: Not all cinephiles would agree with that.

NK: You don't always ask the patient for an account of his or her particular pathology. What would they think they were doing?

PW: They would think they were just, as the word says, 'loving cinema'. They would not necessarily privilege one aspect of cinema. In a sense that's the problem I'm trying to address through the notion of cinephilia. Cinephilia itself describes simultaneously a particular relationship to cinema (and the question then opens up of what kind of relationship that might be) and it also describes a particular historical period of relating to cinema. The heyday of cinephilia runs roughly from the early 1950s to the late 1960s. In that sense 1968 was more or less the end of cinephilia. So one could describe cinephilia in terms of a particular kind of classic narrative cinema (its parody included) which would go from, say, film noir (and whatever antecedents you can construct for it in the United States or elsewhere) to Godard's parodies or recontructions of his notion of cinephilia: that is, of his experience of relating to that kind of cinema. And both of those would be part of the cinephiliac moment, the cinephilic moment I should say. Actually the cinephiliac moment is my preferred description because of its overtones of necrophilia, of relating to something that is dead, past, but alive in memory. So there is a kind of necrophilia involved, and I don't mean that negatively.

NK: What would be the option? What would be a relation to cinema that wasn't necrophiliac in some way?

PW: One would historicise it. I would say that cinephilia describes a relationship to cinema that is still uncontaminated by a relationship to television although it was constructed within the period when television became a cultural presence. This is not how I would have put it at the time. With hindsight, that historical period can be seen to relate to that moment of transition until the late 60s when there was a massive focus on the so-called 'mediatic society', involving the need to take account of the daily and political impact of the mediatic environment in relation to which our thoughts are formed. And the so-called major discovery of ideology in the late 60s is then no more, also no less, than the taking into account of a condition of living and thinking which is deeply imbricated in a massive proliferation of industrialised messages. It's a process of industrialisation that is still going on, with television and advertising as the most obvious formats. It involves the proliferation of, not necessarily the written press in general, but certainly the periodical press. The massive importance of newspapers has always been recognised, but the situation of the periodical press is crucial. It is related to the economic boom of the 1950s. All those aspects suddenly become problems in the culture, and in the politics of culture. The best-known reference point here would be Guy Debord's *Society of the Spectacle*[2] and the Situationists. Its a kind of reactivation of Surrealism in the light of the emergence of this different kind of mediatic society. So I'm also using slogans such as 'the mediatic society' to refer to something vague that is perceived as happening in the culture without knowing exactly what it is. But the fact that there is an obscure feeling that something has shifted, and that it is in the area of relationships to media, becomes an issue which is then discussed in terms of ideology, subjectivity and (eventually) pleasure. Consequently one could say that something to do with cinephilia is involved with that pre-televisual, pre-68 relationship to an incipient mediatisation of the social. And at that time the medium of cinema is simultaneously the most widespread and the most visible, the most immediately relevant, to people growing up. It's also bound up with the post-war period of economic boom, with certain notions of liberation still very prevalent in the exit from a war-time period when all kinds of cinema were not accessible. Films flooded into Europe immediately after the war and became a larger or more obvious cultural presence than they had been before the war precisely because of that gap in between. So the return of cinema made an impression which is qualitatively different from the pre-war period.

NK: Two things about that. Is it a problem for your historical periodising that television begins in North America in 1946? And secondly, given my understanding of cinephilia as a particular critical practice, what interests me is that the fetishistic cinephilic gaze can be transposed quite happily to TV. Different generations of television viewers watch and valorise different television programmes, from *Bonanza* to *The Avengers* and *The Addams Family*. So why wouldn't those televisual objects perform the same function or be implicated in the same sorts of critical operations that are going on in cinephilia?

PW: Let's make a distinction. Let's split that relation to television from the start. First of all, the relationship to television in the post-war period was deeply implicated in the history of the cinema. This was particularly the case during the live period, the so-called 'golden-age' when a notion of 'liveness' was fetishised in its own terms. Actually, at that time, television was on the edge between theatre and cinema and as such was available to an aspect of cinephilia, as I understand it. That availability was destroyed a few years later when the golden age of live drama in the States was replaced by pro-grammed, short, filmed dramas which came from Hollywood. Tele-vision recycled many of the same fantasies as Hollywood and tried to put the same utopias into play. There was, consequently, a moment in the 60s and early 70s when telephilia was proposed as an equivalent to cinephilia. The concept didn't take off. You can tell why by look-ing at the main book on/of the telephiliac moment, Chris Wicking's and Tise Vahimagi's *The American Vein*. There they try to do an Andrew Sarris on television.[3] The people they talk about are either minor Hollywood figures or wannabe Hollywood figures. In either case, they are talking about directors measured by the standards of an old but still dominant model. Once again there is a notion of retros-pection, a sense of a bygone era clinging to that book. By the time it's born this particular notion of television is already telephiliac, necro-philiac. It is not a description of a contemporary relationship to contemporary television. In the wake of that development, one finds an attempt at a weakened replay of a memory of cinephilia on the part of certain people who used to harbour fantasies of being pro-gressive. Then, when these radical critics become dutiful sons, daughters, fathers, mothers, they stay home watching television and, predictably or oddly enough, they try to replay, in terms of television, the retrospective fantasy of a once-upon-a-time relationship to an image-discourse that is no longer available to them. Of course, I am generalising, but although it would probably be libellous, it certainly wouldn't be difficult to reel you off a list of names of TV critics and 'theorists' who would fit that description. There are, therefore, two ways in which telephilia and cinephilia are linked. One involves the notion of pastness, an element of nostalgia, which is not strictly personal but actually relates to a notion of the periodisation of mediatic forms, with telephilia trying to recapture a previous phase of the relationship to the industrialisation of culture. The second shared aspect is the replay of a relationship to Hollywood cinema. The question simply returns: what element of the relationship to the screen or to cinematic narrative is being designated by the notion of cinephilia and is being re-evoked in the notion of telephilia? The question just returns and stays there. I don't think telephilia is an alternative. Besides, as a critical discourse, telephilia only relates to television drama. It doesn't relate to game shows or to gardening programmes, which are thought to be the domain of sociology and politics. It doesn't relate to news programmes either. It relates overwhelmingly to drama, and that's worth pointing out in terms of the filiation from cinephilia to telephilia.

NK: I want to ask about the way the cinephilic/cinephiliac description of a particular cinematic moment introduces the notion of a representational limit. You claim that it is the identification of a moment in which something (a gesture, a voice), some element within the representational system, evokes a sense of its own 'beyond'. That it is a kind of moment of representational *aufhebung*, supersession.

PW: In working on cinephilia, I'm increasingly trying to focus not on the terms which people use to describe things, or on the rationalisations given, but rather on the vague sense of change that seems to underpin a desire for a shift in terminology. It's clear that certain terms (postmodernism and so on) routinely come into and go out of fashion. Some of these terms have different life-spans and something is being gestured towards by these shifts in terminology. It is an obscurely perceived notion of change. I stress 'obscurely perceived' because I don't believe that what is being designated by the people who try to legitimate their usage of the terms, who try to define the terms, actually is what it is all about. For instance, an art historical 'ism' is never about what those who define it say it is about. Such an 'ism' is either a bundle of characteristics which can always be detected in a wide variety of historical periods and places (that is to say, it never coincides with the historical placement of the label), or it designates a cultural-historical moment at the cost of abusively simplifying and reducing the phenomena one is trying to describe. Procrustes comes to mind in that context. I increasingly suspect that we don't know what we're talking about.

NK: When we talk about ... ?

PW: When we begin to talk in different terms, having sensed that it is necessary to shift terminology. We do that in response to an obscurely perceived shift in periodisation that is occurring somewhere, without actually knowing where that is. Is it an economic shift, an historical watershed, a cultural modification or mutation, a shift in regimes of perception? Is it manipulated by the State, the party, industry, whatever? There are various, as I say, 'obscurely perceived' shifts, 'through-a-glass darkly' senses of shifts, to which people like us, the semi-professionals of discourse, try to point. But all we do is point in a general direction. We don't actually know what we're pointing at. We know there's something happening over there, somewhere, and it's in trying to give an account of that 'something happening' that the terminology shifts. But the new terms merely repeat the gesture of pointing, they do not clarify much at all. As I said, their use value probably is precisely in their inability to produce clarity: people can use them in all kinds of ways, even contradictory ones. The mere fact of using the new terms allows us to signal, or to fantasise, that we too have sensed the shift. That is all.

NK: What is happening in the shift to the notion of cinephilia and the shift out of it? What is at stake in its circulation as something to defend or criticise, having its death declared or its fitful survival announced?

PW: In order to try to give an account of what is meant by notions of cinephilia, we have to think about resistance via the notion of the Lacanian Real. There's probably nothing there but something keeps resisting. There is the sense of a repetition, of a persistence within a discourse which we point to with the term cinephilia. Cinephilia doesn't do anything other than designate something which resists, which escapes existing networks of critical discourse and theoretical frameworks. What is this thing that keeps cropping up in all these different forms and keeps being called cinephilia? What is the discourse of cinephilia hovering around? It has never been a coherent discourse. It has always been a semi-journalistic, publicistic, sloganised discourse. And in thinking about what cinephilia might loosely be pointing towards, we first of all have to realise that it is a French term, located in a particular rationalisation or attempted explanation of a relationship to cinema that is embedded in French cultural discourses.

The privileged moment of that history seems to me to be the notion of *photogénie*. *Photogénie* was the first major attempt to theorise a relationship to the screen. It was a notion that was in solidarity with a polemic about the cinema conducted by the Surrealists. Although it was opposed to the Surrealists, the *photogénie* discourse was part of a battery of terms which were in play, being contested in relation to an argument dominated by the Surrealists as cultural consumers and activists. These terms were also deemed relevant by film-makers and critics who were not necessarily themselves Surrealists, but who were engaged with that same thing towards which the Surrealists were pointing and which they also talked about in relation to the photograph: the capturing of fleeting, evanescent moments.

The second over-determination in play is a whole discourse about the industrialisation and mechanisation of the visible. This discourse talks about the revelatory powers of the photograph and of the image-in-movement, from the late nineteenth century onwards. It includes Marey and Muybridge and their notions of chrono-photography, of movement constituted in time: all the things that Deleuze talks about in his *Movement-Image* book and that Virilio talks about in terms of shifts in regimes of perception which happen under the impact of the mechanisation, the industrialisation of image-production.[4] Basically, it's the shift out of painting. This attempt to grasp what was happening to regimes of perception was itself highly inflected by a set of Catholic concepts which were already very widespread in the culture, and had been for a long time. Principally this is the discourse of revelation. It's a discourse which takes many forms in relation to cinema. The whole argument around realism hinges on a discourse of revelation just as the whole *Cahiers du Cinéma* auteur polemic basically was a discourse of revelation, the revelation of the soul. Whether it was the soul of the viewer being projected onto the screen, the soul of the actress being revealed in Rossellini's *Stromboli* or the soul of Hitchcock being revealed in *I Confess*, there was always a discourse of revelation under it all in different modalities.

In 50s and 60s France, cinephilia was particularly incarnated in the debates around *Positif*, *Cahiers du Cinéma* and MacMahon, with the MacMahonists, who were, in a sense, the radical wing of the French cinephiliacs and congregated around the Cinema MacMahon, which, at the time, primarily programmed recent past Hollywood cinema. Their main journal was *Présence du cinéma*. Cinephilia became part of a discourse that unified the relationship to the cinema of groups of people who otherwise had positions quite opposed to one another. *Positif* and *Cahiers du Cinéma* were very opposed to each other but also unified by a notion of cinephilia. The MacMahonist and *Cahiers* groups had many debates, schisms, fall-outs, but what unified them was that notion of cinephilia, anecdotally represented by the fact that they all saw one another in the front rows of the cinema, grooving on their relationship to cinema which they then went away and rationalised into different types of positions.[5]

The only thing that persists, the only resistance, the only trace of the Real in this discourse of cinephilia has something to do with what you perceive to be the privileged, pleasure-giving, fascinating moment of a relationship to what's happening on a screen. Almost by necessity, it becomes a question of something being revealed in a social relationship, because the relationship to cinema is a social relationship. Something is being activated and revealed in that relationship. A revelation is being delegated to the screen in the same sense that *photogénie* delegated certain privileged moments to the screen. For example, Sessue Hayakawa coming into the room in *The Cheat*, his body at a certain angle, in a particular position, opening the door, entering with a particular body language, was isolated by Epstein as a particular moment of *photogénie*. It was seen to be something that escaped rationalised, critical-theoretical discourse. Epstein perceived something in that moment which he built into a theory. He also found this thing in faces as they were reproduced on the screen (some faces, not others). Later critics, whether writing in *Positif*, *Cahiers* or *Présence du Cinéma*, reproduced in a professional and sometimes pleasurably stylistic way aspects which the non-critics (of which I was a part at that time) reproduced in their daily conversations. When school friends and I talked about the films we had seen, there was an overlap between the way we did that and the professional, stylised public performance of critical discourse as circulated by film magazines. And there again, I think film magazines created their following in areas of obscurely perceived overlaps which were translated into the way we say: 'I like that magazine and I hate that magazine.' Very loosely articulated, short-hand designations were in play which were actually covering the complex processes in which a multitude of possible pleasures were imbricated, of obscurely perceived coincidences of relationships which you felt this magazine shared and that magazine inflected in a way you were out of sympathy with. These were shorthand terms. One could use the word 'emotional' to describe them, but I don't, because it's a combination of affect, pleasure, intensity, neuroses and their forms of rationalisation, all of which go hand in hand. They are obscure, experiential, shorthand ways of designating at least a partial overlap of a mode of understanding and a mode of experiencing. It is not strictly 'emotional' but it has the same vagueness with which one uses emotional terminology.

In asking myself what exactly it is that all these people have in common when they talk cinephiliacly about cinema, all I can answer is that they have a 'love of cinema' in the same way that you can love any kind of collecting activity. And perhaps that notion of collecting objects is not a bad analogy in the sense that you are there talking about discrete objects, moments, which are being serialised in your mind into collections, which is how Walter Benjamin talked about it, I seem to remember. In the end, perhaps, the moment of cinephilia has to do with the serialisation of moments of revelation. That is the conclusion I draw from locating it in that nexus of discourses and cultural practices.

NK: The obvious question to ask now is, what is being revealed?

PW: I can't detect any consistency amongst cinephiles, beyond a broad selection of similar 'good objects'. Basically that means Hollywood cinema between the Korean war and the Bay of Pigs.[6] That seems to be the privileged object of cinephilia, but it spills over on either side of Hollywood and it spills across the Atlantic. What is being revealed is not the same to all critics. All critics do not select the same privileged moments to which they attach their cinephilia. It's the same when people talk on street corners after seeing a film, saying which moments they liked. The moments are different but each is talking about a pleasurable relation to that particular film. The difference in selection is less important than the fact that you are signalling the relationship of pleasures generated between you and the screen, generated by that particular film (because its not just any old film). I think one example that is dear to your heart is the scene in *On the Waterfront* involving Brando, Eva Marie Saint and the gloves, and the fact that critics focus on that set of gloves rather than the use of gloves in the later scene between Brando and Steiger.

NK: Let me remind you of my obsession in that particular regard. The famous dropped glove scene between Brando and Eva Marie Saint is usually cited as an example of the way an adventitious, unrehearsed event occurring in the performance of the script provides an occasion for Brando's method training or intuitive genius (you can go either way) to exhibit itself. He puts the 'accident' to use. Watching that scene, having read *Kazan on Kazan*,[7] I tend to notice the number of times Eva Marie Saint tries to retrieve the glove and the things Brando does to delay this happening. But would I 'see' or 'find' such a representational aspect if I hadn't read *Kazan on Kazan*? For me, that scene shows Brando performing a familar anti-romantic yet romantic trope. I don't know if it could be said to be distinctively American but it's a situation in which we are presented with the paradox of the eloquent inarticulateness of the working-class figure. Remember his speech describing her when she was younger: she had 'wire' on her teeth, her hair was 'like rope', she was 'a real mess'. And this is followed by: 'All I mean to say, you turned out real nice.' That scene obviously made possible the Stallone/Talia Shire scenes in *Rocky*. But why do I concentrate on this part of this scene? Romance is performed elsewhere in the scene, when he asks her whether she remembers him and she says yes. He says 'Some people got faces you remember' and touches his nose, turning his head to the side. Or the later scene where he takes her to the bar and says 'You're sore at me', before delivering the famous 'I got the rest of my life to drink' line. I realise I'm privileging lines of dialogue but it's always dialogue accompanied by a facial or bodily gesture. For example the presentation of Brando's eyebrows, scarred from boxing, in the bar scene as he hunches his face into his hand. When I fetishise those sorts of scenes it's usually because of dialogue performed via bodily gesture, a mix-

234

ture of vocality and *mise en scène*. And in the very famous cab scene between Brando and Steiger, a scene also involving some play (on Steiger's part) with a glove, but never remembered for that in the way the earlier park scene always is, Kazan claims the scene is 'made' by the tone of voice Brando uses in saying 'Aw Charlie', even before he gets onto the 'I coulda been a contender' speech that is reprised in Scorsese's *Raging Bull*. As a cinephile, I could as readily fetishise, to name some favourites, Jean Arthur's voice, Henry Fonda's way of walking in *My Darling Clementine*, Barbara Stanwyck's performance in *The Lady Eve*. If it is the function of the cinephile to identify an epiphanic moment, how many forms can the epiphany take?

PW: I'm glad you used the word 'epiphanic'. If you read the early *Cahiers* stuff that Truffaut and Godard were writing, you see that they were responding to films. They were not doing criticism but were doing written responses to films. They were formulating a rationalisation of a highly Catholic, somewhat right-wing *politique* in France at that time, which came to be known as the *politique des auteurs*. What they were writing at that time was a highly impressionistic account; in T. S. Eliot's terms, an 'evocative equivalent' of moments which, to them, were privileged moments of the film. You have just listed a number of such moments that characterise your particular cinephilia. These are moments which, when encountered in a film, spark something which then produces the energy and the desire to write, to find formulations to convey something about the intensity of that spark. And that intensity is then translated and, to some extent, rationalised, secondarised, in the writing, into a *politique* which later on, in Britain, became a theory. But the rationalisation into theory did not make the sparks go away. On the contrary: the theory gave us a keener sense of the dimensions the theory was gesturing towards but which kept escaping it.

NK: Another example would be the way both Truffaut and Godard loved the 'Lie to me' scene from *Johnny Guitar*. That's quoting dialogue again but you'll recall that the scene moves from the kitchen to the bar-room accompanied by the swirling, circling camera movement.

PW: Most film criticism and much journalistic film criticism tends to feel under an obligation to isolate such a moment or a scene; in Anglo-Saxon countries, it is increasingly a line of dialogue rather than an image or a scene, and that's interesting to reflect on. The cinephiliac discourse tends to work on scenes, on moments of gesture, on looks. For example, on Ava Gardner walking barefoot in *The Barefoot Contessa*, or Brigitte Bardot in a particular pose or dress. These are the kinds of moments that are privileged, although people might not agree on the films within which they occur. I remember Ado Kyrou writing about a particular moment in an Italian film by Matarazzo, involving a group of scantily dressed women sweating on a kind of slave ship. It's a real exploitation film, *La Nave delle donne maladette* (1954). But that particular image grabbed Kyrou. Kyrou was the mentor for *Positif* and his books on Surrealism and on *l'amour fou*[8] are crammed full of moments like that. This exemplifies the filiation of Surrealism to cinephilia. At the same time, Kyrou engages tangentially with a notion of a *politique des auteurs*. He too tends to collect certain moments and attribute them to authors. The result of Kyrou getting off on that moment in a Matarazzo film is to say that Matarazzo is an auteur. Similarly, the MacMahonists talk about Ricardo Freda[9] equally enthusiastically. Various other people were being promoted as authors (Don Weiss, for heaven's sake) because they had been the occasion on which a film sparked something in its encounter with a particular set of viewers. The moment of revelation is unstable. You cannot predict with any certainty that this moment will be the cinephiliac moment. Although, again, there is a remarkable convergence of the moments that are isolated.

Maybe all this can only be seen with hindsight. The sheer repetition of some of these moments makes us forget that when these films were written about or talked about on their release in Europe, various other moments were mentioned as well, by different people. It's just the repetition of particular moments, like the *On the Waterfront* one, which become culturally embedded and symbolic in some way. If you look at Godard's early criticism he talks about a Tashlin film, and various other films, by mentioning certain things that anchor his memory of the film and which is then conveyed in the form of an enthusiasm for that film. And he's still doing it in his book on the history of the cinema by reframing photographs.[10] These are almost always details of images. Godard hardly ever uses a still which reproduces the whole of a frame. He will reframe the look or the turn of a face, or the bend of an arm or a shoulder or a neck or whatever. It's the fragment of the image that he focuses on.

So I think one can draw two general conclusions concerning the discourse of cinephilia in relation to what it points to. One is the moment of revelation. Secondly, what is being revealed is subjective, fleeting, variable, depending on a set of desires and the subjective constitution that is involved in a specific encounter with a specific film. And because subjectivities and networks are themselves social, historically variable and so on, there will be both overlaps and similarities between different people reacting, say, in Paris to a particular American film. Nevertheless, there is something that persists, which is the moment of revelation. How is that moment of revelation talked about? You can make a list of the moments that cinephiliacs select. I tend to think that the selection is done, on the one hand, in good

Catholic terms and, on the other hand, in fetishistic terms. Both of them being very valid terms, especially the fetishistic one. The notion of revelation is not peculiar to Catholicism but is embedded very clearly in that particular influential critical discourse we call cinephilia. Its Catholic roots are as relevant as its fetishistic aspects.

When the cinephile selects a fragment, a net is being cast over the film which trawls up particular moments. To persist in my Catholic imagery, we can say there are different fishes of different sizes. One way of accounting for the cinephiliac description would be to say that it has to be an aspect of cinema that is not strictly programmable in terms of aesthetic strategies. What is being looked for is a moment or, given that a moment is too unitary, a dimension of a moment which triggers for the viewer either the realisation or the illusion of a realisation that what is being seen is in excess of what is being shown. Consequently you see something that is revelatory. It reveals an aspect or a dimension of a person, whether it's the actor or the director, which is not choreographed for you to see. It is produced *en plus*, in excess or in addition, almost involuntarily. In a sense, the voluntarism of it is neither here nor there. And if you read the critical discourses about actors, the voluntariness of the ability to produce those signs of excess or revelation can well be designated as the particular genius of a particular actor. So whether or not it's voluntary doesn't particularly matter. If you can systematise the production of these voluntary/involuntary moments, then you become a genius screen presence or a genius director (as in the directorial touches of a Lubitsch or Hitchcock).

NK: Does the category of 'surprise' or the aleatory operate in all this?

PW: In the sense that revelation presupposes surprise or presupposes a moment that is not programmed, then the spark can happen that activates the cinephiliac's pleasures. I don't think, though, that 'surprise' itself is a definitive characteristic because you can go back time and again and reconsume it almost ad infinitum. What you are reconsuming is the moment of revelation experienced in an encounter between you and cinema, which may be different from the person sitting next to you, in which case you have to dig him or her in the ribs with your elbow to alert them to the fact that you've just had a cinephiliac moment. This is a mode of ordinary consumption containing a critical dimension which is quite valid in its own terms and which is actually being relayed in more rationalised film critical discourses. There is a theory of cinema implicit in the dig of the elbow into the ribs just as much as there is in Metz's work. Theoretical networks are involved and I think cinephilia relates to a dimension of that network, a dimension of a theory of cinema. It's a theory that is premised on notions of revelation, on the notion of excess. However, in order for notions of revelation and excess to happen, to be noticeable at all, they have to be demarcated or demarcatable, in some sense, from what else is happening in the film. So it is no accident, indeed it is highly necessary, that cinephilia should operate particularly strongly in relation to a form of cinema that is perceived as being highly coded, highly commercial, formalised and ritualised. For it is only there that the moment of revelation or excess, a dimension other than what is being programmed, becomes noticeable. If that in itself is the system of the film, as, say, in a Stan Brakhage film, you don't have a cinephiliac moment precisely because it's no longer demarcatable. You can't perform the critical trawling operation because the whole film tries to be 'it'. You can fetishise the whole of a Brakhage film (this has been done) but it is hard to fetishise a moment of a Brakhage film. Well, you could but it would require a lot more work than does the fetishising of moments in a Jacques Tourneur or a Fritz Lang film. In those cases, it's precisely the machinic aspect of the cinema which allows you to privilege certain moments more readily and then transpose them into other analogous moments in cinema. For example, in some accounts of neo-realism, Rossellini becomes someone who is able to produce, in the way he conducts his camera and directs his actors in *Stromboli* (especially in his direction of Ingrid Bergman), for our pleasure, certain moments of excess: namely the moment when Bergman reaches the top of the volcano and has a religious experience. Personally, I don't see the religious experience but when the *Cahiers* critics discuss the film, that is what they latch onto and therefore there is something there that is worth thinking about.

NK: What is it?

PW: It's certainly not what they say it is, a religious experience. Why did they choose that moment? Because they can attribute to it a *mise en scène* of excess or point to the genius of Rossellini in his ability to get from a highly professional Hollywood actress something which goes beyond the scenography, the dramaturgy and the stylistics of cinematic narration? Something which is of the same order as an actor making a particular gesture, having a particular body posture, the grain in the voice? One can't be sure, but such things probably are taken into account in casting decisions, as one of those imponderable impressions that you want to mobilise in your film but which is not strictly controllable in terms of the detail of a performance. Therefore, for instance, in relation to the gloves in *On the Waterfront*, one could say that it is the moment of Brando's method training coming through in the film in excess of the role he is playing. Where he gets it from does not really matter. What matters is that something should

238

be perceived as in excess of the film's register of performance, as potentially undesigned, unprogrammed.

NK: But if we were to take seriously some of the discourses and practices of method acting, then those two things you mention might not be separable. For example, the notion of 'emotional memory'. Think of the way some writing on Brando's performance in *Last Tango in Paris* linked it to Brando's anecdote about getting shit on his shoes because he had to do some chores immediately before going on a date one evening when he was young. How could anyone ever see that, spontaneously, in the film? Isn't it rather the case that there exists a film consumer who also reads other things relating to the film? Maybe the cinephilic act of 'reading' a film involves aligning the film's image-discourse with other more or less fanzine writings that attach to, or can be attached to, the film. You don't have to read *Sight and Sound* and *Film Comment* on Eastwood's *Unforgiven* but a cinephile probably would. And perhaps it is that sort of combinatory act that goes some way to defining the reproduction of the cinephile. One account of the history of cinephilia might say that, in the 50s or whenever, cinephilia produces the institution of the magazine/fanzine which in its turn helps recruit future cinephiles.

PW: Yes, magazines have something to do with it, but not so much for those who read them. More for those who write in them: that is where the rationalisations of cinematic pleasure are to be found most readily. Cinephilia has more to do with writing in magazines than with reading them. It is as if cinephilia demands a gestural outlet in writing: if not in magazines then on index cards or in list making. The excess experienced needs an extra, physical ritual, a gesture, in addition to watching and talking. Perhaps it has also something to do with bearing witness: the need to proclaim what has been experienced, to draw attention to what has been seen by 'the elect' but which may not have been noticed by 'routine' viewers. There is always something proselitising about cinephiliac writing, a barely contained impatience with those who have eyes but do not see. The elitist dimension of cinephilia is too well known to require further comment. The important point is that such writing brings us back to the quasi-religious discourse of revelation. As for the emotional aspect of the acting, in the case of Brando and the gloves, the main point is that at that moment he does something which allows you to glimpse Brando incarnating a character. There is a moment of doubling, of ghosting, as they would say in photography, or of double-voicing as Bakhtin would say. Brando emerges from behind the character and does something which is in the function of the character but which the character doesn't necessarily have to do. It's not coded or programmed for the character to do that; consequently there is a moment of hesitation. You cannot say this is Kazan telling Brando to do something which he then more or less competently executes, nor can you say it is Brando doing something that surprises Kazan who then leaves it in. That may well have been the case, but you cannot tell by watching the film. Besides, critical viewing should be immune to the lies a director or an actor or a publicity agent might want to spread: Kazan's decisions can only be known to Kazan and are thus irrelevant for us. It's relatively visible that Brando surprises Eva Marie Saint but, then again, it could be choreographed. The moment of excess is fundamentally undecidable. There is a moment of undecidability, of hesitation, which is inherent in fetishism. It's a fetish precisely because it could be either thing.

NK: How does all this fit into that aspect of cinephilia we discussed earlier, that notion of reaching a representational limit? Could you also say whether in such a fetishising moment one is isolating something in the film that is supposed to be essentially cinematic or something that is alleged to be a quintessential element in a particular film. It would then be a condensation or an expressive detail. Call this the ontology question as it relates to cinephilia. And could you also make some comments on certain representational moments of undecidability, since this seems to be an important part of your account of cinephilia?

PW: There is a moment of potential dislocation, of seeing something beyond what is given to you to see. What is given to you to see, for example, might be Brando acting that role. Then suddenly there is a bit of Brando the person, an aspect of his personal biography or subjectivity coming through, in the same way that there is allegedly something of Ingrid Bergman coming through in the scene on the top of the volcano, or in a gesture of Humphrey Bogart, or in a facial expression of Robert Mitchum, or in the bare feet of Ava Gardner. One could multiply these things ad infinitum but what they have in common is that they are moments of excess which are fished up by particular people in order to designate their relationship of pleasure to a particular film. What is important is that they dig up moments which can only be seen as designating, for those people, something in excess of the representation. So that cinephilia becomes itself a vague label pointing to the fact that, in the encounter between people and cinema, pleasure can be generated in particular moments. And these moments show you where the cinematic institution itself vacillates, where it might tip over or allow you a glimpse of the edge of its representation. The cinematic apparatus, which includes image and viewer, induces pleasure in its viewer by getting you to believe or to see something that is impossible to program into the representation. Therefore it points to that which exceeds the logic of the film, some-

240

thing which is not, in that sense, part of representation as such. It is the symptomatic, the dangerous moment of representation which points to an elsewhere. For the cinephile, there is a moment in a film (and it happens more often in certain kinds of films) when cinema, in showing you one thing, allows you to glimpse something else that you are not meant to see. There again, you cannot designate in any particular film the something you are not meant to see. This is a highly individual, and therefore highly social, process. There is a whole cultural history and cultural analysis at play there. Cinephilia designates that process, indicating that this is an issue in the relationship, a kind of matrix which says that, in the relationship between film and viewer, the film allows you to think or to fantasise a 'beyond' of cinema, a world beyond representation which only shimmers through in certain moments of the film. Where you see it shimmering is largely, but not exclusively, up to you. The cinephiliac claim is that cinema can do this.

NK: For me, some of those comments recall Balazs' *Theory of the Film*,[11] which has a section called 'The Face of Man' in which there is a subsection called 'I can see that I cannot see'. It's where Balazs is discussing the 'microphysiognomics' of early cinema. He talks about Asta Nielsen's face 'registering a pretence that is a lie. She is lying that she is lying.' He then goes on to say of a piece of Sessue Hayakawa's acting that 'we can see that there is something that we cannot see'. But putting that to one side, what you've been describing so far is the way a certain kind of critical practice renders particular moments in particular films. Do you have anything to say about the practice of cinephilia within cinema? For example, Belmondo in Godard's *Breathless*, in front of the Bogart cinema poster, running his finger across his mouth and saying 'Bogie'. What is the status of that gesture? And if I point out that moment of cinephilia, calling it citation, quotation, homage, intertextuality or whatever, is my act of criticism in some sense redundant?

PW: Cinephilia being designated in cinema is an activation of complicity. Cinephilia as a component of a film culture which is then recycled in the film and which therefore bonds viewer and film in a particular moment of complicity. Whether you grasp that or not, the fact that Belmondo has to double-code it indicates the possibility that people wouldn't share the moment simply by him doing the gesture. He has to say 'Bogie' in exactly the same way that Orson Welles has to double-code the negative aspect of the singing in *Citizen Kane*. The fact that Susan sings badly in an opera is not sufficient for an audience to recognise that she's singing badly. Welles has to go up to the workmen in the rafters and have them tell us: 'This is bad.' That is double coding. The Belmondo example is the same. He makes the gesture which is the cinephiliac reference, the gesture of bonding, and then, in case we dont get it, he has to double-code and say 'Bogie' to anchor the cinephiliac dimension. I prefer the word 'dimension' to 'moment' to allow for things like the vague impression a viewer, let's say a teenage viewer, may get seeing American teenagers move across the screen. A whole world is evoked by their body language, which is not necessarily part of acting (Mamie Van Doren may have it just as much as Eddie Cochran). This is a world evoked by a body language which has to do with clothes, with whether they wear sneakers and leather jackets or a stetson hat and jeans. Different body languages and therefore different belief worlds are evoked.

A lot of pleasure can be derived from minor programme fillers made by nonentity Hollywood directors, the *Hollywood Confidential* sort of thing. Some early Roger Corman films are badly scripted, atrociously acted, not well shot. And partly because of that lack of polish and the cavalier attitude to the shooting, some of these revelatory dimensions come along more than they do in highly rehearsed films that had twenty different takes in order to get the gesture right. So in the low-budget, hurriedly produced formula films, it's more likely to come through as an impressionistic evocation of a particular world incarnated in nothing more than gesture or intonation. Then there are the landscapes and the light in the image, they too evoke worlds that are surreal, as in photorealist painting, even in the most banal films provided they are shot with a bit of care, early travelogues, say. There too you can have a kind of excess of 'the seen' beyond 'the shown'. These films evoke worlds that people can relate to as much as they do to more obviously present aspects of the narrative: say, the various ideological, moral and ethical lessons proposed by the narrative and the characters.

Those dimensions are also part of the cinephiliac phenomenon. Perhaps they are even the most important part of cinephilia, evoking half-submerged fantasies which themselves were shaped under the impact of industrial and propagandistic imagery (for instance, the Belgian imaginary of 'America', for people of my generation, was decisively shaped by a myriad impressions derived from Hollywood films, rock and jazz music and images, American soldiers hanging about after the Second World War and during the Korean War, advertising imagery, and so on. The things that matter about those impressions is not so much their generic importance (everyone of my generation shared that exposure to the effects of the US aggressive imperial aspirations in the wake of Europe's devastation), but which precise images and sounds and products were sedimented in an Antwerp teenager's fantasy. By putting it like that, I hope I am also indicating that we are talking about a hybrid process: local history and personal neuroses.

NK: If I could pursue an aspect of an earlier question. When the cinephilic description occurs, to what extent do you think it is a form of ontologising cinema?

PW: One of the presuppositons of cinephilia is what André Bazin theorised in terms of an ontology of cinema. I think the two concepts are in solidarity with each other. You can, and most people do, reject an ontology of cinema as formulated by Bazin or as glossed by Peter Wollen in his brilliant *Screen* essay.[12] Obviously you can reject that and remain thoroughly soaked in cinephilia in terms of your responses to cinema, as you recycle them in your critical writing or speech. Nevertheless I think it's a contradiction. The ontology of cinema, as voiced by Bazin, claims that, because a mechanical reproduction is involved, there is a privileged relation between cinema and the real. That is to say, there is something which is being reproduced and therefore there is an unfilmed world before the camera came along and pointed to it, some of which (and the more the better, as far as Bazin is concerned) transpires into the recorded and projected image. And what people like Bazin want you to relate to in their polemic is precisely the dimension of revelation that is obtained by pointing your camera at something that hasn't been staged for the camera.

That's the whole aesthetic of neo-realism and it's why the melodramatic aspects of De Sica or Rossellini are neither here nor there as far as Bazin is concerned. The fact that they shot on location, without much rehearsal, in difficult conditions, meant that something shone through into the film. There again, these are mystical notions of revelation. That aesthetic can be talked about, polemicised about, in a hundred different ways. The ontology argument underpins them all. You can value Ophuls because he does something else (fetishises the frame, screens off the real) or you can fetishise that dimension of the real which shines through, with the camera merely trying to follow there where it allegedly appears. The camera is led by the profilmic rather than the profilmic being arranged in function of the filmic.

Both of these arguments share the same assumption of ontology but do different things in relation to it. The cinephile shares the notion of an ontology of cinema and the less the image has a Bazinian ontological relation to the real (the death-mask notion of the real), the more the image gets electronified, with each pixil becoming programmable in its own terms, the less appropriate cinephilia becomes. This is where we shade over into television in so far as it is a medium that is on the way towards the electronified image. Television has a short history, emerging out of cinematic notions of visual dramatic narrative and into the possibility (at the moment it is no more than that) contained in the whole discourse around virtual reality and synthesised images. Television has a short history but all of it is on that edge of moving from one thing to the other. Cinema is still perceived as being completely locked into the 'before' of the electronification of the image. It doesn't necessarily have to be locked into that moment, but cinephilia is one of the discourses that says cinema is locked into it. And I agree with the cinephiles.

NK: When someone focuses on, say, *mise en scène* in a Douglas Sirk film and reads it as an ironised rendering of script material, is that being cinephiliac? It should be work that's familar to you![13] What's going on there? In the case of Welles it might be a camera-angle, depth-of-field in Renoir, re-framing in Ophuls. What's the relation of that kind of critical writing to the forms of critical description you've been discussing?

PW: Sirk is a notoriously difficult case. I'd first draw attention to two different Sirks. One is Fassbinder's Sirk and the other, I'm tempted to say, is my Sirk, our Sirk. They're both equally cinephiliac. You must remember that I'm not using cinephiliac as a negative term. It relates to something which is potentially productive. It doesnt have to be at all times, but I would argue that today it is. Fassbinder's Sirk talks a lot about acting, about Jane Wyman and her frustrations. There is a projection onto the Sirk-film by Fassbinder about the enactment of frustration which he focuses on actorial performance and psychologises in terms of character. This may have to do with his own preoccupations as a theatre director, with the direction of actors. Fassbinder's question concerned how one could render these profoundly social moments – Jane Wyman's character is frustrated in Eisenhower's America because of a whole parcel of specific notions of sexuality, marriage, consumption, psychiatry, and so on – which Fassbinder sees at work in Sirk's films and which he is concerned to reproduce in his own films. It relates to Fassbinder's desire to provide some sort of X-ray of the various frustrating and frustrated currents at play in the fabric of his own society. Fassbinder focuses on that aspect of Sirk's films from the point of view of being a director of actors. How do you get that dimension through, in your films, the way Sirk did in his? The question remains whether or not Sirk did do this or whether it is just Fassbinder seeing it.

NK: Which is what I'm getting at. You know the notorious slogan, 'A discourse produces its own object'. To what extent is that happening here?

PW: But, you see, a different discourse, my Sirk, produces the same object but for totally different reasons, and locates it in a completely different part of Sirk's films. I find the acting in Sirk's films, for the most part, boring, and the characters completely uninteresting. One

244

of the reasons I like Sirk's films, one of the reasons they talk to me, is because the characters become supremely irrelevant. Characters are totally flattened out, are simply strings of clichés put together. And the moments in Sirk which I and other people fetishise are things like the television set gift or the little Bambi in front of the window (both in *All That Heaven Allows*) or the moment when the toy falls off the table in *There's Always Tomorrow*. One could say that Sirk's films confirm the fact that all fictional characters are always concatenations of clichés, which makes them so 'realistic' and so suitable for demonstrations of the fact that social existence determines consciousness. There is no cliché quite as obnoxious as the cliché of the 'unique' or 'rounded character'.

My Sirk can be synopsised in the credit sequence of *Imitation of Life*, a credit sequence the design of which he suggested. It has cut-glass diamonds falling and filling up the screen. In that credit sequence, seeing 'through the glass darkly' is suggested, which summarises a lot of Sirk. I see it as the metonym of all Sirk's films. Many of Roger Corman's Edgar Alan Poe films have similarly abstract credit sequences which, to my mind, actually summarise the films in an abstract but evocative manner. In the end, why I fetishise Sirk comes closer to why Fassbinder does the same, in the sense that I'm preoccupied by the same problem, although not from the same position. I'm not a director of actors but I'm equally concerned to read a kind of a social pathology, as it transpires, into or through a film. The reason for the fetishisation of it involves a shift in temporal and geographic location. I did see Sirk's films in Europe, when they first came out. I couldn't bear them. They affected me very deeply but I couldn't stand them. Ten years or so later, located in a different historical conjuncture, in Britain, preoccupied by notions of film theory, politics, Vietnam having intervened in our fantasies of the United States (it was no longer the land of Coca-Cola, blue jeans and sex), I read Sirk's films quite differently. And the same went for feminists who were looking for different moments of revelation in these films. We were all concerned to explain the way a Sirk film allowed us to glimpse, at work in American society, 'through the glass darkly', a whole set of frustrations, problems and pathologies. Their existence was revealed, together with a mode of narrativising, socialising and of sweeping those dynamics under the carpet. Both these dimensions were presented to us in Sirk. Some people did the same thing through Minnelli, less successfully I think, and certainly with less reverberation. That was probably because Minnelli shifted genres, doing musicals and melodramas. Nevertheless, there was some dimension, some aspect of Minnelli that activated the same string. Especially in films like *Home from the Hill* and *The Cobweb*. We couldn't as readily disengage Sirk's kind of stereographic vision in melodramas by other directors.

So in the end, both Fassbinder's Sirk and our Sirk coincided from different positions. We both perceived something in Sirk which in the end has to do with the ontological argument in relation to cinema. What was shining through, in the form of people's gestures, intonations and the like, was a whole X-ray view of American middle-class disintegration. Why we should have seen it in Sirk rather than in others, that's the whole question of film theory as far as I'm concerned. What is to be made of the fact that one can systematise it, point quite easily to it in Sirk, although without much power of conviction, I might add. People who don't see it are not convinced by it. But to the extent that those writings and arguments around Sirk did have reverberations, a sufficient number of other people must have seen something similar. The similarity of perception is prior to the adherence to the writing; it enables the spread of the writing. I don't think that the writing alone has a power of conviction. It merely allows you to recognise that you too have seen something. If you haven't seen it in the first place, the writing won't convince you. So in a sense there was something to be seen in Sirk's films by a relatively diverse set of people with diverse interests. They saw it in relation to Sirk and not in relation to John Stahl or John Brahm, to name two directors whose films Sirk remade. Some people tried desperately to see it there too and might have come up with the odd moment. But they couldn't account for a system or a logic that runs through a majority of the work of those directors, whereas one can talk about it in Sirk from his German to his American films, from the way he uses Zara Leander to the way he uses Jane Wyman or Dorothy Malone. I would say that the dimension of Sirk as author resides in that ability of critical discourse to show that, intentionally or not, his films have an X-ray power for a relatively large number of people, whereas other films don't. The whole critical discourse is an attempt to pinpoint the particular aspects and moments of the films which would justify this fairly large number of people privileging Sirk in this way at that time.

NK: In the case of Sirk, one thing to say is that it is the identification of a European intellectual going into a North American cultural context, carrying the capacity for critique with him, and carrying it out in a particular way. But another person who made films around that time is Samuel Fuller who is sometimes classified as one of the so-called 'American primitives', and who seems less likely to produce an intellectual critique of that kind of the American cultural context. And yet Fuller has been identified as having produced, however ambivalently, similar cinematic statements.

PW: True, but Fuller was talking about other aspects of America and in those other areas he too was producing a kind of stereographic view of social disintegration, except that it made him angry while Sirk became sad and probably frightened (with good reason, if you remember that he was a lefty in Hollywood during the witch hunts). Also, Sirk was able to rationalise his approach sufficiently to transmit it for instance to the students of the Munich Film School. His practice in relation to film students underlined and legitimated our, that is, Fassbinder's and the Anglo-American critics' intuitions. Sirk was able to transmit an attitude, an approach to cinema to his students, which resulted in the films he supervised at the Munich Film School, all of which were focused precisely on the limits of cinema. You remember his teaching method? He would give students a series of literary texts for cinematic adaptation, and would ask them which one they regarded as the least possible to adapt to cinema, and that is the one they would work on.

NK: As would have been clear from the line of my questioning, my interest in cinephilia is in its status as a particular form of critical description. Hence my desire to focus on its discursive regularities, its repetitive turns. It does seem to me to be an instance of criticism performed as an 'aesthetic occasion'. It's a particular kind of uptake on a cultural object which perhaps has no essential necessity in terms of the medium being addressed, the 'cine' aspect aside. So I have two questions which relate to the ontology issue of cinephilia in particular ways. First, would you agree that equivalent critical descriptions have been applied to things that predate and postdate cinema? For example, particular gestures and forms of performance in theatre must have received similar description, and there is also the case of descriptions of sporting performance: cricket, soccer, rugby, tennis, boxing have all been rendered into aesthetic occasions containing sublime revelatory moments. This leads to my second question. If this is the case does it mean that the critical practice of cinephilia needs to be placed in a larger realm of 'aestheticising discourses' in which the particularity of the object, here the specificity of the medium of cinema, is less important than we have been implying?

PW: As for the larger realm, I don't know. But all critical descriptions of theatrical performance that I have so far come across have always been highly coded in terms of expectations of gestural range or codified notions of expressivity. The example that comes most readily to mind is that of the Irish Abbey Theatre Players at the beginning of the century. They were hailed as innovative, partly because they refused to move whenever possible. Therefore their theatrical style became very subservient to the articulated word, to speech. Body movement was kept to an absolute minimum. This was partly a direct criticism of what was perceived to be happening on the English stage and what was recognised there as levels of expertise, which had to do with mastery of gesture and the skilful display of one's range of both vocal and physical gesture. It was calculated to be the opposite of that. Even a minimal gestural presence on the stage, although recognised as extremely charismatic and glorified by critics, even the relative absence of the artificial codes of theatrical performance meant that the codes were still there, in an inverted form. I've never come across any description of a major theatrical actor or actress where what was being praised was not in fact a highly coded form of presence rather than the non-coded or the slippage out of the code (which is what I'm talking about in cinema). I've never heard that being elevated into a positive feature in theatrical criticism. This may have to do with the condition of physical performance, the fact that you are quite a long distance away from the performer. Therefore the text in the theatre, the vocal performance, the exaggerated gestural performance (which is only naturalised by distance), the physical performance conditions, don't allow you to catch the revelatory glimpse beyond the code because the code itself is geared precisely towards bridging that gap of distance. So it becomes all about the skill with which the code is performed. And those codes can adopt various stylistic conventions, from non-movement combined with an emphasis on the voice through to song-and-dance and what we now describe as the over-the-top acting of the nineteenth-century English stage. I'm not saying it is not possible to have the revelatory dimension to acting in the theatre. I'm just saying there is no pressure on me to find an explanatory account of something that recurs in the discourse of theatrical criticism. Because, in the theatrical criticism I've read, I simply can't find a similar regularity of something to be explained in terms of revelatory moments as that which I've labelled the cinephiliac pressure, which occurs all the time in film criticism. And although my knowledge of theatrical criticism is far from exhaustive, I'm sure I'd have come across it by now if it had been so persistent in the critical discourse.

NK: What about sport?

PW: I'd have to make a distinction between the discourse of the star and the manifestation of star quality in journalistic discourse. This is part of a regime of commodification of sport, one which requires star performers for the box office, for the business side of sporting spectacles. There is much pressure on sports commentators to identify star quality because that's what sells. That is not the equivalent of cinema because the star discourse of film is not the same as the cinephiliac discourse. It's actually very difficult to sell cinephilia. What would you be selling? If it's a broad impression of a cultural atmosphere that is disengaged from, say, a 1950s American teenpic, and which imbues the screen in the way jackets are worn, etc., then you can't sell it. What is sold is plot, action, spectacle, star quality. What is sold in

248

sport is not the same kind of stardom. But I don't want to exclude the possibility of the revelatory dimension in sport. I would imagine it could occur around the fact that the body, although subjected to highly codified rules of the game, rules of skill, etc., can reveal moments of 'non-necessary skill'. I have in mind Johan Cruyff playing soccer. This would be a situation in which there is a surplus of bodily agility on display which goes beyond the standards of skill, and where notions of intuition and mastery of the body itself (as opposed to mastery of the game) come into play. But I'd rather relate that excess to a narcissistic pleasure of bodily control, mastery of the body. I would link it to the mirror phase and the anticipatory pleasures of an ideal ego rather than to some 'philia'.

NK: What would you make of such things as the fetishising of TV music programmes such as *The Old Grey Whistle Test* in Britain or *Countdown* in Australia?

PW: For each television example that you give I would be able to point to a cinephiliac antecedent in cinema. There is a whole slew of American music movies which anticipate that particular format, with a loose narrative woven into it. And in the case of something like *Shindig*, one has to ask what the fascination of the go-go dancers is that it can help produce the popularity of that musical programme as opposed to another one. You also have to look at the interface between the radio pop programme presentation of music (for instance, by Alan Freed) and the televisual presentation of music. Something happens in that shift which reactivates already existing patterns of pleasure and expectation which have been calibrated on cinema but adapted to different formats. I'm not saying that these programmes are cinema, only that they reactualise something in a pleasure-producing relationship which I would argue deserves to be looked at before one reaches a conclusion which says that this is radically different. I don't think it is radically different. Pleasure is a complex phenomenon of interlinked relationships. It derives its energies from memory and then translates, transfers those to aspects of other experiences, a process that is culturally determined and socially inflected. And if you take a relation to cinema or television as a bundle of different potential relationships actualised in particular narrative or programme formats, then it's simply moronic to designate one of these formats as giving one kind of pleasure and opposing that type of pleasure to another one. Pleasure is multiform and complex. Different elements of a relationship to an image-discourse are rearticulated in other forms of relationships. It is misguided to claim that cinematic and televisual pleasures do not overlap. There are aspects of the relationship to television which overlap with aspects of the relationship to cinema. The pleasure derived from watching a film on television is deeply implicated in our memories of watching films, our memory of the experience of watching a film in a cinema. I would argue that we unconsciously re-translate the perceived television image back onto a screen in a cinema. It does not really matter whether we have seen the film before or not: we simply compensate in our imaginary. And I think that the shift from cinephilia to telephilia, the very attempt to introduce the notion of telephilia, indicates (symptomatically) an area of overlap at the same time as it indicates a non-total coverage of the two areas. My profound disagreement with some notions of telephilia precisely turns on the fact that areas of non-overlap are elided, with the consequence that areas of overlap are misunderstood. And so, for every example provided of a relationship to television (especially in the 50s and 60s), I think a lot more analysis has to be undertaken, many more questions asked, before one can say something intelligent about television. People are beginning to try, but then, the one who seemed to be getting a grip on the medium, Serge Daney, died recently.

But by addressing the notion of cinephilia, I'm trying to get at something else, something I came to think about because of my dis-agreement with notions of pleasure as currently proposed in aca-demic-critical discourses. It's undeniable that there are pleasures, in the plural, involved in one's relationship to cinema and television. It's important to stress the plurality of pleasure. One has to accept the historical, geo-cultural variability of pleasures. The pleasures an Aus-tralian teenager derives from a particular programme will differ from those taken by an American teenager in an archetypal American town or by a Belgian teenager in a provincial Belgian town. If one allies that to the complexity of pleasure-generation itself, then there is a lot to be analysed rather than prematurely foreclosed by simply asserting that something is good because it gives a lot of people pleasure.

NK: You seem to be using the category of pleasure rather differently from the way it figures in a variety of writing on popular cultural objects and practices (for example, some of the claims for transforma-tive readings/consumptions). Could you say a bit more about how your use of the term differs from these other usages?

PW: Thank you for exempting me from the garbage being talked about pleasure since the late 70s. First of all, pleasures are generated via a variety of possible fantasy scenarios, involving patterns of psychic investment, energy displacement, etc. However one accounts for this, there are varieties of pleasures to be had. It could be the pleasure of narcissism, the pleasure of subordination, the pleasure of mastery, the pleasure of disintegration, etc. There is a multiple array of possible pleasures depending on psychic scenarios. I think none of these pleasures, in itself, is either good or bad, positive or negative.

There is nothing wrong with pleasures of sadism just as there is nothing wrong with pleasures of masochism, narcissism or whatever. Each of them is required for survival. The problem with current discourses of pleasure is precisely the way they make pleasure into a monolith. It is essentialised into a singular, unitary reaction, regardless of the scenario involved. Secondly, current academic discourses ignore that cinema or any other representational practice binds a variety of possible pleasures into narrative structures in such a way that the pleasures come to function as positive or negative indicators *vis-à-vis* a particular social representation. It is not the fact that Rambo gives pleasure that is important. It is the fact that some pleasures for some people are attached to that particular character taking those actions in that circumstance: militarised, individualised, brutalised. The binding process is the problem: which aspects of representations are we supposed to find pleasurable and according to whom?

NK: Why is the binding process the problem? Why isn't it, to put it crudely, the 'content' of the representation?

PW: The binding process presupposes that there are two different things being bound together. Pleasures are one sort of thing and they can be articulated with, bound into, a host of different types of representations. The pleasure of understanding is one of these pleasures that is systematically denigrated and denied, whereas pleasures of emotional identification with demonstrations of physical violence or power are constantly presented as attractive pleasures. The way they are stitched into the narrative and the way the psychic economy is distributed across the narrative means that pleasures are attached to that rather than to something else. Feelings of displeasure are associated with particular scenes and feelings of pleasure and release are associated with other things. So the question becomes, to which of these types of narrative economies and narrative distribution of energies do you attach pleasure? If you start analysing that question you quickly perceive that some types of pleasure are systematically denied whereas other types of narrative event are constantly presented as available to be experienced as pleasurable. What I find reprehensible about the notion of pleasure operating in current popular-cultural critical discourse is its denial of complexity, its denial of the fact that pleasure is articulated to narrative events, to a narratological dynamic. The distribution of pleasures is an orchestration of the relationship between viewer and image. And it is in that orchestration that pleasure is defined and socially sanctioned and some other pleasure is denied and socially denigrated. That dimension of articulation is absent from the popular culture notion of pleasure. There are certain things, such as witnessing public executions, which can be highly pleasurable. Is that therefore a pleasure one would want to see legitimised? There are ambivalences in relation to pleasure which are not permitted to be explored, which, at the moment, have to do primarily with so-called perversions: sado-masochistic circulations of alternating, oscillating, sometimes ambivalent forms of identification within which there is no longer the category of 'victim'. And those kinds of oscillating pleasures and identifications also take individual characters on the screen as themselves multiple and available for multiple types of psychic engagement. Claire Johnston was talking about those things in the 70s when she analysed *Double Indemnity*,[14] but nobody seems to have taken any notice.

NK: Well, as Liz Cowie puts it in her 'Fantasia' article,[15] a piece which follows on from your writing on Raoul Walsh's *Pursued*,[16] a viewer doesn't have to engage with every aspect of a particular character. A female character might, on occasion, be available to what are socially coded as male pleasures.

PW: So even the physical gender of the character on the screen doesn't necessarily predetermine the pleasures of identification and non-identification that are available. All that is part of the orchestration of the complex webs of meaning that run through a film as a whole. Therefore the question of how you articulate pleasures to particular moments is something to be taken into account rather than to be flattened out into a singular alternative of pleasure/non-pleasure. What the popular culture discourse does is legitimate as pleasure whatever increases the balance sheets of the major companies. Pleasure is quantifiable in terms of dollars and cents; the more successful, the more pleasurable. That is the dead-end of that popular cultural studies notion of pleasure. People who claim radical intentions wind up giving academic legitimacy to the most cynically commercial, profit-oriented sales strategies.

NK: I don't think you'll agree with this. What would you say if I pursued my suggestion that cinephilia should be seen as a subset of a larger discursive practice, one involving a kind of 'aesthetic occasion' in which a critical apparatus is brought to bear on, say, a cricket game (for example, Pinter writing on the 1948 Australian touring cricket team) or some aspect of popular culture, or a film?[17]

PW: I don't think cinephilia is to be equated with aestheticisation.

NK: That's why I thought you wouldn't agree!

PW: There again, in terms of aestheticisation, you have to make some distinctions. There is the aestheticisation of the image in, let's say, something like Carné's *Les Enfants du Paradis* or in René Clair or in Olivier's *Hamlet*. There is a form of stylisation in cinema which is actually equivalent to academicism in critical discourses. The whole new wave and the discourse of cinephilia, in France at least, was quite specifically against the academic notion of 'the aesthetic, of what was thought to be a beautiful image, from Autant-Lara to Cayatte, the whole *cinéma de papa*. A whole tradition of quite self-consciously aestheticised French art cinema was explicitly opposed by the discourse of cinephilia, with its predilection for things which did not appear to be stylised or aestheticised. In a sense, cinephiliac discourse appeared to privilege absence of aestheticisation, where something shines through beyond the aestheticised. And this is mythified in terms of the soul in the early *Cahiers* or is mystically designated in terms of the real coming through, as in Rossellini's statement that cinema expresses the real by means of itself. Aestheticisation is fundamentally different from cinephilia. Therefore, I don't think one can be a subset of the other.

NK: Towards the end of your '*Photogénie* and Epstein', you contrast Epstein's refusal of psychoanalysis to the Surrealists' position and you provide a kind of cost-benefit analysis of Epstein's refusal. The critical description offered in this interview, as an assemblage of a particular-kind, is both a psychoanalytic cultural history (you speak of neurotic knots, secondarisation, the Lacanian Real, and so on) and a quite detailed textual account of the cinephiliac mode of targeting a film or a dimension of a moment in a film. Perhaps in deference to what you know to be my particular interest in cinephilia, that is to say, a form of critical practice or description predicated on the isolation of an epiphanic moment (for me) or a revelatory fragment (for you), you've come some way from saying that cinephilia simply describes someone who loves cinema. You've begun to identify some of the modes that form of loving takes. Are you in a position to perform a little self-reflexive agonistic and comment on why you find this to be the most appropriate way of thinking through the issues cinephilia raises for you?

PW: Firstly, don't forget this stuff is work in progress. I really am not at all sure that this line of thought about cinephilia hits the mark. But it is possible to talk about cinephilia without invoking a psychoanalytic framework. It's possible to talk about it in religious terms or in phenomenological terms. There are various possible philosophical frameworks available. I choose to deploy a psychoanalytical one. Nevertheless all of us are circling around a knot which is felt to be in need of identification and explanation and which is seen as a driving force, as a source of energy. Obviously, I think my terminology has a greater illuminatory power than either religion or phenomenology. In a sense, all of us are circling around something which I choose to designate as the Real in Lacanian terms, and for which others might choose another term. Were still talking about something which is revelatory, which is an energising factor in the relation between the screen and the viewer. But I don't think psychoanalysis is absolutely necessary to gesture towards what I'm trying to explain.

NK: I've indicated fairly often now that I'm interested in cinephilia to the extent that it constitutes a particular discursive practice whose contours can be mapped. I get the strong impression that it's much more than that for you. For you, it's important because you think it describes an actual, lived, real moment in cinematic consumption. You're interested in the presence of that 'thing' that occurs in the cinema whereas I've 'deadened' it into simply being another practice of critical writing.

PW: I am interested in cinephilia now because the dominance of television is destroying cinema: increasibly, film-makers, especially British ones, seem unable even to remember cinema. I have no principled objections to televisual discourse: I do protest, though, against the impoverishment of cinema (both in its making and in its viewing) being advocated in Anglo cultures. That is a crime against culture. Thinking about cinephilia allows us (me) to put onto the agenda what could well be lost if the current media criticism is allowed to remain unchallenged. There definitely is that 'thing' that insists in different modalities, different discourses, different critical writings. The importance of pointing to it now rather than simply taking it for granted, as I used to do, is because, as you know, most recently I've been thinking about the way historical complexities are representable in film. In that context, I've been struck by the fact that it is not sufficient for the film-maker simply to be an intelligent analyst of a cultural formation, and then to transcode that understanding into a filmic narrative. That kind of analytical film-making has proved to be bankrupt. The films which I identify as being particularly successful in the way they 'inhabit' (in Raymond Williams' terms), in diagnostic ways, their own cultural situation, are films which mobilise this ontological dimension of cinema in various ways, either through notions of lighting, *mise en scène* or camera movement. I'm thinking of Solanas, of some aspects of Cinema-Action's movies, of Raoul Ruiz, Ousmane Senbene, Nelson Pereira dos Santos, Guney, Amos Gitai. All those people inhabit their cultures in very complex manners and that complexity is translated into a representational practice that goes beyond the narrative.

NK: I don't want this remark to derail your train of thought, but is it

254

really there? Think of your earlier remarks on the interpretations of Sirk's films.

PW: It is there, for instance, in the density of the use of architecture and landscape in films, which are no longer simply background. There is something in the relation between camera and scene, what the camera films, which transpires into the filming and which is activated by these other dimensions of the film, which are highly intelligently, deliberately, structured as narratives, as analysis, as allegory. The fact that these other dimensions of the film are structured in that way activates these areas of surplus. In a Rossellini film these areas would not be activated in that way because the narrative itself is still too conventionally within the melodramatic mode. It's not analytical enough, it's too skewed towards human universals and does not pay sufficient attention to concrete, local, historical detail. This is a broader version of the 'ghosting' example we discussed earlier, of something shimmering through. I am having some difficulty in labelling exactly what shimmers through, in identifying the particular signifiers or aesthetic strategies which cause those other dimensions, the second of Bakthin's double voice, to come through. At present, it's all still rather vague, on the level of an intuition. But there is a linkage between my interest in 'Third Cinema' and cinephilia: each one is a case of double-voicing. With cinephilia, we are talking about a shadow of the limits of cinema. With Third Cinema, we are talking about the articulation between representation and history in cinema. The concrete, local, historical detail shines through, as does the 'beyond' of, say, a character in the Brando example for the cinephiliac. But it does so only when activated by other dimensions of the film. That means that the whole of the film has to be available to this kind of cross-fertilisation. Such a dimension requires a representational practice that works not only in terms of interacting sound and vision but also involves being able to use, in a concentrated manner, different levels of composition, in terms of depth or width (in relation to the edges of the frame). It also requires, for its manifestation, a density of the image which is absent in current forms of television because of the lack of resolution of the television image compared to the film image. Fast stock, used increasingly in most routine commercial productions, also destroys that potential opening up of the space within which the analytical dimensions of a film can activate, fertilise, other dimensions which usually go by the board as picturesque background or whatever. Because of the systems or patterns of meaning organised in narrative events (character, choices of location, and so on), other aspects of the image, almost by contagion, are activated so that the whole image, the whole space, is infused with a sense of history. It's a sense of history which is not explicitly signified to the viewer. There is no arrow pointing, saying look at this tree in the background. But there is something that comes through because of the cinema's ontological dimension and because of the nature of the attention and the relationship of pleasure which is catered for between the image and the viewer. Those things have a technological and a cultural basis, both of which are absent in television. Therefore it's important to talk about that now because there is a dimension of visual impoverishment which is related only to current forms of television. There is no technological limit, other than commerically imposed ones, which would constitute a reason why television wouldn't be able to achieve the same density and size of image. You could have the same libidinal relationship with it. Current television doesn't have it and I deplore the increasing internalisation by film-makers of the knowledge that their films will be seen primarily on video and television. They seem to content themselves all too readily with a lack of attention to the productivity of the cinematic image and indeed to its pleasures. This involves a set of debates concerning film and television now, but it also concerns the moment of potential convergence of cinema and television. A new breed of director will have to come on the scene when the television image is of sufficient density and resolution to enable those cinephiliac dimensions to be activated again. That moment might be ten years or so from now. In the meantime, there is the very real danger of losing a whole generation of film viewers, film-makers and critics, by going along with, even celebrating, a cultural critical discourse which legitimates what I can only understand as the brutalisation and the impoverishment of cinema's potential. For this potential is, as yet, by no means exhausted.

NK: One last question. Early in the interview you were describing something and you said, 'This is not the way I would have put it when I was a cinephile.' When did you stop being a cinephile and how did you stop?

PW: Although I no longer see fifty films a month, I am still a cinephile. I get many cinephiliac pleasures not only from some of the recognised masters but also from watching the films of Terence Fisher, Koji Wakamatsu, Jose Mojica Marins, 1950s and 60s German Edgar Wallace and Mabuse films or even downright sleaze movies like those of Jesus Franco. I am enough of a cinephile still to wonder about cinephilia.

Notes

1. See pp. 124–33 in this volume.
2. *La Société du spectacle* (Paris: Buchet-Chastel, 1967). For an illuminating account of Situationism and Debord's role in it, see Peter Wollen, *Raiding the*

Icebox: Reflections on Twentieth Century Culture (London: Verso, 1993), pp. 120–57.

3. *The American Vein: Directors and Directions in Television* (London: Talisman Books, 1979) and Andrew Sarris, *The American Cinema: Directors and Directions 1929–1968* (New York: E. P. Dutton, 1968).

4. Gilles Deleuze, *Cinema 1: The Movement-Image*, trans. Hugh Tomlinson and Barbara Habberjam (London: The Athlone Press, 1986), first published in France in 1983. See also Paul Virilio, *The Vision Machine*, transl. Liz Heron (London: British Film Institute, 1994), first published in France in 1989.

5. See Antoine de Baecque, *Les Cahiers du cinéma: Histoire d'une revue*, vol. 1: *À l'assaut du cinéma 1951–1959* (Paris: Cahiers du cinéma, 1991).

6. See Paul Willemen, 'The limitations and strengths of a cultural policy' in *Framework*, nos. 15/16/17, 1981, pp. 96–8.

7. Michel Ciment (ed.), *Kazan on Kazan* (London: Secker & Warburg, 1974), first published in France in 1972.

8. Ado Kyrou, *Le Surréalisme au cinéma* (Paris: Arcanes, 1953); *Amour-érotisme et cinéma* (Paris: Le Terrain Vague, 1957).

9. See *Présence du cinéma*, no. 17, 1963.

10. See Tom Milne (ed.) *Godard on Godard* (London: Secker & Warburg, 1968); *Introduction a une véritable histoire du cinéma* (Paris: Albatros, 1980).

11. *Theory of the Film* (New York: Dover, 1970).

12. See *Screen*, vol. 17 no. 1 (1976); reprinted in Peter Wollen, *Readings and Writings. Semiotic Counter-Strategies* (London: Verso, 1982), pp. 189–207.

13. See pp. 87–98 in this volume.

14. Claire Johnston, '*Double Indemnity*', in E. Ann Kaplan (ed.), *Women in Film Noir* (London: British Film Institute, 1978), pp. 100–12.

15. E. Cowie, 'Fantasia' in *m/f*, no. 9, 1984.

16. Paul Willemen, 'The Fugitive Subject', in Phil Hardy (ed.), *Raoul Walsh* (Edinburgh: EIFF, 1974), pp. 63–92.

17. Harold Pinter, 'Hunter and the Past' in *Poems and Prose 1949–1977* (London: Eyre Methuen, 1978), pp. 87–90.

Index